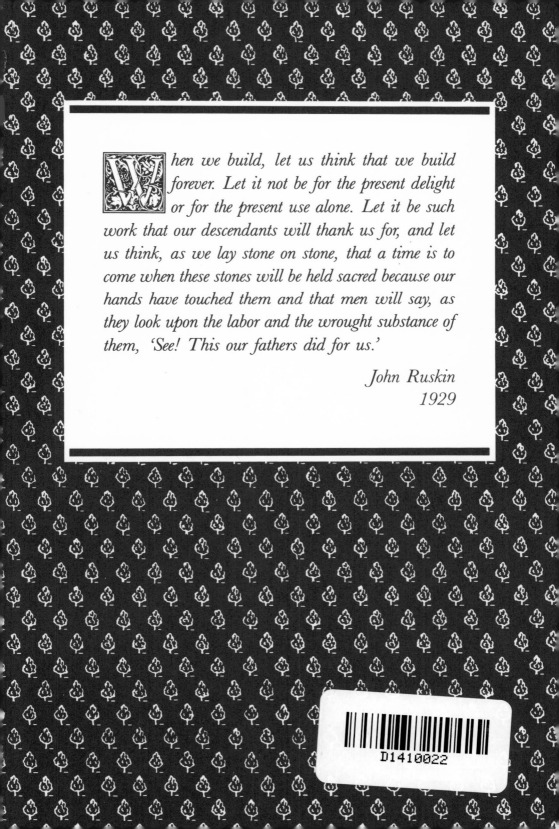

When we build, let us think that we build forever. Let it not be for the present delight or for the present use alone. Let it be such work that our descendants will thank us for, and let us think, as we lay stone on stone, that a time is to come when these stones will be held sacred because our hands have touched them and that men will say, as they look upon the labor and the wrought substance of them, 'See! This our fathers did for us.'

John Ruskin
1929

On the Corner of
Main and Texas A
HOUSTON
LEGACY

On the Corner of Main and Texas A HOUSTON LEGACY

Marie Phelps McAshan
Edited by Mary Jo Bell

HUTCHINS
HOUSE

Distributed by Gulf Publishing Company, Houston, Texas

A HOUSTON LEGACY

Library of Congress Cataloging in Publication Data
McAshan, Marie Phelps.
  A Houston Legacy

  Bibliography: p.
  Includes index.
  I. Houston (Tex.)—History. I. Title.
F394.H857M29   1985   976.4'235   85-21926
ISBN 0-87201-407-X

ACKNOWLEDGMENTS

I am greatly indebted to my good friend, Mary Jo Bell, who edited *A Houston Legacy* with expertise and sensitivity. From the first reading, she believed in the book.

I also can never repay my husband, Samuel Alexander McAshan, for listening to my countless revisions as if for the first time. But he, too, believed in *A Houston Legacy*. A fourth generation Houstonian, he told me many stories of old Houston. Two of his forebears were early Mayors, Alexander McGowan (1867) and Sam Houston Brashear (1898) who set aside Sam Houston Park as a perpetual reminder of the days when Texas was a Republic.

The third person to whom I am indebted, who encouraged me long ago to keep on writing, to one day tell the story of Houston, was Harriet Dickson Reynolds, head of the Houston Public Library (1956–1967).

DEDICATION

This book is dedicated to my husband, Samuel Alexander McAshan and to our grandchildren:

Stuart Lee Phelps, Jr.
John Merrick Phelps
William Clark Phelps
Merrick Phelps Murdock
Marie Lee Murdock
Alexander McGuire Neuman
Whitney Celeste Neuman
Douglas Clay Neuman
Lillie Celeste Ruschell

PREFACE

I have worked on *A Houston Legacy,* for the past 10 years. Writing days were rarely consecutive. I wrote in bed, at the kitchen table in Washington County, in the garden where there was no sound but the cicadas, in the Colorado mountains and on the Texas prairie. There was no cloistered room with my lunch left at a locked door. Family, plumbers, electricians, TV man, civic and social commitments of a life time seemed to be ever in evidence.

But the strong feeling that each of us has a different voice with a different story to tell in one form or another, never left me. I wanted to tell mine of Houston where I was born and my father before me, of the trouble free days when children galloped horses down the green esplanades on Main Street and sat on the curb seeing who could count the most cars on Main Street. My story is for grandchildren and their children who will grow up never having known that Buffalo Bayou was once for swimming, fishing and boating. It is for the new Houstonian to catch a glimpse of the roots of this fascinating mosaic of people, sky towers, freeways, big business and the arts of a city called Houston.

Marie Phelps McAshan

*O*NCE only Indians and buffalo roamed over what is now downtown Houston and drank from its clear stream. A snow white bull with a magnificent hide like velvet led the buffalo herd. The Indians believed he was an emissary of the Great Spirit, and thus sacred. They killed other buffalo for food, but the white bull went untouched.

One day a white hunter killed the sacred buffalo, stripped off its beautiful hide and carried it away.

The frightened Indians cried out to the Great Spirit that they were innocent of the crime, and they wailed the loss of the great bull through long nights.

But, one morning a splendid tree with glorious white flowers appeared on the bayou bank. They felt that the Great Spirit had placed it there to flourish with the soul of the buffalo in the pure white blossoms.

The Indians were comforted. They named the stream Buffalo Bayou, and for many years thereafter the beautiful Magnolia was called the Buffalo Tree.

Learned souls have thought that the bayou's name derived from the buffalo fish, and it is true that the stream teemed with them. But it is also true that archeologists have found bison bones over a large area on either side of the stream.

As a native and long-time Houstonian, I'll take the great white bull and the Buffalo Tree.

———————————◁ ▷———————————

For centuries, Buffalo Bayou, known only to Indians, twisted its way through sycamores, water oaks, gum, pine and magnolia; it was silent save for owls, doves, possums and squirrels cheetering up thick grape vines.

In the spring, buttercups, Indian paint brush, black-eyed Susans, Queen Anne's lace, sparkled through the fields down to the bayou's edge. Field larks, blue jays, doves, huge black crows, chicken hawks filled the white fleeced sky with their cries, the mockingbirds were quick to add to their repertory. Hooty owls blinked silently down at sand cranes one-legging it at the bayou's edge. But this is not the beginning.

———————————◁ ▷———————————

The story of Houston is the story of Buffalo Bayou, the people and Main Street. Buffalo Bayou rose in the northern part of what is now Fort Bend County and flowed eastward across southern Harris County to mingle with the waters of Galveston Bay and the Gulf of Mexico. Along the way it was strengthened by two other bayous. One, Whiteoak Bayou, rose in northwestern Harris County and flowed some 20 miles to join Buffalo Bayou at the point where Houston would be born. The other, Brays Bayou, joined Buffalo Bayou eight miles downstream from its juncture with Whiteoak Bayou.

Where Buffalo and Brays Bayous meet, John Richardson Harris established a settlement in 1824. It quickly grew into a prosperous port and trading center, named Harrisburg in his honor. The county also would bear his name. Harris died in 1829 believing that his town was situated at the head of tidewater on Buffalo Bayou, and that it would be the most important city in Texas.

He was wrong!

Three years before Harris' death a wealthy planter, Jared Groce, had transported 100 bales of cotton by wagon from his plantation near the present site of Hempstead to where Buffalo Bayou and Whiteoak Bayou meet. He loaded the cotton on what were little more than steam-powered rafts taking it past Harrisburg on to Galveston. Groce had found the head of tidewater, but the significance of his discovery would not be realized for a decade.

Groce had been in the first wave of settlers invited to Texas shortly after Mexico won independence from Spain in 1821. He had his own train of 50 wagons. He brought family, slaves, farming equipment and a large herd of cattle from Alabama. He also brought seed, and planted the first cotton in Texas. And in 1825 he built the first cotton gin.

Eleven years later, when Texas declared its independence from Mexico, Groce outfitted and provisioned men for the Texas army. More, General Sam Houston and his ragged band bivouacked at Groce's plantation from March 31 to April 14 as they retreated from General Antonio Lopez de Santa Anna's Mexican regulars. A week after Houston's men broke camp, the two armies met in battle at San Jacinto—but not before Santa Anna paused long enough to put Harrisburg to the torch. At San Jacinto the Texans defeated the Mexican army, and a republic was born.

In the wake of victory, the Allen brothers, Augustus Chapman and John Kirby, were swept into the roles of Founding Fathers of the City of Houston.

Historically in pioneer days, crossroads grew into villages, villages into towns, towns into cities. But Houston — from the first moment of vision — was conceived by its founders as a city.

The Allens were two New York City promoters. Augustus was 30, John Kirby 27. They had traveled to San Augustine, Texas in 1832 and on to Nacogdoches a year later. There Augustus married wealthy Charlotte Baldwin, and the brothers invested much of her inheritance speculating in land certificates. When war with Mexico began they became sutlers to Houston's army. It was widely reported that they also outfitted a schooner to help guard the Texas coast.

War's end found them living in a tiny settlement near the ruins of Harrisburg. The brothers had plans to purchase the site and rebuild the town, but its ownership was in litigation.

As they dallied, Augustus heard that a planter a decade earlier had brought 100 bales of cotton down the bayou from a point farther upstream. Electrified, the brothers hired a small steamboat and made their way up the heavily tree-shaded bayou. The water ran deep and obstructions were minor. When they reached the mouth of Whiteoak Bayou, they moored their boat to the opposite bank.

Augustus stepped ashore. *Here* was the head of tidewater! *Here,* with his brother's help, he would build a city!

There are varying versions of how the city got its name, some quite fanciful. One had Charlotte Allen naming it while toasting General Houston at a dinner party, and the Allen brothers never denied it. They had become friendly with Houston while they acted as provisioners to the Texas Army. But a sequence of events suggests strongly that the Allens simply were aware of the promotional value of the General's name.

On August 26, 1836, the brothers dealt with Mrs. T. F. L. Parrot for half a league on the south and west sides of the bayou, part of a land grant which had been obtained from the Mexican government in 1824 by her first husband, John Austin. They paid her $1,000 cash and signed a note for $4,000, due in 18 months.

Only four days later they announced the opening of their townsite—calling it Houston—in the pages of the *Telegraph and Texas Register,* which was being published at nearby Columbia.

———————————————

Sam Houston was elected president of the new republic two days later. There was a mystique about this indecipherable man that stirred the imagination of all men and women. Standing six foot three, he was tall, strong and commanding.

Sam Houston was born in Virginia March 2, 1793 but moved to Tennessee in 1807 where he received very little schooling. He preferred to live with the Indians rather than in the new settlement. He became the adopted son of a Cherokee chief. He took the name "Raven."

In 1813 he served under Andrew Jackson, which was the beginning of a life long friendship. He was persuaded by Jackson to practice law and subsequently ventured into politics. Sam Houston won the vote as governor of Tennessee but resigned for no apparent reason and after divorcing his bride of a few weeks, Eliza Allen, he traveled to Arkansas.

He crossed the river into Talaquah, Oklahoma, home of the Cherokee Nation and resumed his former Indian life. He married Tiara Rogers whose mother was de-

scended from the greatest Cherokee Chief, Sequoyah,
United States interpreter. Tiara's father was John
Rogers.

Descendants of Tiara Rogers include famous humor-
ist Will Rogers. In this decade, they are W. W. Keeler,
former Chairman of the Board, Phillips Petroleum and
Blanch Keeler Adams' children who reside in Houston
today. They are K. S. "Bud" Adams and Mary Louise
Adams Pickrell. (Courtesy W. W. Keeler, Chief of
Cherokee Nation 1949–1975)

Sam Houston lived in Talaquah for four years and as
Ambassador of the Cherokee Nation to the United
States, was frequently in Washington as guest of his
friend Andrew Jackson. President Jackson commissioned Houston to go to Texas and to return with an ac-
curate report on Indian affairs. While in Texas he successfully arbitrated a treaty with the Comanches to cease
their raids on Americans east of the Texas border across
the Sabine. He went back to Washington and on to Talaquah, but in one year he returned to Texas to stay. His
presence here became history where he confirmed the
Allens' avowed belief in him.

Beginning with a precocity which was to prove charac-
teristic, Houston—still unbuilt—succeeded in being
chosen capital of the Republic of Texas.

While still in Columbia, the Allens engaged the publishers of the *Telegraph and Texas Register,* Gail Borden and
Moses Lapham, to lay out their town. The newspaper-
men, before the war, had been publishing in San Felipe,
and had fled with their press before Santa Anna's ad-
vancing army. They were almost captured in Harrisburg, but escaped to Galveston while Santa Anna

burned the town—and threw their press in the bayou. They obtained a new press after the war and set up shop in Columbia.

Borden also was an engineer. He had laid out the town of Covington, Kentucky, platted San Felipe for Stephen F. Austin, and had prepared the first topographical map of Texas. (Years after his work in Houston he would become wealthy and renowned for devising a method to condense milk.)

Borden mapped and Lapham surveyed 128 acres, dividing the area into 62 blocks. A downtown was divided by named streets, the remainder held in reserve for future expansion. Borden was not stingy with the Allens' land. He mapped Texas Avenue as the chief thoroughfare, running east-west with a width of 100 feet. Other streets, including Main, were plotted 80 feet wide. Those widths would have seemed extravagant to the builders of other major Texas cities, but the Allens did not complain.

Indeed, they had other things on their minds. On October 2, 1836 the Congress of 14 senators and 29 representatives met in Columbia in their first session. Sam Houston was on hand. So were the Brothers Allen. With not so much as a privy standing on their land, and with Borden still busy at his drafting board, they sought to sell their town as the capital of Texas. Sam Houston offered no discouragement.

Like other promoters, past and future, the Allens were not quite truthful about the climate and other facilities, but they promised to build a statehouse at their expense and to provide housing for legislators at nominal costs. Augustus pointed out Houston's location at the head of tidewater and the accruing advantages for international commerce. General Houston enthusiastically agreed.

On the fourth ballot, the Congress selected Houston over 15 other aspirants as the capital city. "It was a grand *coup,* and it set a pattern never to be broken. Each passing decade had its moonshooters as Sam Houston's town rose out of the swamp to become the most dynamic city in the Western Hemisphere . . . ''

———————————————>◄ ►<———————————————

Main and Texas, where the Capitol was erected, was the most famous corner, the heartbeat of the town. When the Congress was in session, Main and Texas wasn't normal without a fight. Every man wore the national weapon, the Bowie knife, on one hip, a revolver on the other. But Dr. Ashbel Smith, Surgeon General of the Republic of Texas, during one recess, used his buggy whip on Senator S. H. Everett, who had the temerity to disagree with him. Dr. Smith said later that he had a knife and revolver he could have used on Senator Everett, but the buggy whip was handier. Senator Everett's post-whipping remarks were not recorded for posterity.

The Capitol had been built hastily. (When the two houses of Congress first met, the Capitol Building still lacked a roof, but President Houston opened the session wearing a velvet suit.) And in January 1837, Houston was designated the county seat. So the Allens began construction of a courthouse at Fannin and Congress on the northwest corner of Courthouse Square, and a long building on the north side of Congress, fronting Market Square between Milam and Travis. This latter section was divided into stores and stalls for business activity. An area on Texas Avenue between San Jacinto and Fannin was marked "School Reserve." It was sold as the site of Christ Episcopal Church, now Christ Church Cathedral.

By 1837, Houston was a town of 500 people, though many of the residents were still living in tents staked in the mud along Main Street which was the trail that ran to the bayou. Things looked so good that the *Telegraph and Texas Register* was moved from Columbia to Houston, and the first Houston issue was on the streets on May 2. Dr. Francis Moore, the editor, was a one-armed New Yorker who had been a surgeon in Houston's army. He was famed as a duelist, but later he would condemn the popular practice and press for its abolition.

The city was incorporated on June 5, 1837. Colonel Andrew Briscoe, a signer of the Texas Declaration of Independence and the county's first judge, ordered a city election for mayor, eight aldermen, tax collector, secretary-treasurer and constable. Touted to win the mayor's race was Francis R. Lubbock. He and his beautiful Creole bride were early settlers from New Orleans. He operated a thriving general store on Main Street, and sold the first barrel of flour in town for $30.

Lubbock was opposed by James S. Holman and Thomas William Ward. Ward was typical of the men of this time—at the center of the action. He had lost his right leg at the battle at Bexar, but that didn't stop him from organizing a company which he led at San Jacinto. He was a builder, and had erected the Capitol Building for the Allens. When the city celebrated the first anniversary of Texas independence, Ward fired off a cannon and, in his excitement, blew off his right arm!

Nevertheless, the colorless Holman, a town lot salesman, won the race. He got 12 votes, Lubbock 11, Ward 10. Holman apparently was not an impressive chief executive. Five months later, at a new election, Dr. Moore, the newspaper editor, was elected mayor.

———————————⊃⊷ ⊶⊂———————————

Buffalo Bayou was the main artery for the settlers and goods coming to the new town. The boats, often little more than rafts with cabins, brought in machinery, clothes, seeds, medicines, furnishings, U.S. newspapers and the inevitable barrels of whiskey. They took back to the States cotton, hides, sugar, and timber.

The little steam packet, *Laura,* navigated Buffalo Bayou up as far as Houston. In 1837, General Sam Houston wrote to a friend that the steamboat *Yellowstone,* 120 feet long, had arrived with a cargo of goods and 140 passengers. At that time it was quite a problem to navigate one of those river boats up the narrow channel with overhanging trees to the site of the present city of Houston.

New arrivals on their trip up Buffalo Bayou marveled at such magnolias, eighty feet high with a girth like huge forest trees. There were laurel, bay, and firs, rhododendrons, asters and arbutus. The trees and shrubs grew to prodigious heights and often met over the steamer.

Many women landed in a state of semi-shock, not only from the groundings coming up the narrow twisting Bayou but fearful of what their husbands—drinking and gambling in the cabin below—had lost. What cherished possession? How much of their land grant? One woman watched her beloved piano slide into the bayou after a grounding.

The first sight of Houston was not encouraging. Main Street's deep mud, the pools of water breeding future yellow fever epidemics, the scattered tents, the crude cabins of split pine boards and dirt floors, the astonishing number of saloons, were not inspiring to a woman with six children.

The foot of Main at Texas became an extremely active transfer point where mule and ox teams met the incoming vessels to exchange cargos and passengers.

Stagecoaches and wagons brought families overland with provisions and furnishings. The slaves walked, driving a mule or a cow; the head of the family rode a good horse. The whole procession often bogged down for days in the muddy sea of the prairie. But they kept on coming, from New England, Virginia, the Carolinas, Georgia, Tennessee, Kentucky, England, France, and Germany.

———————————————

Buffalo Bayou also was the social artery of early Houston. Children swam in its fresh waters where their fathers fished. Later, pleasure launches carried families to enjoy the wild jungle of the bayou's banks. A doe and her fawn, a big antlered buck, herons and cranes stood in the shade of towering pines, oaks, magnolias, sycamores and grapevines big enough to swing a man.

Early Houstonians were able to take advantage of their environment. Cat-tails, growing in the shallows, were pounded between stones, then mixed with water to provide flour rich in protein. The heavy Spanish moss, festooning the bayou oaks, was the raw material for mattress stuffing. The town's mattress maker would bury the moss in the earth near his shop. After a period of time the moss was dug up. The grey loops of the moss were gone. What remained were fine black hairs for his mattresses.

The dagger-like point of the Yucca plant was a life saver against the bite of the water moccasin. The Indians had taught that a jab into a snake bite would make the blood flow freely. But some believed it was the poison of this Spanish dagger that counteracted the snake's venom.

While Buffalo Bayou was the main artery of early Houston, Main Street was the heart. Large, heavily loaded oxwagon trains rumbling in from the prairies; a stage coach full of visitors clattering to a halt at the City Hotel; traps and buggies of families trotting down to the end of Main to watch a boat come in. The boys of the town were likely to stage a horse race, scattering dogs, people and mud as a dignified judge in his broad brimmed, black hat and a nervous drunk swung hurriedly through a saloon door.

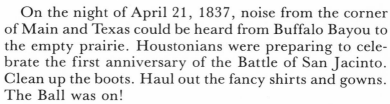

On the night of April 21, 1837, noise from the corner of Main and Texas could be heard from Buffalo Bayou to the empty prairie. Houstonians were preparing to celebrate the first anniversary of the Battle of San Jacinto. Clean up the boots. Haul out the fancy shirts and gowns. The Ball was on!

Every woman in town had spent weeks gussying up the only ballgown she had brought from the States. Buggies and traps full of young women from the plantations on Oyster Creek and the San Bernard River, came rattling into town. Mary Jane Harris, the "Belle of Buffalo Bayou," came by boat from Harrisburg, bringing her maid. Many found the Bayou easier travel than riding through the deep woods and heavy underbrush to Houston.

Captain Mosely Baker, one of San Jacinto's heroes, lived with his wife and child in a clapboard house with one big room. Carpet draperies divided it into a bedroom, parlor and dining room. Baker and Sam Houston were bitter, political adversaries. But on this night of the Ball, Captain Baker invited the President of the Republic along with other friends to his home beforehand.

Houston then diplomatically invited Mrs. Baker to lead the first cotillion with him. Clad in a handsome ballgown of satin with black lace overdress, she gracefully accepted. Houston was equally splendid in ruffled shirt, scarlet cassimere waistcoat and suit of black velvet, corded with gold.

Ladies, resplendent in their white mull and vari-colored satins, were staring disapprovingly at one young woman. She had stepped down from her trap and had gone up to her knees in mud. Furious with the whole town, she had returned home to put on what ordinarily no virgin would wear in public, a defiant black!

The Ball swung out in an unfurnished, roofless, frame building, originally built for a store. All ages had helped to build a temporary roof of oak, yaupon and magnolia limbs. They had tied wax candles to barrel hoops and hung them, lighted, to the rafters. On this night, everybody stepped out high and swung wide to "Oh Resin the Bow!" At midnight, they went to Ben Fort Smith's City Hotel, to dine on turkey, ducks, rabbit, flounder, candied yams and champagne.

Over on Market Square, the San Jacinto veterans couldn't care less about satin and ruffled shirts. They were celebrating to the explosion of guns and dancing around a big bonfire while oxen pawed at the mud, bellowing and jangling their bells. The Vets filled the night with raucous singing of "Will you Come to the Bower?"

Houston town was on its way!

New Englander Mary Austin Holley, visiting Houston in 1837, wrote in her famous *Diary* that Main Street ". . . extends from the landing into the prairie . . . two large hotels, two stories, painted white, one block of eleven stores, rent $500 each, some two-story dwelling houses . . . streets designated by stakes."

Ben Fort Smith's City Hotel was constructed of hand-hewn logs. It consisted of one big room with a bar and gaming tables, a long shed with a dirt floor. The shed was dining room by day, sleeping room by night. Beds were blankets over moss mattresses, $1.50–$2.00 per day. The hotel was short on water closets and running water, but long on gambling rooms and bars. It was Sam Houston's favorite hostelry. When it collapsed from its pleasurable sins in 1855, every man in town mourned.

Ben Fort Smith's mother, Obedience Smith, followed her immigrant son to Houston with children, grandchildren and slaves. This first Houston real estate lady tycoon bought up land around the burgeoning village like this century's R. E. (Bob) Smith (unrelated). Many deeds of Houston property are traced back to her ownership, from Old Indian Trail and the San Felipe Stage Route to include all of what is now West University Place and River Oaks.

———————————————————

In May, 1837, the first session of the Second Congress of the Republic of Texas was held in the Capitol at Main and Texas. The building was 70 feet wide, 140 feet deep, and painted peach blossom!

Sober voices of lawmakers held steady against shouts of drunk San Jacinto veterans. The cultivated Virginian talked to the escapee from U.S. law, the Methodist minister to the gambler, the U.S. botanist to the illiterate wagon wheelwright, the Baptist to the saloon keeper. Outside, the women, in the best bonnets and dresses they had brought from the States, averted their eyes from a noisy group of prostitutes.

Lawyer William Fairfax Gray, of Virginia, a member of the first session, swung through the doors of the building. Gray had brought his wife, Mollie, his flute, and his 250 volume library to the new village. On the east side of Travis, between Preston and Prairie, he set up a law office which today has become Baker Botts (*From Virginia to Texas,* William Fairfax Gray.)

Both Grays kept diaries. Mollie wrote that she was depressed leaving the cultured refinements of their Virginia home. But she was quite surprised at the new town, a "precocious city," and that her husband's flute, interest in law, religion and philosophy were stimulated.

But Gray, the intellectual and philosopher, was still a man of his own time. He wrote of the slave smuggler,

Monroe Edwards: "He . . . imported the Guinea negroes from Cuba about a month ago. About fifty of those
poor wretches are now living out of doors like cattle.
They are all young, the oldest not twenty-five, the
youngest perhaps not more than ten; boys and girls huddled together. They are diminutive, feeble, spare,
squalid, nasty and beastly in their habits."

Slavery had been outlawed in Texas by Spain, then by
Mexico. But neither had interfered with immigrants
bringing in their slaves as servants indentured for 99
years.

As the aristocrat Gray swung through the doors of the
new Capitol, he left behind, for the moment, the smell of
mud, horse dung, tar dripping from ox-wagon wheels,
stagnant ditch water and the rollicking peal of a Calliope
at the foot of Main. An Irish captain preferred it to whistle blowing. Immigrants from France, Germany,
Czechoslovakia, Holland, England, the United States,
wandered along Main, hopeful, bewildered as to tomorrow. But they spoke with one tongue:

"Long live the Republic of Texas!"

———————————————

When the session of the Second Congress ended, President Houston rode his horse slowly down Main Street,
to his cabin near the steamboat landing . . . "a double-
pen log house with a windway through the center . . .
the dirt floor cabin with blankets over the windows is so
crude that . . . when wearied past endurance, he goes
out and sits down on the prairie in back of the cabin
which makes his palace." (*Texas Diary,* Mary Austin Holley)

Some looked on him as primitive in his personal habits. Yet, when famed naturalist John J. Audubon called
on him in his cabin on Main, he found him, " . . .
dressed in a fancy velvet coat and trousers trimmed with

gold lace; around his neck was tied a cravat somewhat in the style of '76.''

———————————————————⟩⊣ ⊢⟨———————————————————

The best-known, most-talked-about woman in town was the owner of the Mansion House Hotel, Pamela Mann. She could drive oxen, fork a bronco, use a Bowie knife or derringer as expertly, so it was said, as she could make love. Pamela and her "girls" at the Mansion House provided spirited companionship for the town's robust males. But the hotel's other guests obviously enjoyed their stays there because more routine business was brisk. And Pamela, in the rough, frontier atmosphere of the town, found few doors in any social strata closed to her despite police charges of counterfeiting, immorality, larceny and assault to murder. She went where she pleased and generally was well received.

It will be recalled that General Houston and his army rested for a fortnight at Jared Groce's plantation while being pursued by General Santa Anna and his Mexican regulars. The plantation was crowded with refugees who had fled ahead of the Mexicans. Pamela was among them, and it was at Groce's that she first met Sam Houston.

Pamela, her husband Marshall and two sons, Sam Allen and Flournoy, had come to Texas from Louisiana in 1824. They had settled on a farm in the Robertson Colony. When war came, they were in the path of the Mexican advance. With other colonists, they headed north for Nacogdoches, but paused at Groce's plantation.

General Houston needed a pair of oxen to use in pulling the "Twin Sisters," a pair of cannons. Pamela offered hers—with the understanding that the Texas army was marching to Nacogdoches.

But once across the Brazos River, General Houston headed in the direction of Harrisburg. Pamela forked her bronco and raced in pursuit. Exactly what she said to the startled soldiers once she caught up with them is subject to debate, but it was sufficient to convince them to meekly relinquish the oxen. General Houston had to find some other way to move the "Twin Sisters."

After the war, the Mann family moved to Houston. On the northwest corner of Congress and Milam, Pamela established the Mansion House. For all of her escapades, Pamela maintained friends in the power structure. When Flournoy Mann was married in 1838, Sam Houston and Dr. Ashbel Smith were among his attendants.

And when Pamela was finally convicted of something—forgery—Houston's successor, President Mirabeau B. Lamar, granted her executive clemency. She died in 1840, leaving the Mansion House, slaves and considerable property to her progeny. And to the wild buckos of the town, she left some pleasant memories.

———————————————◆◀ ▶◆———————————————

Few, if any, Houstonians have heard of Frost Town. Yet the pretty little German settlement on Buffalo Bayou, on the northeast, was the home of some early settlers before Houston was incorporated.

On April 13, 1837, Jonathan B. Frost bought 15 acres of land from Augustus and John Allen. Samuel M. Frost, the next owner, divided the land into lots, selling them to 20 or more families.

In 1847, the Deed Records of Harris County described the settlement as "Frost Town, a suburb of Houston." Its main streets were Ark, Spruce, Race, Bremble. Frost Town cemetery covered two blocks bordering Buffalo Bayou. Nearby were the homes of these early Germans, the grocer, barrel maker and Klopper's barn, where, every Saturday night, they danced to German music.

Each small gabled house had its carefully tended flower and vegetable garden. Frost Town jealously guarded its German customs and simple family life. After school, the boys walked through the narrow, wood-planked streets, selling milk from the family cow. No young person went anywhere at night without his parents.

On the day Michael Floeck's new brewery was finished, the owner invited everybody for free beer. Just before dawn, a reveler kicked over one of the lanterns and Floeck's brand new brewery burned to the ground.

"Chivaree" is a word foreign to Houston today. In Frost Town, no one could get married and escape one. Celebrants would gather in front of the bride's house, jangling cow bells, exploding firecrackers, and building a big bonfire. The groom, finally smoked out of the house, had to pay off with free beer at Floeck's Brewery.

One bridegroom made the mistake of following his bride's advice not to give in to the celebrants. At this news, a cannon was dragged in front of the bride's house. Loading it with sawdust, the celebrants kept up a continuous blasting. The bride, in wild tears, called her new husband a coward. The bewildered groom decided to rush out and announce free beer for everybody!

The many yellow fever epidemics took their terrible toll of the little settlement. The most famous horror tale of the times was of the little girl with long golden hair whose body lay rotting in the street, slowly being devoured by rats. Nobody would run the risk of contamination to bury her. Finally, one compassionate man whom history regretfully left nameless, could stand the sight no longer. He leaned down, gently took her in his arms and carried her away to bury her.

Many prominent Houstonians began their Texas lives in Frost Town. John T. Browne, later Mayor of Houston, lived there in 1871. He owned a rent house he leased for $10 a month. One of his renters was J. J.

Sweeney who paid his rent in sweet potatoes. Sweeney was to become a leading jeweler and his descendants prominent citizens of Houston.

In 1954, bulldozers, preparing for the East-Tex Freeway, were demolishing the gable-roofed cottages, ripping up Frost Town's streets with their original signs, Spruce, Bremble, Gable. A square-headed, handmade nail lay apart from the rubble, all that was left of a simple, unique way of life in Houston. (Author's column, *The Houston Post*. Reprinted with permission.)

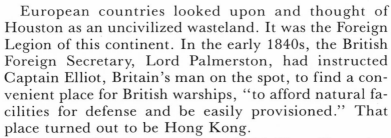

European countries looked upon and thought of Houston as an uncivilized wasteland. It was the Foreign Legion of this continent. In the early 1840s, the British Foreign Secretary, Lord Palmerston, had instructed Captain Elliot, Britain's man on the spot, to find a convenient place for British warships, "to afford natural facilities for defense and be easily provisioned." That place turned out to be Hong Kong.

Captain Elliot was so impressed with Hong Kong that he included its acquisition as part of the peace agreement between China and the United Kingdom following the opium wars. Apparently, Queen Victoria was not amused at being handed, "a barren island with barely a house on it." She quickly recalled the far-sighted Captain Elliott and history records that he was effectively banished to Houston, Texas. (Private communication, Clayton A. Umbach, Jr.)

All British subjects assigned to work in Houston have received a hardship allowance, the same as allowed for enduring the climate in Calcutta. This "hardship allowance" was lifted in the late 1960s.

CHAPTER TWO

*"By the end of 1837, Houston
had 1200 residents, a theatre, 50 gambling houses, nearly 100
saloons, and no house of worship."*

THE ROAR and rumble
of the wagons rang out
from the prairie to the landing at the foot of Main Street.
Cracking his long whip over the head of each of his oxen,
shouting at each by name, the wagoneer drove into town
loaded with timber, flour, meal, honey, hides, chickens,
eggs, cotton. He left, loaded with sugar, salt, coffee, cotton cloths, beef.

"The wagoneer's home is his wagon . . . his oxen feed
on the grass, he eats and sleeps at home. Time is no object. He penetrates the most remote parts of the Republic. For a consideration, he can get his wagon loaded; if
not, he loads himself. He is free as air and cares for nobody. These men form a class of themselves, but with
their useful branch of industry are destined to fade away
(like the old bargemen of the Mississippi) when the snort
of the iron horse shall awaken the solitude of the prai-

ries." (*Texas and Her Resources and Her Men* by Jacob de Cordova)

According to the late Dr. Andrew Forest Muir, Rice University history professor and writer, professional men—attorneys, physicians, clerks in Holy Orders and ministers—were numerous in Houston but in general (with only notable exceptions) were men of mediocre talents.

One of the notable exceptions was Dr. Ashbel Smith, newly appointed by President Houston to be Surgeon General of the Republic. This Renaissance man, a dapper little figure in his stovepipe hat and Prince Albert Coat, a Phi Beta Kappa key dangling from a heavy gold watch chain, eyes glinting above a scanty beard, was a familiar sight on Main Street.

He lived on his 2,000-acre homestead, "Evergreen," on Galveston Bay, about 25 miles from Houston. The recurring yellow fever epidemics kept a servant busy rowing him up the bayou to Houston. If they landed before dawn, he simply wrapped up in his blanket and slept under a tree until time to make his call. Dr. Smith suspected that the mosquito was the chief cause of the dreaded yellow fever epidemics that took so many lives, but he could never gather enough scientific proof. He also knew that Houston's climate was a contributing factor and he relentlessly sought the cooperation of the people who lived in Houston as well as support from the State.

What prompted this native of Hartford, Connecticut, a Latin and Greek scholar, Yale graduate in medicine with three years of post graduate work in Great Britain and on the continent, to forsake his civilized world for the uncertainty and unknown of Texas?

Smith was small and frail, but as audacious against an enemy or the unknown as David against Goliath. He was as quick to taste the "black vomit" of yellow fever to see if it was contagious as he was to accept a challenge to fight a duel with Bowie knives. One day, every inch of his 115 pounds was geared for a duel when Sam Houston galloped up and thundered, "Halt!" Whereupon, both parties halted.

As Captain during the Civil War, Ashbel Smith placed a cannon on the bridge over Galveston Bay and defied his mutinous company to cross. He reported later, "It stopped the Mutiny and every Mother's son went back to the barracks!"

Smith was an incomparable braggart about any animal he owned. He had a common, half-grown hog whose virtues he bragged about to his friend Sam Houston. Fed up with Smith's bragging, Houston invited him for breakfast one morning. Smith eloquently thanked him for the most delicious pork he had ever tasted. With a twinkle in his eye, Houston said he was glad to hear it because the pig was Smith's own!

Smith often bragged about a horse he owned named Glencoe. One day Cornelius Vanderbilt and his wife docked at Smith's landing on Galveston Bay. During their visit, Mrs. Vanderbilt asked to see Smith's famous horse. Mrs. Anson Jones took her out to the pasture and pointed to a sorry nag. "There he is, 'Bag of Bones!'"

However, Dr. Ashbel Smith acquired titles bigger than his body, less than his intellect: "Minister Plenipotentiary to England and Envoy Extraordinary from the Republic of Texas to the Court of St. James and St. Cloud France" and was the last Secretary of State under the last President of the Republic of Texas, Anson Jones. Dr. Smith was president of the Board of Examiners at West Point and was the first Superintendent of Schools of Harris County in 1874. He negotiated the first treaty with the bloody Comanches who rarely left Austin and San Antonio in peace. That this most savage of all Texas tribes honored no treaties didn't take away from the success of the moment.

On April 11, 1861, Smith also opened a medical
school in Houston where he planned to teach as Professor of Surgery. But the next day, the cannons at Fort
Sumter were heard loud and clear all the way to Texas.
He signed up to go to war. In his later years, he used his
rich intellect to collaborate on a revision of the King
James version of the Holy Bible, which was published in
1885. On his death at "Evergreen" on January 21,
1886, he left to the University of Texas, which he had
helped to establish and had served as the first Regent,
his library of 4,000 volumes. (*A Biographical Sketch of Dr.
Ashbel Smith,* Dr. S. C. Red.)

By the end of 1837 the city boasted an estimated 1,200
residents. There were 30 saloons and gambling halls.
The *Nation,* a U.S. publication, went farther, saying that
Houston had "a theatre, 50 gambling houses, nearly 100
grog shops, and no house of worship!"

The *Telegraph and Texas Register,* incensed by what it
considered a slur, ran an editorial asking Houstonians to
give a rousing welcome to a newly-arrived representative
of a Bible Society ". . . in order to destroy those un-
founded prejudices which exist in the minds of many
persons in the States and elsewhere as to our moral character!"

But the ministers who visited the city in 1837 agreed
wholeheartedly with the *Nation's* implied criticism. One,
Reverend Littleton Fowler, confided to his journal:
"Here I find much vice, gaming, drunkenness, and profanity the commonest." Nevertheless, he took an "eye
opening" voyage to Galveston and back with President
Houston, members of his cabinet, and others. He told
his Journal: "Saw great men in high life. If what I saw
and heard were a fair representation, may God keep me
from such scenes in the future! On our return on Sunday

afternoon, about one-half on board got mildly drunk and stripped themselves to their linen and pantaloons. Their Bacchanalian revels and blood-curdling profanity made the pleasure boat a floating hell. . . ."

Fowler was just one of the itinerant preachers who came and went, conducting services under a great oak on Market Square and occasionally in the Capitol Building. Fowler even served briefly as the chaplain of the Senate.

The *Nation* and the preachers were correct in saying that Houston had many saloons and no churches, but this did not necessarily mean that it was a bad town. Many a good man in this frontier settlement went to a saloon as much for conversation and comradeship as for imbibing. A large number of them were single, and others had not yet fetched their families from their points of origin. A saloon then, was a place to read one's mail, to read a newspaper, to catch up on the gossip as well as heft a glass.

There *was* a dearth of churches, and apparently there was no strong inclination to erect any. The various denominations gathered at one place or another and appeared to be satisfied with such arrangements. The Allens sold a half block on the north side of Texas between Travis and Milam to the Methodists in 1837, but a church was not erected until 1843. Charles Shearn, a merchant from England, almost single-handedly pushed that church to reality.

The Episcopalians organized in 1839, when Reverend R. M. Chapman came to Houston as a missionary of the Church. He and 39 Houston men led by William Fairfax Gray united to form this small congregation. Charles Gillett, parish priest in the early 1840s, called on one of his communicants, a man with two orphans he and his wife were raising in a one-room house. He hadn't as yet been able to afford a good floor but he told Gillett that he would give two of his cows to the new church. God's house was his house, too.

Christ Church, a small brick building with tinted windows and a belfry wasn't to rise on Texas and Fannin until 1845. William Fairfax Gray did not live to see it. In the early days, most of the parishioners lived nearby. In 1893, the present Christ Church Cathedral was built on the site of the first little church. The ivy to cover it was brought from the vines of Westminster Abbey in London.

The cornerstone of the first Jewish Synagogue was laid on Franklin Street in 1870. The first Baptist Church was on the corner of Texas and Fannin.

Roman Catholic missionaries came early to Houston. Father Joseph Querat from Lyons, France, a Texas missionary from 1852 to 1878, purchased a quarter of a block on Franklin and Caroline. He built a small wooden church there in the 1860s. The property was sold and the block on Texas and Crawford bought. Here, the beautiful Annunciation Church was begun in 1867. It was designed by the famous Galveston architect, Nicholas Clayton.

The bricks for its foundation came from the purchase of the old Harris County Court House. It was completed in 1874, the sacristy and steeple added in 1881–84. The doors of this most imposing structure of Houston's past open on an interior similar to an 18th century European Cathedral.

Directly across Texas Avenue the old Union Station still stands, a beached whale of dignified stone, its vaulted ceilings empty of the trains' thrilling echoes. Here, Houstonians came daily just to see who was arriving. From here, boys and girls departed for boarding school for the first time, standing on the rear platform of the train as it pulled out, waving goodbye to their families with that awful plunge of heart that comes from leaving all that is loved and familiar, the forms ever receding as the train wheels ground faster down the track away from the Union Station until the sight of it was gone altogether.

Equally emotional was coming home at Christmas, when the shout went up in every car, "We're backing in!" The train always backed in to Union Station. A great deal of warm, human exchange, unknown to the Houston Intercontinental Airport today, was lost when Union Station closed. The only travelers around Texas and Crawford now are the drunken, hopeless vagrants on the sidewalks, waiting to go nowhere.

The dock at the foot of Main Street also was a meeting place for early Houstonians, saying goodbye or welcoming new arrivals. The unexpected was always expected. Such as the day the English naturalist, William P. Smith, tried to load his collection of antelope, panther, fox, coyote, crows, wild hogs, prairie hens and 1,400 Texas plants on board the steamboat *Mustang*. The Earl of Derby had sent Smith to Texas to bring back to England a collection of wildlife.

The corner of Main and Texas was specially volatile on December 10, 1838. Mirabeau B. Lamar was about to be inaugurated as second President of the Republic of Texas; David G. Burnet, the "pious politician," vice president.

Lamar sat in the gallery of the Capitol holding his carefully prepared speech tight in his hands. He was a poet, a literary man. He could write a good speech. But outgoing President Sam Houston was getting all of the attention! The men had long been political enemies. The rumor that Lamar intended to move the Capital of the Republic to Austin had outraged Houston.

Inauguration day which should have belonged to Lamar was stolen by Houston. "Old Sam all diked out in knee britches and a powdered wig, elocuted, waving the sword he carried at the battle of San Jacinto." (*The Day Old Sam Stole Lamar's Thunder,* R. Henderson Shuffler) At the end, Lamar was too upset to make his speech. He handed it to a clerk to read.

Those in the wildly assorted crowd couldn't help but notice a handsome general in San Jacinto battle dress. He was General Sidney Sherman, native of Marlboro, Massachusetts, hero of the Battle of San Jacinto, and originator of the famous Texan yell, "Remember the Alamo!"

This dashing general was to influence every facet of Houston's growth as organizer and first President of the first railroad in Texas—the Buffalo Bayou, Brazos and Colorado. He would be one of the developers of the Houston Ship Channel. Later his commanding portrait hung on the living room wall of his granddaughter, the late Mrs. William Sperry Hunt of Houston. She recalled that Sherman tied the long, white glove of his future bride, Catherine Isabel Cox, to the staff of the only flag carried in the Battle of San Jacinto. There it waved above the 52 volunteers he had equipped. The flag had been made by ladies of Newport, Kentucky, and Cincinnati, Ohio, and was of white silk with a scarlet-robed goddess inscribed, "Liberty or Death!" Played with for years by Sherman's young descendants, it now hangs nobly frayed in the Capitol at Austin.

At Lamar's inaugural, this day, was a young baker from Shropshire, England, Thomas William House. Who could foretell that his descendant, Edward House, would become advisor to Presidents Woodrow Wilson and Franklin Roosevelt? House and another Englishman, Charles Shearn (the Methodist), had a general store on Main. On one side was fresh baked bread and cakes; on the other, whiskey, hides, guns, axes, blacksmith supplies. Shearn had escaped execution at the massacre of Goliad only because he was a British subject.

And here came Dr. C. B. Stewart galloping his old horse down Main, reining him to a halt in front of the Capitol. The horse had carried Stewart through the wilderness for six weeks to get to Texas in time for the battle of San Jacinto. Stewart was a member of Sam Houston's first cabinet. He received land grants until he eventually owned 186,000 acres. His great, great granddaughter, Laura Beth Moody Knight, now lives in Houston.

The spirit of Lorenzo de Zavala, the earth not yet hardened over his grave, probably hovered in the thoughts of many on this inaugural day. Colonel William Fairfax Gray, in his *Diary,* called de Zavala the most interesting man in Texas. This native of Yucatan had been Governor of his Mexican state for five years. In 1829, he received an Impresario contract to bring 500 families into Texas. In 1832, he was again Governor of Yucatan. In 1833, President Santa Anna appointed him Minister to France. But he and Stephen F. Austin, another loyal Mexican subject, grew to have much in common. They realized that President Santa Anna would never honor the Constitution of 1824, nor concede that the Texas Colonists had any rights.

Unafraid to change his loyalties when convinced they were wrong, Lorenzo left Mexico and brought his family to the wilds of Texas to live. He signed the Declaration of Independence at the Convention of 1836 at Washington-on-the-Brazos, then was elected Vice President of the Republic of Texas.

He built a home at the junction of Buffalo Bayou and the old San Jacinto River. The house consisted of one large room, three small "bed closets," a kitchen and a porch. Mrs. de Zavala, a tall, beautiful 27-year-old New Yorker, his second wife, bore him three children. De

Zavala's son by his first wife, a native of Yucatan, was back from serving in the Texas Army (having taken along his French valet).

Lorenzo de Zavala, after giving the best of himself to two Republics, died on November 15, 1836.

James Morgan was another face in the crowd on Lamar's Inauguration day. Morgan, a native of Philadelphia, came to Anahuac, Texas in 1830 and set up a mercantile business. He brought with him 16 slaves. To get around the Mexican law against slavery, he bound them as indentured servants for 99 years. In 1835, de Zavala appointed Morgan as an agent for himself and several New York financiers, among them Samuel Swarthout, a friend of Sam Houston, to buy up Texas real estate. The group also planned to set up a colony of free Negroes in Texas. It is ironical that slave owner Morgan was selected to organize it.

Another Morgan, Charles, was owner of the Morgan Lines, the first steamship line in Texas. He would be called "Father of the Houston Ship Channel." His steamships, the *Constitution, New York,* and *Neptune,* ran between New Orleans and Galveston.

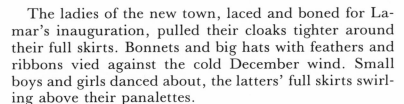

The ladies of the new town, laced and boned for Lamar's inauguration, pulled their cloaks tighter around their full skirts. Bonnets and big hats with feathers and ribbons vied against the cold December wind. Small boys and girls danced about, the latters' full skirts swirling above their panalettes.

As usual on grand occasions, Pamela Mann was drawing most of the male attention. She was a handsome, well-dressed woman and, when on public display, conducted herself as imperiously as any dowager. She kept her "girls" safely stowed away in the Mansion House.

It was no wild rumor floating about the windy corner that the capital of the Republic would be moving to Austin. The following year would see it occur. "It requires no other argument . . . than barely to look at this wretched mud hole . . . this graveyard, the city of Houston. It would be better to legislate or live in tents or the open air in a high, healthy section of country than to inhale the poisonous atmosphere, drink the bad water, and be subjected to the privations and want of comfort incident to life in Houston. . . ." (*To Wear a City's Crown* by Kenneth W. Wheeler)

The town *did* have a barber shop, the first in the state. The owner, T. C. Leconte, called it "Barber Shop Extraordinary." He advertised thusly: "It is the greatest gratitude that I make myself a pleasure to thank the people of Houston of the encouragement that I have received of them during my stay in Houston. I can assure them that no pains shall be spared to render my dressing room as comfortable as possible. *Being the First Barber in Houston and this Republic* I am sure the good people will not pass by one of their fellow citizens and a good soldier. My price is 25¢ for shaving, 75¢ for hair cutting and no charge if the person is not well pleased." (*Morning Star,* May 10, 1839) Monsieur Leconte resided at No. 2 Anderson Building on Main Street by the City Hotel.

The move of the capital represented a major blow to Houston's prestige, but a yellow fever outbreak shortly thereafter almost made the city a ghost town. Houston newspapers first denied the existence of the pestilence and boasted of the town's fine health. But eventually they had to admit the grim truth—1,000 cases of fever, 200 dead, out of a population of 2,000.

Colonel William Fairfax Gray grew weary with reading burial services of all denominations; he did not exclude the atheists from his pleas to heaven.

It would not be the last yellow fever epidemic to ravage Houston. "Everybody believed in water and garbage sanitation, in the abstract. But don't tell a man what to do with his own back yard privy, stable, personal garbage!" (*The Houston Review,* Vol. 2, No. 3)

But the city had achieved a momentum not even such a disaster could slow. Main Street had a row of 10 shops—small, one-story frame buildings (reproduced in Sam Houston Park by the Harris County Heritage Society). There was H. F. Byrne at No. 1 Long Row with his Stationery and Fancy Store, the Circulating Library that carried everything from seven volumes of the *London Quarterly Review* to half kegs of nutmeg. D. Gray at No. 6 Long Row boasted a "New York Piano Forte of superior tone." One merchant advertised "thousands of papers of garden seeds," along with clothing, crockery and glassware.

Tom Dunn's Hardware & Cutlery Shop was also on Main. His descendants live in Houston today. Among them are civic leaders Dorothy Dunn Davis; Marjorie Dunn Jacobe; Orline Dunn Maer; Virginia Dunn Whitley, Dewitt C. Dunn Jr., Tom C. Dunn; and Steve and Dow Dunn, sons of the late John S. Dunn who generously contributed one floor as well as the Freeman Dunn Sanctuary to M.D. Anderson Hospital, and the Dunn Heliport to Hermann Hospital.

Despite mud and depression, Hungarian George Fisher, a commission merchant, was living in fine style on Main near the corner of Preston " . . . with hundreds of imposing possessions, among them a large gilt frame mirror valued at $300, pier table with marble top, 13 mahogany chairs hair bottomed, 2 large mahogany sofas hair bottomed, 2 testers, 4 dozen German silver forks and tablespoons, one green tin painted foot tub, many brass candlesticks, 14 feather pillows, 8 double hair mattresses, 2 moss bolsters, 1 double carriage harness, plated mountings for a span of horses complete." (*Furniture Used in Days of Republic of Texas,* Alice Kilman for Harris County Heritage Society)

Mary Austin Holley in her *Diary* reported that "Mr. Allen, the proprietor of the land on which the city is built . . . is of course wealthy . . . they are genteel people and live well. Have a good house and elegant furniture (mahogany hair sofas, red velvet rocking chairs . . .)."

On the other hand, there was carriage maker Joseph Gagne and his 15-year-old bride. He set up a home and carriage shop on Prairie and Fannin. "Their total equipment consisted of a great amount of determination, 1 wagon, 5 horses, 1 slave, 2 rawhide bottomed chairs, a handmade wardrobe and a few other household articles and clothing." (*Furniture Used in Days of Republic of Texas,* Alice Kilman for Harris County Heritage Society.)

Many a Houston woman bought her sack of sweet potatoes at one particular store because the owner handed out a recipe for Sweet Potato Pone with each sack. He didn't insult her with measurements. Just told her to use a "right smart" of yams, brown sugar, unsulphured molasses, hunk of butter, couple of eggs, pinch of soda, salt, cinnamon; put it altogether and bake slowly for nearly 35 minutes.

The *Morning Star* was advertising an amazing invention with this ad: "In shape, a refrigerator is a large square chest. The inside is lined with zinc. With $3 worth of ice per year, a family may have all things cool and delicious." (Harris County Heritage Society.) An ad for whiskey at $2 per barrel made housewives furious when they were paying $6 for a pair of chickens, $1 for a pound of butter and $3 for a dozen fresh yard eggs!

Scholibo's Bakery at 202 Franklin Street, would remain the favorite shop for fresh bread, its one great oven faithfully glowing until 1954. Scholibo commissioned the blacksmiths, Stewart & Stevenson, around the corner, to build him a fine little white wagon and letter the sides in fancy gold script, "Scholibo's Bakery." Pulled by his gray mare, her harness jingling sleighbells, he announced his coming from afar in plenty of time for housewives to have their coins ready.

Scholibo's bread was bread that only the Europeans knew about, the kind you bite into with good strong teeth, bread that nourishes the spirit as well as the body.

On Scholibo's death, John and William Oberholz, whose father had been an apprentice to the old German, took over the little bakery. Refusing to give in to Houston's megalomania, they would not enlarge but kept the fire going in the same ancient oven, turning out the same fine bread.

Near the turn of the century, fine carriages were still rolling regularly out Franklin for their mistresses to enjoy buying breads and pastries in the quaint little shop. But the early 20th century grocery stores with their fast turnover of tasteless breads, were transforming Houston. The last customers of the old bakery were the employees of nearby Kress & Co. and the inmates of the City Jail.

In 1954 when Scholibo's Bakery was to be demolished, I paid a farewell visit. Its fame had been long before my time, but the symbol of bread links us to all generations. The deep brick oven in the little room still held one or two small, fierce embers which refused to die. In the center of the room a cistern to catch rain water from an opening in the roof for the baker to mix with his dough had been closed over. The long-handled spatula to turn the loaves, polished fine from long use, stood forgotten in one corner. The thick, whitewashed walls that had absorbed aromas of fine breads for more than 100 years, would in moments crumble under the bulldozer, now roaring beyond the open door.

Meanwhile, T. W. House, the young baker from Shropshire, England, was advertising: "Attention Public . . . Fancy Bakery . . . Loveridge & House will be found at our Bakery on Main Street where we will keep constantly on hand . . . ornamental pound and sponge cakes; fancy sweet biscuits . . . confectionaries of all kinds, equal to any made in the United States . . . orders for Ball and Marriage suppers thankfully received and promptly dispatched."

House, a man of vision and imagination, would be one of Houston's most stalwart citizens. He was only 23 when he established his bakery. A year later he formed a partnership with Charles Shearn, later to become chief justice of Texas, and launched into the dry goods business. He married his partner's daughter, Mary Shearn, in 1840.

Shearn withdrew from the business shortly thereafter and House paid $40,000 cash for the James H. Stevens & Company, dealers in wholesale dry goods and groceries. It was the largest single cash transaction in early Texas history.

As a sideline, he already had entered the cotton business. In time, it became his chief interest, out of which a bank was to grow. He had started accepting bank deposits as an accommodation to his dealers and customers. In 1850, when the town's population stood at 2,396, House received a charter for the city's first commercial bank.

During the Civil War, House's ox teams moved regularly to and from the Rio Grande River, transporting cotton to Mexican ports for shipment to England, and coming back with desperately needed military and civilian supplies.

His skill and experience allowed him to guide his bank through the Civil War and the financial terrors of Reconstruction, aided by his cashier, Samuel M. McAshan who with his descendants would become prominent in Houston's future years. Samuel Maurice McAshan left the T. W. House Bank to become founder and first president of South Texas Commercial National Bank, located in the second block of Main Street. He was also to become one of the first six trustees of Rice Institute appointed by William Marsh Rice in 1893.

Mr. McAshan's son, James Everett McAshan assumed the presidency of his father's bank, which was later called Texas National Bank. One of his grandsons, named Samuel Maurice McAshan, married Susan Clayton, daughter of Will Clayton who would one day "be" the Marshall Plan. There are many descendants of this family living in Houston today. Harris McAshan had three daughters, Arlene, Martha and Anne McAshan Baker (Mrs. Robert Lee). In 1985 the seventh generation, little James Everett McAshan was born in Kerrville, son of Maurice and Karen McAshan.

House was one of the organizers of the Houston & Galveston Navigation Company in 1851. He served as Houston's mayor in 1862. After the Civil War, he created the Houston Gas Company, the city's first public utility, and he was involved in the laying of the first street railway. Admired and respected, he died in 1880.

———————————————————————————————

Transportation in and out of Houston was definitely a problem. In 1848, General Sam French wrote to his niece about earlier days: "I remember Houston, only a few houses on the bayou. One Sunday morning I wanted to fit out nine government wagons. I sent out a clever Texan and before sundown, he brot in 54 mules and 4 horses and had the teams all ready. We started, General Twiggs and I, in the stage for Austin, drove through a solid sheet of water 25 miles . . . it rained three days. Monday at 2 a.m. on the third day, the stage sank down and the body rested on the ground out on the prairie away on over the Brazos River near a place called Round Top (now a center of restoration)."

Mary Austin Holley found her fourth visit to Houston disappointing and dull since the capital of the Republic was in Austin. But the Municipal Market House, a long one-story frame building, was going up on Travis, and the city fathers were adding a second floor at City Hall. The town's first grist mill, owned by Elim Stockbridge, and worked by three oxen on a treadmill rose at the foot of Texas Avenue. John Kennedy also had a grist mill at Congress and Dry Gulley, a huge hole at the foot of San Jacinto and Caroline. Kennedy was a daily spectre, walking about streets covered from head to toe with cornmeal.

Even more important, N. T. Davis had built the first cotton compress in the town with a process that compressed a bale in 15 minutes. Before that, cotton was shipped in bales as they came from the gins, a space-consuming problem for both wagoneers and boatmen.

So the town refused to roll over and die, capital or no capital. Its ego had been bruised by the move of the seat of government to Austin, but not its spirit.

CHAPTER THREE

"On February 19, 1846, Anson Jones, the last President of the Republic of Texas, solemnly declared to an emotional crowd: 'The Republic of Texas is no more.' The Lone Star flag of the Republic of Texas slowly lowered. The flag of the United States of America rose. A deep silence fell."

A N UNEASY peace lay over Houston and the rest of Texas after the battle at San Jacinto. The treaty signed with Mexico didn't abolish the fear that the Mexicans would again ride against them in force.

That fear was well grounded.

In March, 1842 a Mexican army crossed the Rio Grande without fanfare and seized San Antonio, Victoria, Goliad and other towns. The Mexicans just as suddenly retired across the border before the Texans could muster military opposition.

Sam Houston, back as President after defeating David G. Burnet in the 1841 election, ordered the seat of government moved back to Houston from Austin. The Congress convened in June 1842, the Senate meeting in Odd

Fellows Hall and the House in the Presbyterian Church on Main opposite the Masonic Building.

In September 1842, the Mexicans once again surprised the Texans. Mexican General Adrian Woll and 1,500 regulars captured San Antonio. Once again the Mexicans left their prize and headed back for Mexico. Pursuing Texans defeated a small detachment of Woll's troops, but a company of Texans was surrounded by Woll's men. Of the 55 Texans, 33 were killed and the remainder executed or sent to die in captivity.

Houstonians gathered in the Presbyterian Church to hear Sam Houston address the House and Senate. Old Sam was in fine form and he made it clear he was in favor of invading Mexico. Inspired by the speech, the Houston Independent Light Guard quickly organized in Market Square, each man bringing his own firearm, hatchet and blanket.

A force under command of General Alexander Somervell marched to the Rio Grande to mount an invasion, but Sam Houston apparently had undergone a change of mind. The troops were ordered to turn back.

Houstonians gathered in Kessler's Arcade and other Market Square establishments to talk about Sam Houston's ambivalence. Many thought his fire had cooled because the U.S. government had frowned at invasion.

In any event, a group of 300 Texans under Colonel W. S. Fisher crossed the river into Mexico independently and attacked the garrison at Mier. Fighting was fierce, but the Texans were defeated and captured. They escaped as they were being marched deeper into Mexico, but were recaptured and every 10th man was executed. The others were marched to Mexico City and prison. Eventually 35 of them were released.

Meanwhile, Houston and Austin were caught in a tug-of-war over the site of the capital. Sam Houston finally ordered government archives moved to Washington-on-the-Brazos, and the seat of government was maintained there until 1844. It was moved back to Austin by President Anson Jones, who succeeded Houston.

―――――――――――――――

Among the men to return from the Mier Expedition was Charles S. Longcope. He had brought the first Japanese persimmon and the first dahlia to grow in Houston. He had been a Mississippi riverboat captain. He would emerge as one of Houston's leading commission merchants, founder of the Houston Cotton Exchange and a director of early railroads.

His home on Chenevert Street was one of Houston's most charming dwellings, with verandahs of exquisite wrought iron railings from New Orleans. It had belonged originally to Peter Paul Floeck who came from Millheim on Rhein Germany, in 1844.

Longcope stood on his front verandah at the end of the Civil War and read to his slaves the proclamation of their freedom. He gave each of them a building lot in the 4th Ward. But only three of his ex-slaves accepted his offer. The rest stayed with him until his death 16 years later.

―――――――――――――――

John K. Allen died of congestive fever August 15, 1838. He was only 29. His brother Augustus Allen, in 1843, packed his bags and departed the city he had founded, never to return. Charlotte Allen, though separated from her husband, became influential in Houston until her death in 1895. Her home was demolished in the early 1900s, and the Gulf Building now stands on its site.

Augustus died in the U.S. capital, of pneumonia on June 11, 1864. He lies buried in Greenwood Cemetery in Brooklyn, New York.

———————————◄ ►———————————

Matilda Charlotte Houstoun was among the visitors in the early days. An adventurous Englishwoman, she hit town just as Mexican General Adrian Woll crossed the Rio Grande to seize San Antonio. Despite the talk of war, Mrs. Houstoun captured the public's attention. She later would write of her experiences in a book titled *Texas and the Gulf Coast or Yachting in the New World*. She had arrived in Texas waters with her husband aboard their yacht, *Dolphin*. They took a small steamer, *Captain Kelsey*, up Buffalo Bayou to Houston.

Texas hospitality on board was an eye-opener to the English woman, "Do you liquor, Ma'am?" she was asked. She nodded, and was handed a tumbler of "eggnoggy." She raised her brows at the Texans' boast of having invented it. "I believe the British Navy claims the merit of its invention!" she exclaimed.

Her first glimpse of Houston thrilled Mrs. Houstoun. "There were beautiful shrubs growing close to the water's edge and down the steep acclivities had trickled rills of water. The land was high and interspersed with hill and valley on either bank."

To eat and sleep in the town was another matter. "There are plenty of Inns at Houston, such as they are. We took up our quarters at the Houston House, a large shambling wooden building. Our landlord had a great many bad debts. Only that morning, having asked a gentleman to pay his bill, the reply was, 'If you come to insult me again, sir, by damn I'll shoot you!' Breakfast consisted of tough beef steaks, each as large as a good sized dish, eggs hardly warmed through and emptied over the meat, and squirrels!"

For dinner, she dined on "pork dodgers and 'dough doings,' corn bread, chicken fixings and sausages." Dodger was southern slang for a corn cake. Corn cake with pork was called pork dodgers. Rosetta, a Black woman with rings on every finger, waited on the Houstoun's, ". . . and a hideous creature she was!"

But Mrs. Houstoun couldn't know about the variety of home cooking that was going on. At the Theodore Berings', who had newly arrived from Bering, Germany, she might have enjoyed some of their favorite hot buttered grits, small light biscuits, charlotte russe. The Eugene Pillots and their twelve children might have offered her some of their delicious Oyster soup.

Sam Houston's bride, Margaret Lea, whom he brought to Houston in 1840, would be cooking her favorite dish for him, fried green tomatoes.

Mrs. Zerviah Noble could have been found making her favorite "English Trifle, a wondrous custard of eggs, sugar, milk, one-half poured over thin slices of pound cake, spread with plum jelly, grated nutmeg, rest of custard, the whole covered with whipped cream, drops of wild plum jelly sprinkled with chopped pecans!" (*Harris County Heritage Society Cookbook.*)

The Houstouns not only left the town hungry, they didn't get any sleep. They were ". . . obliged to fix an umbrella over the bed while I (Mrs. Houstoun) watched the feet of a restless cat as she wandered over our heads, her paws finding their way through the holes in our sail cloth covering."

The next morning, undaunted by the expected Mexican invasion of Houston, she hired a wagon "drawn by two stout horses." Off they set "in spite of wind and weather," to visit the interior of Texas. On leaving Houston, she wrote, "We ascended a hill so steep as to seem almost impossible for a carriage, however slight, to be drawn up it."

When Mrs. Houstoun returned to England, she gave Houston a retaliatory slap. "Houston, proud as the Texans are of it as a City, does not bear close inspection; there is but one brick house in it, and I could not quite make out what its inhabitants meant when they talked of it as a great city!"

Mrs. Houstoun should have visited John D. Andrews' three-story Greek revival home at 410 Austin Street. Andrews was not a rough and ready immigrant but a cultivated Virginia gentleman who was said to have resembled Sir Walter Scott. He landed in Galveston in 1837 with his wife, Eugenia, and two small daughters by a previous marriage.

He brought along a fine library as well as white pine from Maine, cypress, solid walnut handrails, posts, bannisters and a marble mantel for the house he planned to build in Houston. The family traveled to Houston from Galveston by coach and oxwagon. Because their ship was so storm-tossed in the Gulf, Eugenia swore on a Bible that she would never again cross any body of water by boat or bridge!

Her great granddaughter, artist Eugenia Howard Hunt is a native Houstonian.

Andrews made a deal with another newcomer, Thomas M. League, who already owned some lots. He built a big two and one-half story house on League's land and gave the second story to the League family. The third half-story was used by both families as a recreation room and for Andrews' passion: collecting antiques.

League and Andrews became partners in a general mercantile trading and commission firm and also built an overnight inn for stage coach passengers. But in 1840 the partnership was dissolved and Andrews retained some lots and the big house as part of the settlement. The following year Andrews became Houston's fifth mayor.

Andrews' house was called the Castle because of its size and architecture. There was an orchard of peach, pear, plum, thick grapevines at the rear. Cape jasmine and a rose garden with brick walls scented the front yard. Sam Houston, Anson Jones, Dr. Ashbel Smith, and French Ambassador M. de Saligny came often to have a whiskey on the porch or around a fire with its fine marble mantel in the big living room.

Sam Houston had a cabin at the rear of the house. He came often to dine with the Andrews'. He delighted in playing jokes on the Andrews' small daughter. She sat in her high chair at meals, with her small puppy being served his plate at the table beside her. Houston would switch their plates, roaring with laughter at the child's howl of outrage. The puppy, who had been taught to eat only from his own plate, would sit stricken until he got his plate back.

Andrews never missed the auctions held at the foot of Main by Frances R. Lubbock, later Governor of Texas. As a result, his house and attic were crammed with antiques. Once when he was visiting one of his plantations near Richmond, Mrs. Andrews called some draymen and had them load everything out of the attic. Off they went to the auction to be held the next day.

Arriving back in Houston sooner than he was expected, Andrews heard of the auction. He was just in time to make it to the foot of Main. Not recognizing his own antiques, he made the highest bid for the entire lot. A dumbfounded Mrs. Andrews watched the loaded drays come back up the drive. When the house was remodeled in 1878, Mrs. Andrews eliminated the attic.

In 1928 or 29, Colonel Andrews' great-granddaughter, Nancy Flewellen Howard (Mrs. A. Philo) refused $37,500 for the house at 410 Austin. In 1937 Olshan Demolishing Company tore down the famous landmark.

There were other nice homes, but Mrs. Houstoun was correct about the lack of brick structures. It would be the late 1840s before Ebenezer B. Nichols would erect the first brick building on Main Street between Franklin and Commerce. The more well-to-do would follow suit with brick homes on Quality Hill, the area south of the Courthouse Square extending eastward from Main to Crawford. The houses sat well back off the streets and generally were surrounded by brick walls.

Other construction had been done or was underway. A bridge 100 feet long spanned the bayou at the foot of Preston Avenue to make it easier for wagon trains from Hempstead and the plantations along the upper Brazos and Colorado Rivers to reach Market Square.

The Capitol, vacant after the departure of the Legislature, was converted into the Capitol Hotel. There was an Opera House, and city fathers had enacted an ordinance calling for 12-foot-wide sidewalks of brick to get the city out of the mud.

Some thoroughfares were cobblestoned, and some were paved with wooden blocks. When it rained, the blocks buckled up and had to be hammered down again.

There was a Chamber of Commerce and a Port of Houston had been created. Besides the Opera House, there was a theatre and reputable eating establishments. In addition to the grist mills and cotton compress there was a brick factory, steam mill, two sawmills, a cotton warehouse, livery stable, tannery, mule barn, blacksmith and ship repair shops, and three newspapers.

And . . . there was a school!

Of course there were still the saloons and prostitutes. No "lewd woman" was allowed in the city limits by law, and if one were found she was to be fined $10. The ban was ignored, and the fines were levied only at politically proper times.

Texans had talked for and against annexation to the U.S. since the dawn of the republic. With Anson Jones succeeding Sam Houston as President, annexation moved closer to reality. Merchants in Long Row, who favored annexation, were eagerly awaiting the flow of U.S. currency to Houston and their coffers.

And one morning in March, 1845, Houstonians awakened to a cannon's firing in Market Square.

The muddy streets quickly filled with all ages in all states of dress. Somebody climbed on an ox-wagon and shouted out the big news. The United States Congress had passed a resolution offering Statehood to Texas!

Celebrations, like a prairie fire out of control, took over the town. The following April 21, 1845 a county-wide meeting was held at the Presbyterian Church in Houston. The vote was to accept the invitation for Texas to join the United States, declaring, "In signifying our willingness to enter the American Union, we would also testify our full confidence in the honor and justice of the American people."

Those for annexation celebrated the great news, each in his own way. In the back rooms of hotels men in bright colored blanket coats sat around the pot-bellied stoves with tumblers of whiskey, chewing tobacco or rolling it in corn shucks and talking about what annexation was going to do to prices. In the parlors, men in frock coats, vests, black string cravats, wide-brimmed hats were talking the change in politics and telling old Sam Houston stories.

Some thought since the U.S., France, Great Britain and the Netherlands had recognized the Republic of Texas, it should have stayed independent. A slave standing by his master's horse on the corner of Main and Texas felt the excitement like a far-off thunderstorm. Only a few years earlier he had been put up for auction with one likely gentle mule, 100 head of cattle, a rifle and a shotgun.

In the following months cotton was King on Main Street. Long ox-wagon trains, loaded with cotton from inland plantations, rumbled toward the wholesale stores on the bayou. Ads ran in the newspapers offering to trade one or more Negro boys for cotton.

But prosperity and celebrations aside, Texas couldn't be admitted to the Union until it adopted a State Constitution acceptable to the United States Congress. David G. Burnet was elected the Harris County delegate to the State Convention in July. Sam Houston was the delegate from Montgomery County. But he never got there. He went to the United States to be at the bedside of his close friend, Andrew Jackson, who was dying.

The Convention finally framed a satisfactory constitution. On February 19, 1846, Anson Jones, the last President of the Republic of Texas, solemnly declared to an emotional crowd in Austin, "The Republic of Texas is no more!"

The Lone Star Flag of the Republic of Texas slowly lowered. The flag of the United States of America rose. A deep silence fell, every man locked within his own thoughts and memories.

On February 21, 1846, the Texas Legislature elected Sam Houston and Thomas J. Rusk to the United States Senate, where Houston would serve almost 14 years. J. Pinckney Henderson was elected the first Governor of Texas.

Annexation caused Mexico to break relations with the U.S. War followed. It ended with signing of the Treaty of Guadalupe Hidalgo on February 2, 1848, and Mexico gave up all claims to Texas.

With the exception of increased traffic through the port, the war had little effect on Houston. But another terrible yellow fever epidemic killed hundreds. Stores closed. Streets were deserted. Those who could afford it fled to the countryside. And once again the tar barrels smoked and lime was strewn across the town like sleet in winter. But as in the past, cooler weather of fall brought respite from the pestilence.

———————————◅ ▻———————————

Even before annexation, Houston would fill up day by day with eager strangers—some of them strange-looking foreigners. "A large number of French people disembarked and formed a procession, and at their head walked a tall gentleman in a velvet coat, wearing a three-cornered hat. He carried a drawn sword in his hand; a tri-colored flag of France floated above his shoulders!"

The world was coming to Main Street!

———————————◅ ▻———————————

And the Germans came also. The largest number was sent to Southeast Texas in 1844–47 by the Adelsverien, a colonizing enterprise which founded New Braunfels and Fredericksburg. Texas was also regarded in Germany as a likely spot for a penal colony. One entire family had been sentenced to Texas because a son had killed a German Prince in a duel.

On October 10, 1848, two German families, the Wilhelm Rummels and Siegesmund Bauers, landed in Galveston. Loading their possessions on oxcarts, they traveled slowly across trackless prairies, through heavy forests to Houston. Main Street confirmed their worst fears. It looked raw, brawling and dangerous to these sober, devout Germans.

They drove their wagons right on west of town. Nine miles later they were overjoyed to come upon five German families camped on a wooded creek known today as Spring Branch. That night, as one of the men read aloud to the group from his Bible, the Rummels and Bauers decided that here was where they would start their new life.

First things first. They felled the big pines and cut logs for their cabins. Next, they wanted to build a house for God. They cut more great pines and left the logs in the woods to season. They wanted a church in time for their first Thanksgiving. But, one year later, when they went to gather the logs, they were gone. Shocked and mystified as to who the thieves could be in such a wilderness, some feared the hand of God was against them. Their descendants were to speculate that the logs were probably stolen to be sold as cross-ties for the Houston and Texas Central Railroad, then under construction.

Once again, the men went deep in the woods to fell tall pines, hauling the logs into Rummel's yard for safekeeping. At last, a simple church rose in which these German families worshipped for the next 10 years.

Rummel worked in a nearby saw mill. It worried him that the community hadn't given God a finer house when He had done so much for them. One day, running his hands over a beautiful 12-inch heart of pine, Rummel said to himself, "This will go into God's House."

From then on he set aside the finest pieces of pine to come out of the mill, paying for each out of his own scant funds. At last there were enough fine pieces of lumber to build the small church of simple beauty and dignity that still stands today in Spring Branch—Saint Peter's Lutheran Evangelical Church. It has been added to, but the spirit of these early Germans, who believed in putting first things first, still hovers over the altar, stark and simple, and the oak pews, a few of which are original. The peal of the church bells is drowned out today by traffic roaring down I-10 to and from the megalopolis of downtown Houston. But the church has its own distinction. It has stood there since 1858.

Among the many Germans coming to Houston in 1855 were Frederick William Heitmann and his wife Mathilda. They set up housekeeping in Shrimpf Alley, on the edge of Frost Town. Here, their son Frederick August was born.

Heitmann was partner in a cotton and freight forwarding business, Allen and Heitmann, at the corner of Main and Commerce. Freight forwarding was a prosperous business in Houston's early days. In 1865, Heitmann changed to hardware, building the town's first hardware store on the block bounded by Main, Franklin, Fannin, and Commerce. In 1956, I went down to bid the old store goodbye. It was being moved to old Clinton Drive and Kress Street, where it stands today, Heitmann, Bering, Cortes. One of Heitmann's employees, G. E. Ploeger, had been with the original firm for almost 50 years. He told me of his late employer's lifelong refusal to have a telephone on his desk. Heitmann & Co. had the second non-crank telephone in town. The boss had a soundproof booth built for it in the hall. During the 47 years Heitmann was head of the firm, he refused to talk to anyone by telephone until he walked across the counting room and shut himself in the booth.

Fred A. Heitmann, Jr. told me of the day his grandfather was hauling a 1,000 pound barrel on a flat dray. The keg rolled off and sank out of sight in the mud of Franklin Avenue.

———————————◄ ►———————————

Houston was shocked in 1855 when the City Hotel, built in 1837 and the most popular hostelry in town, collapsed. "The President and his Cabinet and the Senators and Representatives and Officials of the first and second Congress had dined at the City Hotel and so too had foreign ministers." (*Telegraph & Texas Register*, May 16, 1855.)

One of the City Hotel's most famous dinners was given to try to reconcile two old opponents, Sam Houston and Thomas Jefferson Rusk, Houston's former Secretary of War. Both had been elected to the United States Senate in 1846. The champagne dinner was such a rousing success that Rusk jumped up and gave a toast to his old opponent: "Houston, with all thy faults, I love thee still!"

The City Hotel barroom was only one of about 20 in town, but it was famous for its explosiveness and famous guests. Every man there who lifted a glass felt he was rich, brave and chivalrous. Bowie knives and pistols were at-the-ready around the tables of poker, keno, faro. Twenty to fifty thousand dollars was lost and won in one night. Decanters, pitchers, tumbers flew in hot debate. In addition, the City Hotel served hard-to-get fresh chickens at $6 a pound and fresh butter at $4 a pound.

Market Square, like Main Street, spoke with many tongues above the bellows of restless oxen and jangling bells. The smell of hot tar rose on the Travis Street side. Called Greasy Row, the small shops catered to the needs of the wagoneer. In front of each store stood a barrel of tar and a cup to grease the wooden axles of the wagons.

On the Preston Street side, the delicious aroma of fresh-baked bread of "Fox the Baker" and newly-ground coffee beans from "The Coffee Woman" mingled with the odor of wild game.

"In those years, Market Square was like a perennial county fair. Traders and vendors hawked their goods; women in sunbonnets and homespuns, men wearing deerhide jeans, bargained for choice venison, roasts or fat wild turkeys. This noisy, teeming place was so much the center of Houston that businessmen sought sites for their stores." (*Six Decades in Texas*, Francis R. Lubbock.)

Kessler's Arcade, on the west side of Travis between Preston and Prairie, was the popular meeting place. Here the town's leaders met to discuss the contaminated

water ("even the rats have taken to gin"), the latest outbreak of yellow fever, and hogs running loose in the
streets. The Jockey Club held its meetings there. As
early as 1840, Houston had four Jockey Clubs. Six-day
race meets were held twice each year, the horses brought
in by wealthy owners of nearby plantations. Kessler also
had his famed round tent used for serving food and
drinks, and housing betting booths, on Main Street. It
was said to have been more than 100 feet in circumference, and 30 or 40 feet high.

Near Market Square was Houston's first "industrial
center," now Sam Houston Park just off Allen Parkway.
There in 1846–47, Virginian Nathaniel K. Kellum built
a house beneath 15 live oak trees for his 15-year-old
bride, Elmyra Cotton, from Mississippi. He had bought
the eight acres and built a brick kiln on the nearby
bayou. He made the bricks used to build his house. He
also sold 10,000 bricks to President of the Republic,
Mirabeau B. Lamar, for a dwelling house and kitchen.

Kellum was a successful businessman with rent houses
on Main Street. But there were also stories of his heavy
gambling, of fast midnight rides across the prairie to the
safety of his house, of settlements he had started and
then abandoned. The promising moment the newlyweds
were enjoying held no foreshadowing of the dark trouble
to come.

It isn't difficult to picture the Kellums' three children
playing on the encircling upper galleries with Elmyra
and Nathaniel rocking on the veranda below. In the summer, ceiling-high windows opened to soft, salty breezes
fresh from the nearby Gulf. In the winter, the sturdy,
double front and rear doors sealed the hall runway
against blue northers and trespassers. A house just right
for the prairie. (The two-story brick house with its tall
narrow brick columns was the first restoration of the
Harris County Heritage Society. It is the oldest house in
the city on its original site.)

Elmyra, still more child than woman, must have longed to escape the responsibilities thrust on her by an involved, adventurous, older husband. Nathaniel eventually asked his domineering sister, Elizabeth K. Jones, to live with them and help Elmyra take care of their three baby sons. That arrangement was an anathema from the start to the teenage wife. It also didn't help that Elizabeth financed her brother's numerous business ventures. Before long, she controlled the purse strings of the household.

By 1850, time was running out for the Nathaniel K. Kellums' marriage and their home on the bayou. The house that seemed so big became too small for Kellum and all of his woeful problems. His marriage to young Elmyra was in the divorce court. His brother-in-law Ferdinand was threatening to kill him. He had been ordered into court over a fight with a black man. There was nothing to do but clear out of Houston for good.

Kellum sold his house, 13 acres and brick kiln to Benjamin A. Shepherd. Then he bought land in Grimes County where he planned to build a resort near Anderson called Kellum Springs. He persuaded Shepherd and several other Houstonians to invest in it.

But Kellum Springs didn't turn out as he had dreamed. More threats from Ferdinand, on behalf of Elmyra, reached him. He added a codicil to his will: "Should I be assassinated by any person, I desire that my executors shall see that said assassin be vigorously prosecuted to conviction and for that purpose I appropriate $2,000 to be paid out of my estate if it be necessary."

His premonition was well founded. At Kellum Springs one night, as he was walking beyond his house, a shot rang out. The burning explosion in his arm threw him against a nearby tree. When he recovered from his wound, he set out to track his former brother-in-law. At last he cornered him. The two men had a prolonged fist fight before Kellum pulled his gun and shot Ferdinand to death.

Shepherd sold the Kellum house in 1851 to Abram Noble for $2,000. Abram, a widower with five children, married a widow, Zerviah Kelly, who had one daughter. They all lived together happily for awhile in the house on the prairie. Zerviah told the children legends of the friendly Alabama-Coushatta Indians she often let camp beneath their big oak trees.

There is an old superstition that the walls of a house absorb the sorrows and troubles of the previous owner. Their ghosts haunt the lives of those who live there later. Elmyra Kellum's unhappy ghost must have haunted Zerviah Noble. After a hotly contested court battle, she too won a divorce from her husband. She got the house and land. Her daughter Catherine died in the house January 10, 1866, giving birth to her second child. Zerviah was left with the baby and four-year-old Eloise to support. She announced the opening of a private school in her big, airy house in its beautiful location beneath great oak trees near town.

Here, boys and girls under 12 came to learn Greek, Latin, French, math, history, drawing, painting and worsted embroidery. Being a resourceful woman, Zerviah tied the baby in a rocker nearby, sat Eloise down with drawing paper and a cup of purplish water color she had made from the indigo plant, and went about her teaching.

The Alabama-Coushatta Indians camped beneath the big oak tree near her house when they came to town. Always friendly, one of the men made a pair of white beaded mocassins for her granddaughter. During one of the bad yellow fever epidemics, Zerviah Noble put cots on the galleries and nursed victims herself.

When the Kellum-Noble house and land were sold to the city of Houston, then Mayor Sam Brashear promised they would be "twin monuments to remind Houstonians of the days when Texas had a President instead of a Governor, a Congress instead of a Legislature."

But by 1954, it had become clear that none of Brashear's successors had been interested in preserving such a reminder. The Kellum-Noble house was condemned for a parking lot. Floors had buckled, walls cracked, handmade brick crumbling like sand, the foundation was perilous. Tramps had slept in the house, defecated in it, built small fires in its corners for warmth. The house had even been used to house cages of animals from the Houston Zoo. The landmark's infirmity seemed terminal.

One Sunday, I wrote a story on the sad plight of the oldest house in Houston still standing on its original site. Mary Ellen Shipnes sketched the illustration. *The Houston Post* ran the story. A reader called: "Let's save the Kellum-Noble house for future Houstonians."

Out of that one telephone call grew the Harris County Heritage and Conservation Society and the restorations in Sam Houston Park.

Even Sam Houston Park itself, site of Houston's first industrial center, was awaiting destruction. The proposed Allen Parkway was to run through its center. The board members of the new Harris County Heritage and Conservation Society wired then Governor Price Daniel that in no way should the State be allowed to destroy the heritage of Houston! Allen Parkway was diverted to leave Sam Houston Park intact.

The fledgling Society may never have left the talking stage if architect Harvin Moore had not donated his valuable time to the restorations. Today, the Kellum-Noble house, Nichols-Rice-Cherry house, Pillot House, San Felipe Cottage, St. John's Old Place Church, Bandstand, Long Row of Shops and a restaurant are open daily to visitors to Sam Houston Park. Each year, the Society gives a beautiful Ball to support its gifts of history to the city.

The latest addition to Sam Houston Park is the early 20th Century home of the Staiti family which was moved from 421 Westmoreland during the summer of 1985. Built circa 1905, the home was given to the Harris County Heritage Society by the surviving 10 members of the Staiti family. Henry Thomas Staiti was president of the Prairie Oil Company, and was active in early oil fields, including Spindletop.

———————————————

Dr. William C. Griggs, executive director and president of the Harris County Heritage Society, currently working with the Buffalo Bayou Park Program has announced the plans for a world class museum, The Museum of History and Technology. This museum will record the only complete history of Texas from 1519 to the present, and will project visitors into the Texas of tomorrow.

The concept includes the use of vertical, as well as horizontal space, thus utilizing The Time Machine that will enable visitors to experience moving through the centuries of Texas history selectively by eras or years of their choice.

"The charted Texas coast by Alonso Alvarez de Pineda in 1519, a full century before the founding of Jamestown, will be the point of origin. All major eras and events of Texas history will be experienced through a time machine concept," said Dr. June Holly, director of development. The estimated cost of the museum construction is $25,750,000 and is in the advanced planning stage.

———————————————

Ebenezer B. Nichols, who erected the first brick building in Houston, built his home facing Court House

Square. It was an era when men believed in the everlasting permanence of their land and houses. Young Nichols, from Cooperstown, New York, brought such a dream with him when his steamboat landed in Galveston harbor in 1839.

There the wind blew the sands and bent the wild marsh grasses, burying deeper the bones of shipwrecked explorers and Karankawa Indians of 300 years earlier. Some historians say Galveston was the famous Malhado, Isle of Misfortune, where explorer Cabeza de Vaca and his 80 companions were shipwrecked.

For Nichols, the wind carried many ghostly voices, among them the shouts and laughter of the pirate Jean Lafitte's men, gone from the island for ten years. A few grey board houses rimmed the sands. The new life ahead looked foreboding to the ship of immigrants.

But young Nichols seized his fiddle and struck up a lively, defiant polka.

At that moment, the shape of his destiny waited nearby. A homesick young girl, Margaret Clayton Stone, was leaning on the deck rail of her ship, waiting to land. She had come to Texas with her Aunt Millie Richardson Stone Gray, who would write her famous *Diary* on Texas, and her uncle, William Fairfax Gray, who was to found Christ Church in Houston. Homesick, listening hungrily to the lively music, she vowed to meet the fiddler.

For new arrivals on barren Galveston, introductions weren't hard to come by. More than a jaunty tune across the waves must have drawn them together. On August 7, 1842, Margaret and Ebenezer married. In 1845, Nichols bought the lot at San Jacinto and Congress across from Court House Square. But it wasn't until 1850 that he started building the Nichols-Rice-Cherry house (restored in Sam Houston Park by the Harris County Heritage Society).

Nichols' partner in a general merchandise store was William Marsh Rice. Rice married Margaret Bremond, whose father, Paul Bremond, would build the second railroad in Texas, the Galveston and Red River Railroad. In 1856, Nichols moved to Galveston and sold his house to Rice.

The Nichols-Rice-Cherry house has a host of unanswered questions. Who was the skilled craftsman who carved the Ionic columns of the front gallery of the Greek Revival house, the front door, interior cornices, newel posts, stair rails, the fine, interior double doors? Fifteen-year-old August Bering, who was to become one of Houston's leading hardware merchants, is said to have hired out just to sharpen the tools of this unknown master carver. As for the architect, he went on his way, as nameless as the portrait painters who wandered over Texas in those days.

The Rices opened the doors of their house to many teas and receptions, always extending the banquet table the length of the two front parlors. One morning, Mrs. Rice held a ceremony in the front gallery. She presented a banner she had stitched by hand to the brave men of Hook & Ladder Company No. 1 for the efficiency with which they operated the steam pumper to put out the almost daily fires. In August, 1863, a mournful crowd gathered before the same gallery for her funeral service.

William Marsh Rice was one of 10 children of David Rice, skilled mechanic and inventor of the Rice musket, and Patty Hall Rice of Springfield, Massachusetts. Rice landed in Houston in 1839 with $2,700 he had made from his little grocery store in Springfield. By the time he left Houston, he had promoted the Ship Channel, railroads, banks, the Houston Academy, and had endowed Rice Institute, now Rice University. Who could have foretold that William Marsh Rice would be the victim in one of the most famous murders in Texas? (See Chapter 8)

In 1867 Rice married Julia Elizabeth Brown, whose sister, Charlotte Baldwin, was the wife of Frederic Allyn Rice, one of the town's earliest residents. The newly-weds left the Houston mansion to live in New York. In 1873, Rice sold it to the Railroad Real Estate Building & Savings Co. of Texas. In 1886, it was bought by hide merchant John J. Finnegan. (In this same year, Rice bought the Capitol Hotel for back taxes. The hotel would later bear his name.)

John Finnegan leased the house to Captain Charles Evershade of the Morgan Steamship Lines in 1887. For years, it was known as the Evershade Mansion. The City Directory shows that Charles Evershade was still living in the house at the southwest corner of Franklin and San Jacinto Street in 1896.

In July, 1902, Finnegan put the house up for auction. The national depression had hit Houston and only a few people showed up.

The only bid the auctioneer received came by mail. It was $25 for the front door! Sick of the whole business, the auctioneer gave the lone bidder not only the front door but the whole house!

Emma Richardson Cherry, artist, was this high bid-der. She had came to Houston from Aurora, Illinois, by way of New York, Denver, France, and Italy. She moved the house to Fargo Street, far out on the then prairie, and lived there for 57 years. Emma Cherry died in 1959.

Save for a party in the garden of Mr. and Mrs. Charles Bybee, restorationists, the home might not have been restored in Sam Houston Park today. Two guests at the party, philanthropists-financiers Gus Wortham and Wesley West, listened to the story of the imminent de-mise of the house.

Someone asked Wortham, "Why don't you buy it for $5,000?" He said "All right, I will!"

Another asked West, "And why don't you move it to Sam Houston Park?"

He said, "All right, I will."

Such are the ways in which great things were accomplished and still are in Houston. The old landmark, its walls disassembled, every board numbered, took to the road and to its final site in Sam Houston Park.

In the 1950s I went to Dickinson, Texas to see Ebenezer Nichols' great granddaughter, Mrs. H. H. Schelling. She lived in "Nicholstone on the Bayou" which Ebenezer had built for a summer home.

She related how Nichols, wanting to organize the Bank of Galveston, wrote to President Sam Houston asking for a charter. "I propose to find 12 honest men to help me organize a banking corporation," he wrote. Houston wrote back: "If you can find 12 honest men, you'll do more than Jesus Christ was able to do."

She also told of the time Nichols advised Houston, who opposed secession, not to make a speech in outraged Galveston. But old Sam, at 70, after kicking one attacker down a long flight of stairs, did just that!

CHAPTER FOUR

"One early train out of Houston was called the 'Tri-Weekly.' It would go out Monday morning and try all week to get back."

EARLY-DAY Main Street thundered under the hoof beats of ponies of Alabama-Coushatta Indians racing in from their settlements along the Trinity and Neches Rivers. Unlike the Karankawas on Galveston Island—"demons of Hell," Lafitte called them—the Alabama-Coushattas had always been friendly, chiefly because of Sam Houston.

Since he had lived for years with a Cherokee tribe, they called him their "Cherokee brother." He promised to look after the Indians' interests as no white man had. The Alabama-Coushattas had lived under the Spanish Crown, the Republic of Mexico, France and the Republic of Texas. They still had no title to their own lands and were losing more territory daily to unscrupulous white settlers with money and lawyers. But they trusted Sam Houston.

When Texas declared its independence from Mexico, Sam Houston met with the Chiefs of the Alabama-Coushatta tribes. He pulled out all the stops in his eloquent "speechifying" to persuade them to remain neutral. He promised that when Texas got its freedom from Mexico, he would look after them and their lands.

The Chiefs remained neutral. Some of the Alabamas migrated to Oklahoma until the Revolution was over. The Coushattas remained, killing their own cattle to feed refugees in the wake of Sam Houston's retreat to San Jacinto, to assist and befriend him.

After the Revolution, Houston tried to keep his promise. He proposed a treaty to protect the homes and lands of the Alabama-Coushatta Indians from lawless white settlers. In 1840, the Texas Congress was petitioned to assign certain lands between the Neches and Trinity Rivers as a permanent home for the two tribes. The petition was denied; some Texans even thought the Indians should be exterminated altogether.

When Texas joined the Union, the Federal Government proposed moving the Alabama-Coushattas to a reservation set aside in Oklahoma for Indians of the South and Southwest. They refused to leave. Finally, in 1854, Texas at last bought and gave the tribes title to 1,280 acres for a reservation near Livingston, Texas, northeast of Houston.

It remains today. The Alabama-Coushattas have seen their once fiercely-proud tribe of more than 1,000 reduced to 500.

There is no trace of these early Indians on Main Street or in Market Square today. Yet, their artifacts remain. Arrowheads, bones, and pieces of pottery have been found in what was believed to have been one of their burial grounds, near Preston and Louisiana. Today the area is covered by Stelzig's, parking lots and the Lyric Center building.

The Indian was here in Market Square, peddling his fresh-caught catfish and trout, wild game, dressed fur skins, corn, and berries.

It was the Irishman John Kennedy's Trading Post on Congress facing Market Square that was the Indians' favorite trading post. Here they reveled in the shelves of bright calicoes, barrels of Lone Star whiskey, English Porter, Texas wine, pickles, chests of gun powder, tea, cloves, ginger, nutmeg, hominy, beans, dry salt bacon, coffins, iron safes, firearms, snuff.

They spread their wares on Kennedy's floor. When Kennedy had put sufficient money on the counter, the Chief signaled enough. The Indians then pointed to the articles they wanted. The Chief slapped down money until Kennedy signaled enough.

If the Indians had any money left, Kennedy let them put it in his safe while they celebrated, making the rounds of all the saloons. Late in the day, the Indians staged splendid rambunctious races on horseback around Market Square until the deputy sheriff escorted them safely out of town.

Kennedy's Trading Post was also a regular stop for the stagecoach. During the Civil War it was turned into a storehouse for ammunition. Today it is a wine and coffee house, restored by Kennedy's great grandson, Dr. Charles Bruhl, and his wife Adaline. The charming two-story brick building at 813 Congress is the oldest commercial building on its original site in Houston. (Author's column, *The Houston Post.* Used with permission.)

———————————⊐◄ ►⊏———————————

Allen's Landing was crowded that day in 1852, the women in their full skirts and bonnets from Miss Nellis', direct from New York and Boston—the latest Paris fashions. Some men wore narrow trousers, frock coats and top hats; others wore homespun pants and deerhide jackets. But however he was dressed, each man carried a

Bowie knife and sidearm, properly concealed for the occasion.

They were all there to get the first glimpse of the "iron horse" that would "awaken the silence of the prairie." The locomotive *Ebenezer Allen* was being shipped by steamboat up Buffalo Bayou!

But when the steamboat arrived, there was no locomotive to be seen on deck!

Where in the name of Santa Anna was it?

"Oh, it's here, all right," the steamboat captain said. "It just ain't put together."

"Who gives a damn!" someone shouted. "It's an 'iron horse!'"

What did it matter that it came in parts that would have to be assembled? The *Ebenezer Allen* finally thundered down on the solid earth of Main Street.

It was a great new day for the town. Allen's Landing became the scene of a wild celebration. Houstonians would *not* be denied an opportunity to whoop it up and lift a glass . . . and brag a bit. Assembled or disassembled, the locomotive was a Texas first!

Perhaps the happiest man on the Landing that day was Alexander McGowen, who had brought Houston its first heavy industry—an iron foundry. He already was expanding and getting rich by casting great iron kettles for the sugar plantations as well as ornamental grillwork for shops and homes. Now McGowen had visions of railroads sprouting out of Houston like limbs on a tree with his foundry supplying the necessary equipment. McGowen was to become mayor of Houston in 1867.

The railroads did sprout. By 1856 Houston had built the Houston Tap, a link connecting with the Buffalo Bayou, Brazos & Colorado line at Pierce Junction, seven miles from town. The Houston & Texas Central headed toward Hempstead. The Galveston, Houston & Henderson ran 50 miles to Virginia Point. By 1860 the Texas & New Orleans linked Houston with Beaumont and Orange. Houston and Galveston were tied together by a telegraph line!

Back on January 9, 1841, the 5th Congress of the Republic had granted Andrew H. Briscoe, Harris County's first judge, a charter for a railroad. But only two miles out of Harrisburg were surveyed. Because of a possible war with Mexico, Briscoe had been unable to get foreign financing. Texas lacked venture capital. The ambitious dream had had to be abandoned.

Then, in the early 1850s, General Sidney Sherman went to Boston to raise money for what would be Texas' first railroad, the Buffalo Bayou, Brazos and Colorado. He wrote home to one of his backers, "I shall be compelled to let those Boston people have a much larger interest than I had intended . . . to borrow money on Texas securities seems to be entirely out of the question, specially in this section of the country."

In December 1852 the *General Sherman*, a cast-off from a Boston railroad line, arrived by ship at Galveston. It was a little wood burner with a "bulbous haystack" and it could, if fired up high, run 25 miles per hour! When it got up to this awesome speed, everybody called it the "Harrisburg Flyer." The train's most comfortable speed was 10 miles an hour.

It was a great day when the *General Sherman,* its wood stack belching smoke, pulled the small, brightly painted boxcars and coaches along the Buffalo Bayou, Brazos and Colorado tracks, all the way from Harrisburg to Stafford's Point just beyond Houston (20 miles).

The coaches—secondhand streetcars bought in Boston—had long, hard benches on each side which most passengers considered a dubious improvement over the horse. What may have been lacking in the new mode of travel was made up by the celebration at Stafford's Point. Plenty of bourbon and branch water, barbecued beef and *cabrito* (young goat) were consumed to the constant firing of a cannon.

By 1855, the Buffalo Bayou, Brazos and Colorado extended its road to Richmond, a glorious 32 miles. A year later, the track led across a pile bridge six feet above the Brazos at its low stage.

"This bridge was approached on each side by a very steep incline, so that it was necessary for a train of any length to cross with all the speed possible in order to make the opposite hill. The bridge was used from the time it was built in 1856 or 57 until about 1870. I remember only two accidents of any consequence, one in 1860 and the other in 1867. In each case, one of the spans gave way, throwing the train into the river and killing two or three men. To cross the bridge was very trying on the nerves of the passengers." (*A History of Texas Railroads*, St. Clair Griffin Reed.)

In 1859, the Houston Tap and Brazoria was called the Sugar Road because it serviced the sugar plantations south of Houston. The plantations were big customers, producing 10,000 hogshead of sugar and 16,000 barrels of molasses each season that had to go to market. To the west, the Buffalo Bayou, Brazos and Colorado rails extended into cotton and cattle country.

Of course this amazing new kind of transportation called for a celebration. They held it at Pierce Junction where the Houston Tap and Brazoria crossed the Buffalo Bayou, Brazos and Colorado line. The honorees? No less than the four locomotives!

John T. Browne, who came to Houston in 1852 and was later mayor, wrote: "One of the first railroads built out here started at Harrisburg. The bodies were swung by straps on iron springs . . . then came the locomotive that had two driving wheels, one on each side . . . everybody used to call the locomotive the Grasshopper, because it kind of jumped up and down like a grasshopper." The railroad tracks were laid through the prairies. Along the tracks there were numerous waterholes full of alligators. It was great sport for the people on the train to jump off and do some shooting.

One train was called the "Tri-Weekly." It would go out Monday morning and try all week to get back. The maximum speed was about 10 miles per hour.

On one line it was not unusual to hear, "Ike, she's off again!" You see, Ike Filkins was the conductor. Well now, there was one old fellow who had fallen asleep. He woke up, yelled out, "What's the matter?" The brakeman said they were off the track again. The old guy told him to let it stay off, that it ran better off the track than on. He said it was the easiest ride he had ever had on the damn train.

One train from Houston to Angleton, over the Sugar Road servicing the big plantations, was known as "Mr. Bonney's train." Mr. Bonney, the engineer, ran it according to whim. When it ran off the track, he gave the men passengers time to hunt for prairie chickens. In the spring he would bring the train to a jarring halt. Passengers had to wait while he picked wild flowers for his girlfriend in Houston. (*A History of Texas Railroads,* St. Clair Griffin Reed.)

Meanwhile, the stagecoach made weekly trips from Houston to Austin and Washington-on-the Brazos.

———————————

The 1850s also brought an explosion of material goods, private schools and some development of Buffalo Bayou. The Texas Legislature had appropriated $4,000 to clean and improve the bayou. The music of prosperity was in the air.

The *Morning Star,* February 18, 1854, advertised "Music: Lilly Doll, Old Folks at Home, Nelly Bly, Wait for the Wagon, Katy Darling, Annie Laurie, Fare Thee Well, Kitty Dear, Poor Robin's Growing Old, They've Sold Me Down the River—all at Klein & Clarks!"

"Music in Houston dates back to the founding of the City itself, for it is known that the community had a theatre before it acquired its first church. While Houston remained a raw, muddy, frontier town with little or no life in the other arts, it demonstrated surprising vigor and interest in music. Texans who cast their lot with the Allen brothers included pioneers who represented the fashions and tastes of New York, Boston and older cities of the East. A smaller element of the French and Germans from the Rhine country, brought with them a natural feeling for music. Accordingly, once they had built homes on the swampy land, with its scrub oak and the stately magnolia, there was salon music in town. The result of the mixture was that the spirit of fine music was early established.

While Houston was little more than a village, it was visited by some of the great singers of the day, who made the happy discovery that although accommodations were rustic, they had entered no cultural wilderness.

However, all was not music in the new town! Sam Houston took time out of his busy life to fire off a caustic letter to a Mr. Scarla, a commission merchant in Galveston, about none of his furniture arriving in one piece! The letter was found in New York by the late J. S. Cullinan and given to the San Jacinto Museum.

"I have received a small cooking stove without any pipe," Sam wrote. "One large bedstead with Tiester . . . one of the bedposts split at the top and roughly filled with wax or putty . . . no side rails and further I have not looked at the thing. It is of no use as it is to anyone. The bureau came also and the locks all off it. The 'scatchings' of the key holes are handsomely fixed with wax or putty and the joints wonderful; and taking it all in all surpasses anything that I have ever seen, except the sideboard that is infamous beyond all things else. The veneering is broken and split.

"Wherever it needed it, and I should say at least twenty places, has been puttied . . . the looking glass was broken before it left Houston and hardly a splinter reached here. One end of the sideboard was split for near a foot and filled with wax. I passed by the table. It came, the naked stand, without leaves!" (*Harris County Heritage Society Notes*)

But for some in Houston no freedom existed, much less luxuries. In 1850, when the first U.S. Census was taken in Texas, Houston had 2,396 inhabitants, 905 of whom were Negroes.

Ads offering slaves for sale were common in the *Telegraph and Texas Register*, such as this one on February 16, 1850:

> Negro Man for Sale
> A likely Negro fellow, aged 32 years, a brick layer and brick mason by profession, accustomed to working on a farm and a superior cook, for sale low, if applied for immediately. Sampson & Co.

Many in Houston were opposed to slavery. But those who owned nearby cotton and sugar plantations considered their slaves their most valuable possessions. A good slave was valued at $500 to $800. He could produce 10 bales of cotton annually, enough corn to sustain himself, in addition to all of the manpower his owner could use.

Negro women were often mistresses of Houston men. Many oil royalties have been fought over between their progeny and those of legal wives. One prominent Houstonian saw nothing amiss in having his son by a slave girl wait on the table.

While there were some free Negroes in Houston, the ownership of a slave as personal property was regarded as a moral right. A man had an investment in his slave. He expected returns. What's more, the black man couldn't exist without the white man's food, shelter and medical care. For many years, laws would exist in Houston that would ". . . confine, legislate, and punish the black man as no animal was confined, legislated or punished." (*To Wear a City's Crown,* Kenneth Wheeler.)

The average slave was treated kindly, often generously by his owners. But he had no personal rights. The Alabama-Coushatta Indian could sell his fish and game in Market Square. But not the slave. An Indian was free to enter the saloons. But a black man got heavy lashings on his bare back if he was found with liquor. The white man who sold it to him would be fined $20 or more.

When two white men were tried for fighting in the street, May 22, 1858, the jury decreed, "We, the Jury, find both defendants guilty and assess the fine of one cent each." (*Recorders Court,* William Anders) But leniency stopped there. "Negro boy Alfred and Negro girl King are given 50 lashes for fighting in the public street and must pay costs of the suit!"

Nancy, a Negro woman, was fined "five lashes for keeping a disorderly house within the city limits . . . her agents to pay all costs of arrest, punishment." Sometimes, however, justice was dispensed. The court fined James Cook ". . . $2,000 for ill treatment and cruel abuse of a Negro slave woman, Nena." Justice was more likely to be extended to animals. Ferdinand Dietrich was fined $10 and costs for ". . . willfully and wantonly abusing his steers." (April 21, 1859, *Recorders Court.*)

Houstonians who had fought for independence against Mexican tyranny saw nothing contradictory in their approval of the Ordinances Concerning Slaves as passed by the Mayor James H. Stevens and City Council, September 13, 1855. The twelve Ordinances stated that a slave could not be out after 9 p.m. without a written permit from his owner stating where he was going and at what time. He could not play cards or dice. He could not congregate with more than four of his fellow slaves except for worship and then only with one respectable freeholder present.

The Allen brothers shared the belief of white men that black skin could not feel the heat nor snake bites as did white men. They ordered that only slaves be hired to clean and drain the swampy, wooded site where they built Houston. "No white man could have endured the insect bites and malaria, snake bites, impure water and other hardships," wrote the Allen's nephew, Dr. O. F. Allen.

Apparently there was a school for Houston Negroes, as advertised in the *Telegraph & Texas Register*, November 17, 1858: "Mrs. M. L. Capshaw will resume her school in African Methodist Church, Monday, November 22." The curriculum must have been limited. Most blacks could neither read nor write.

———————————————

Members of the German Turnverein Club were among the first to help establish a free school in Houston. Ten young men met at Brewmeister Peter Gable's house on Preston Avenue between San Jacinto and Caroline in 1854, to organize the Turnverein. Their lofty motivation: "The wish of all to belong to a society where each feels as a brother to the other."

In their first year, the members showed so much *esprit de corps* as volunteer fire-fighters that Mayor N. Fuller, in gratitude, sent them two dozen bottles of ale and porter. The Turnverein paid $60 for a piece of land on Caroline between Prairie and Texas in 1856 and put a small house on it.

In 1859, members of the Turnverein organized their well-drilled rifle company, resplendent in snappy uniforms, calling themselves, the Turner Rifles. In 1861, they built their first Turner Hall on Prairie and Caroline. Native Houstonians, now long since gone, told me of the lovely garden behind Turner Hall where entire families once gathered, each to his own white-clothed table, to dine on hearty German dishes, lift their steins and sing robust songs. When the Civil War came, the Turner Rifles would be among the first to enlist.

CHAPTER FIVE

"Any information on sex a young girl got from her mother came mysteriously camouflaged. One mother gave the English Victorian advice: 'Lie still and think of England!'"

R AILROADS and increased boat traffic on the bayou brought prosperity to Houston in the 1850s, but more than once in that decade the boom almost went bust. In 1853 weeks of heavy rain swelled the upper reaches of the bayou. The flood roared down on Houston, tearing away the Preston Avenue bridge and sweeping through the city proper.

While the flood damage was still being toted up, another yellow fever epidemic struck. Once again smoke from the tar barrels rose in the summer sky while the living counted the dead.

Flood, pestilence, and then fire. One roared through the heart of the city, laying waste everything in its path, including T. W. Whitmarsh's warehouse and more than 2,000 bales of cotton. A strong March wind powered another fire that leveled both sides of Main Street between

Congress and Preston. Before it could be extinguished, it broke through to Travis Street. Damage in the second fire alone was estimated at almost $500,000.

There had been other, smaller fires, but the second major conflagration prompted the city leaders to take over control of the fire department.

An impressive tower was added to the Market House, to hold a clock and a fire bell. About time too! Hook and Ladder No. 1, on Franklin and Fannin, needed all the warning it could get. A history of Houston could be written based on where Hook and Ladder No. 1 answered calls: Rice's Stable, Old Capitol, Kennedy's Store, Niggerville, Pillots Building, Macatees.

Judge A. Earl Amerman, Mayor of Houston 1918–21, once recalled the early days when his father and other men harnessed themselves to the hand pumper and pulled it to the fires. The only water available was in the rain-filled cisterns.

For parades, the firemen decorated the engines with the red lilies from the elder Amerman's garden. Children loved the fire horses, especially one big white stallion. When the latter was badly burned because it loyally stood unmoving despite the intense heat of one of the town's worst fires, the children helped to lead the maimed horse to a permanent green pasture near town.

———————————◄ ►———————————

Despite the setbacks, the resilient Houstonians hastened to rebuild. A start was made on a three-story brick courthouse. A new hotel, the four-story Hutchins House, sprang up at Travis and Franklin. It was more elegant than the Mansion House and the Old Capitol.

On the morning of August 29, 1856, everybody was invited to the laying of the cornerstone of Houston Academy. The two-story brick building would house the town's first college preparatory school.

Schooling was becoming a matter of importance. The state of Texas gave Harris County the munificent sum of $1,900 to educate poor children. Liberals and newspapers so fought for more schooling that the Legislature passed an act in 1854–55 setting up a state school system.

Private schools began to open all over the place, primarily because prosperous Houstonians wanted their children in a select economic and social environment. In the *Tri-Weekly* in 1856, John B. Kellogg advertised: "I would hereby inform parents of Houston and adjacent places that I have opened a school in the new Temple Building on Main Street near the Old Capitol." The "safest and wisest plan" was to mix the sexes, "for mutual restraint and moral influence." But if any of the parents felt he was tempting the devil, he would be happy to form a class of girls only, he said. Reading, writing, spelling, $2.00 per month. English, $3.00; Greek, Latin, French, $5.00.

The girl child was fed carefully selected pablum, her freedom as severely restricted as her body in its drawers, long stockings, petticoats, and overdress. One Houston woman later recalled that she was never allowed to play beyond the locked front gate of their big house where One Shell Plaza stands today.

Any information on sex a young girl got from her mother came mysteriously camouflaged. One book was all about the blights that could destroy a rosebud, as if she were a plant. Another mother gave the English Mother's Victorian advice: "Lie still and think of England!"

Boys could roam free as the squirrels, swim naked in the bayou, discover what they came into this world with. They played "Chickamy, Chickamy Cranny Crow" with their black friends. They could learn what was going on in town, especially at Christmas time. They saw the big bear from the San Jacinto River bottoms caged to be killed and sold for his delicious meat. They could watch the Indians and San Jacinto Battle veterans celebrating in Market Square.

Alabama-Coushatta Indians staged races around Market Square on their feisty little ponies while the Veterans marched to each saloon. The boys liked best to follow a man named Tierwester, who took a bullet, not in his body, but in his powderhorn. The drunker he got, the louder he rattled the horn.

The boys also went to Stude's Bakery on Commerce for cakes and hot chocolate. Between bites, they threw firecrackers on the floor. Stude was a tolerant man.

The boys then crossed the bayou on a fallen tree trunk, searching for a pine tree with the right number of holes in the trunk. They inserted gun powder in the holes, lit it, and ran. The adults' relaxed attitude of "boys will be boys" no doubt came from the nearness of open fields and dense woods for them to be boys in.

When Christmas night came, they went to Captain Stanley's celebration for his slaves, to hear Dave play the banjo and Big John sing in a ". . . voice as loud as a steamboat whistle but sweet as a harp." (*True Stories of Old Houston and Houstonians,* Dr. S. O. Young)

The 1858 New Year had scarcely begun when a tragically lonely man went up to his room in the Old Capitol Hotel and put a bullet through his head. He was the last President of the Republic of Texas, Anson Jones, that enigma of courage and failure who had served as Minister to the United States under Sam Houston, Senator of the Republic of Texas under President Mirabeau B. Lamar, Secretary of State under President Sam Houston in 1841, Minister to the United States, and President of the Republic of Texas.

When Texas was annexed under President James K. Polk, Anson Jones had hoped to be elected to the United States Senate. To his great disappointment, his enemy, Sam Houston, and Thomas Jefferson Rusk were elected.

During the last twelve years of his life, Jones had become an embittered hermit, living on his plantation, Barrington, at Washington-on-the-Brazos. His left arm, paralyzed by an injury, increased his depression. He lived chiefly on his memories.

As President of the Republic, he had wanted recognition of Texas independence from Mexico rather than annexation to the United States. As a result, he was burned in effigy. The Convention of 1845 had tried to remove him from office. In the last days before annexation, he had kept his title in name only.

In 1857, he had tried to run again for the United States Senate. He received no votes. Disillusioned, he drifted in a destructive aimlessness in which he felt neither a complete success nor a complete failure, simply a tragically incomplete man. His plantation home is preserved in the State Park at Washington-on-the-Brazos.

In the following year, 1859, still another yellow fever epidemic hit the town. The *Tri-Weekly Telegraph* blamed it on Sam Houston's former White House on Main Street . . . "a yellow fever block with a strong stench. Can not something be done to purify this and the Long Row block before the hot sun of July shall fill the city with their miasma? We had an epidemic here last year and it broke out in the poison atmosphere by the old President's house!"

Beneath the town's daily concerns there moved, with increasing hidden force, the approaching tragedy of the Civil War. On every street corner, in saloons, around dining tables, the debate grew hotter, "Is it to the interest of the South to dissolve the Union?"

Sam Houston, newly elected Governor of Texas, hotly opposed all talk of secession. Two issues brought out every ounce of his fiery eloquence: the denied rights of the Alabama-Coushatta Indians, and the preservation of the Union. Talk of impeaching him grew louder as the days passed.

But the horror of war was still a year away that beautiful day in the spring of 1860 when the first sailing regatta held in Texas set sail at the San Jacinto Yacht Club near Lynchburg on Galveston Bay.

Houstonians went by carriage and boat to enjoy it. The women, in their full skirts, capes and pastel bonnets or wide-brimmed be-ribboned hats, watched the races from pleasure boats or sat on the bank beneath dainty silk parasols.

Eight sailing vessels, their white sails swelling to catch the wind, raced from Lynchburg around the lighthouse on Clopper's Bar. The carefree moment, elusive to hold as the sun sparkling on the white caps, singing with the cries of sea gulls and children running through the shallows, gave the illusion of perpetual joy and security. Forgotten, but perhaps unknown, were the words of Marcus Aurelius, "The past is gone forever; the future is unknown. The present moment is the only permanence we know."

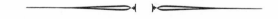

All too swiftly the future no one wanted to face was here and now. Governor Houston was thundering to a large audience at the Houston Academy, demanding "Saner, wiser hearts and minds to prevail against secession." Contemptuous jeers and angry insults answered him. It was the end of the glorious drama which he and the Republic of Texas had played together, and the beginning of his last, brief, bitter years.

To raise funds for the oncoming war against the North, the Galveston, Houston and Henderson Railroad was sold at public auction for $28,000. In the following year, 1861, the Houston and Texas Central was sold to W. J. Hutchins and David H. Page for $10,000. There were ten railroads operating on 469 miles of track. Some of the road routes were maintained to transport troops. But in many places, rails were torn up and made into bullets. When the war ended in 1865, all 10 railroads were bankrupt, all their roadbeds in disrepair except those of the H&TC, Houston and Texas Central.

On January 11, 1861, the *Houston Telegraph* proudly predicted, "Texas will always respond to the movement of South Carolina with votes, with men or gun powder as the occasion may demand!" In spite of its pioneer beginning and though the early settlers were, on the whole, a violent lot, Houston had developed into a Southern town.

Many a Houstonian wore a blue rosette with a silver star on his hat, the symbol of secession. The Lone Star flag, forty feet long, rose on the 100-foot Liberty Pole in Court House Square. On January 14, 1861, Houston voted overwhelmingly for the secession of Texas from the Union. On January 28, 1861, Texas joined the Confederate States of America by act of a Secession Convention in Austin.

When Governor Houston refused to take the Convention's oath, ratified by statewide vote on February 23, he was deposed and succeeded by Lt. Governor Edward Clark. Stormy though the issue had become, many of the old warrior's friends regretted Houston's position.

The tragedy of Sam Houston was that no one listened to the far-seeing wisdom of his final words:

> "I love Texas too well to bring strife and bloodshed upon her . . . it is perhaps meant that my career should close thus. I have seen patriots and states-

men of my youth one by one gathered to their father and the government which they have reared,
rent in twain . . . I stand the last almost of my
race."

————————◁ ▷————————

By 1862, Galveston was in the hands of Union forces.
Houston was the headquarters for the Confederate District of Texas. General John Bankhead Magruder was in
command. Handsome "Prince John" cut a dashing figure on Houston streets. The town was busy with preparations for war. Stores were almost empty of merchandise. John Kennedy's Trading Post on Market Square
was an arsenal for cannon, bombs and small arms.
Frank Foley's merchandise store was making soap and
candles. Tallow Town, the packing settlement adjacent
to Houston, flowed with the blood of thousands of cattle
slaughtered to feed Magruder's forces.

The City Hospital at Austin and McKinney was made
ready to receive the wounded. (Later, during the yellow
fever epidemic of 1867, it would become a grim charnel
house so dreaded that no Negro would walk near it.)
Work was halted on the new courthouse that boasted pil-
lars and porticoes costing $25,000. The uncompleted
building became a cartridge factory with more than 200
boys, girls and older women employed. The basement
became a prison.

Two Houston parents were taking the Federal blockade at Galveston more personally than others. Their
young daughter, trying to get home from New York, was
a prisoner on her ship in Galveston harbor. Finally,
someone conceived the idea of wrapping her in the flag
of the United States and lifting her overboard as a valuable Yankee package. She finally reached Houston, safe
if not feeling altogether sound.

The Confederate Guards, Bayou City Guards and the Turner Rifles drilled daily in Market Square, new faces replacing those who had sailed on down the bayou before the blockade to join the Confederate forces. The Confederate officers' favorite hangout in Houston was the Fannin House on Fannin near Congress. The Old Capitol Hotel also got its share of Confederate uniforms.

Down at the foot of Main Street, secret, momentous plans were budding. The two steamboats, *Bayou City* and the *Neptune*, loaded with cotton, were setting sail down Buffalo Bayou toward Galveston. The ships looked innocent enough. But behind the towering bales of cotton, hidden riflemen crouched. Steaming slowly behind in their wake were the *Lucy Gwinn* and the *John F. Carr*, also loaded with concealed infantrymen.

General Magruder's objective was to rout the Federal ships out of Galveston and recapture the town. His army, stashed between bales of cotton, planned to attack heavily-armed Federal gunboats in Galveston Bay.

As his secret army sailed, Magruder was planning a strong land attack to support the armed steamboats' assault on the Federal gunboats.

Writer Hudson Strode described Magruder's army as a "ragtag force and some improvised gun boats armored with cotton bales."

But what a ragtag force! On New Year's Day of 1863 General Magruder ordered the first cannon fired. The battle was on!

The *Neptune*, guns roaring, rammed the U.S. gunboat *Harriet Lane*. The *Bayou City*, coming along side, kept firing all her cannon balls, killing Union Captain Wainright of the *Harriet Lane*. The Confederates swarmed from behind their cotton bales all over the Federal ship, taking victorious possession.

General Magruder demanded unconditional surrender of the Federal fleet and troops in Galveston, setting a deadline for surrender. But before the hour, the Federal fleet escaped out of Galveston harbor, leaving the *Harriet Lane* and 386 Federal prisoners in General Magruder's hands.

But what a great day for Main Street! By carriage, trap, wagon, on foot, folks massed at the foot of Main. The *Bayou City*, flying at her masthead a cotton hat with the conquered *Harriet Lane*'s ensign and crowded with Federal prisoners, whistled, clanged and bumped against the dock.

Everybody hurrahed like mad. Fifes and drums beat the air. Horses whinnied in shrill protest. Homemade fireworks exploded with terrifying authority.

The Federal prisoners filed slowly off the *Bayou City*, marching in a long line down Main Street. Everybody fell silent, watching intently. But that night was a high old time in Houston with a ball in honor of "Prince John." The walls of Perkins Hall on Franklin Street trembled from all the boot stomping and wild fiddlin' that went on until dawn.

General Magruder, ". . . tall, dark and handsome, a snappy dresser, a fast man with a buck and a lover of beautiful women," apparently could arouse even the most worn-out married woman. To watch the dashing General equally enjoying the collation of ducks, venison, oysters, bourbon, brandy, and one lovely woman after another, made every woman present feel that at any moment "Prince John" might find her desirable. There were whispers that there was a Mrs. Magruder and children somewhere. "However, he never referred to them and most people thought he was a bachelor." ("Rebel Leader Discovered by Kin," Alice Murphy, *The Houston Post,* printed with permission.)

———————————————

Sam Houston, General, President and Founder of the Republic of Texas, friend of the Indians, and named

"Raven" by the Cherokees, died in his home at Huntsville, Texas, July, 1863. He had gone to Sour Lake to rest. But one week later, ill, sad, and scorned by those who had once admired him, he went home to die, in the midst of the war that he had predicted would begin, if the Union were dissolved.

"As the slanting shadows of sunset crept upon Steamboat House, General Houston ceased to breathe. A life so strange and so lonely; whose fingertips had touched stars and felt them change to dust, had slipped away. (*The Raven* by Marquis James)

A difficult man to understand as genius always is, he was a patriot in the oldest, Roman, sense. Three months after he was buried, the Legislature of the State of Texas passed a resolution that stands as his epitaph:

> "His public services through a long and eventful life, his unblemished patriotism, his great private and moral worth, and his untiring, devoted, and zealous regard for the interests of the State of Texas command our highest admiration, and should be held in perpetual remembrance by the people of this State."

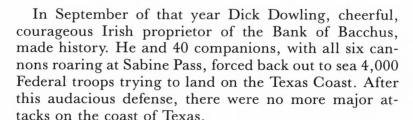

In September of that year Dick Dowling, cheerful, courageous Irish proprietor of the Bank of Bacchus, made history. He and 40 companions, with all six cannons roaring at Sabine Pass, forced back out to sea 4,000 Federal troops trying to land on the Texas Coast. After this audacious defense, there were no more major attacks on the coast of Texas.

For the remaining two years of the war, the Houston woman, like her counterpart throughout the South, had to sharply hone her housekeeping to the barest necessities. Confederate money greatly depreciated—a 100-

pound sack of flour cost $50; a quart of milk, $1; a pair of boots, $100. Beef was cheap at 25¢ a pound, but the lady had better hang onto her old garters. A new pair would cost her $30. Men thirsted for brandy at $20 a pint.

There was no tea or coffee at any price. But the women had picked up practical lore from the Alabama-Coushatta Indians. They gathered the seeds from the flowers of the Texas Ebony tree to make a brew vaguely like coffee. Crushed leaves of the Toothache Tree relieved many a toothache. They gathered purplish berries of the Poke Berry bushes, growing along creeks all through the woods. During the war this was the only source of ink. In the spring, the young Poke Berry shoots were boiled like turnips and mustard greens. Rare was the Texan, black or white, who didn't think a "mess o' poke" was mighty fine. In the fall, the roots were dug up to treat ringworm and rheumatism.

———————————⊳◁ ▷⊲———————————

One of the most fascinating characters of the Civil War, certainly the most inexplicable, lies buried not far off Main Street in the Old German cemetery at 2911 Washington Boulevard. The crusted inscription on the old tombstone reads, "Emma E. Seelye, Army Nurse." No mention of her other self: Frank Thompson, spy in the Grand Army of the Republic.

Sarah Emma Evelyn Edmondson was born in New Brunswick, Canada, in 1841. Her father wanted a son and never got over having a daughter instead. To make it up to him, Emma taught herself to shoot, climb trees, ride unbroken horses. She grew to despise girls—probably even herself.

When she was 18 her father tried to force her to marry a farmer many years older. Emma bundled up her few possessions and took a boat to the United States. Apparently she lived a strange, solitary existence, going from one boarding house to another, working at odd jobs.

Then she made an astonishing decision. She cut off her brown curls. She put on the clothes of a young man. She gave herself the name of Frank Thompson. For a while Frank Thompson worked for the book publishing firm that would one day publish her book, *The Nurse and The Spy*.

On May 17, 1861, in Flint, Michigan, Frank Thompson took his most audacious step of all. One that two years later would astound General Orlando Metcalfe Poe, commander of the Second Michigan Infantry of the Federal Army. Not to say what it would do to Frank's war-time tent mates.

Frank Thompson enlisted as a soldier in the Union forces. For the next two years he served on General Poe's staff as a scout, spy, and brigade postmaster. In those days there were no medical examinations to enter the Army. Frank's only problem was to stay out of the hospital.

It is said that Frank Thompson was given a test in Washington, D.C., to become a member of the Secret Service. One of the Generals conducting the review was George B. McClelland.

"According to government records, Private Thompson passed the test a good shot; a good rider, possessing the ability to keep things secret!" ("Woman Soldier for GAR," *The Houston Post*, February 26, 1967, used with permission.)

Frank was given his first spy mission. Disguising himself as a Negro boy cook, he mingled with General Robert E. Lee's troops, returning to General Poe with highly valuable information on the enemy's fortifications and plans for troop movements.

Emma Seelye-Frank Thompson was said to have penetrated enemy lines as a spy 11 times, once as an old woman selling cakes and pies to the Confederate soldiers. He fought at Bull Run, Williamsburg, Fredericksburg, and Richmond.

One day—and it was a miracle it hadn't happened sooner—Frank was stricken with malaria and ordered to the hospital. Terrified that at last his secret would be exposed, he asked for a furlough. When it was denied, he deserted.

Frank recuperated from the malaria in a boarding house in a small town in Ohio. When he was well he left, destroyed all traces of Frank Thompson, turned back into Emma Edmondson. A few days later, out of some twisted humor, Emma returned to the same boarding house and rented the same room she had lived in as Frank Thompson.

But these years of living a split personality had taken their toll. Emma had a nervous breakdown.

When she recovered, she re-enlisted in the Northern Army as a nurse. Frank Thompson was listed as a deserter.

At the close of the Civil War, Emma Edmondson wrote *The Nurse and the Spy*, an account of her fantastic experiences in the Federal Army. True to her passion for anonymity her book was published anonymously. The book had a sale of 175,000 copies, and she instructed her publisher to give her proceeds to various hospitals.

After the book was published, this extraordinary woman married Linus Seelye. They moved to Saint Mary's Parish in Louisiana. The former soldier had a daughter and two sons. The daughter and one of the infant sons died. The family moved to Missouri and later to Fort Scott, Kansas.

But Emma Seelye was bitter over being called a deserter. She also resented the fact that Frank Thompson had never received the pension owed by the government for his two years of service in the Army as a spy.

She made a trip back to Flint. There she sought out some of the men who had served with her in the Federal Army under General Poe. She wanted their affidavits saying she had served with them.

"Newspaper accounts of the meeting she had with a man with whom she had shared a tent said he 'wilted' when he recognized the woman indeed as his Army buddy Frank Thompson." (*The Houston Post*, February 26, 1967.)

One morning at their home in Fort Scott, Kansas, Emma Seelye read in the town newspaper that Company F of the Second Michigan Infantry was going to hold a reunion. She wrote that she would give anything to attend but had no money. She signed herself, Frank Thompson. Her buddies, delighted to have old Frank, deserter or no, come for the reunion, got up a collection to pay "his" way.

The Houston Post, June 2, 1901, reported, "She attended the reunion in 1884, after 20 years absence, but what a change! Then, they knew her as the affable and soldierly Frank Thompson, now as the mature mother and matron, Mrs. Seelye." What a surprise for Emma's former tent mates!

The United States Congress passed an Act shortly thereafter, removing her disability as a deserter and awarding her a pension of $12 per month.

The Seelyes, their son, Fred, and wife, Lucy, moved to Texas in 1893. Across the Bay from San Jacinto battle ground, the Seelyes bought a small farm. But Emma Seelye was haunted by her strange past. She grew ill in body and mind, spending her days slowly rocking to and fro on her front porch.

One day, the Seelyes sold their farm and took the ferryboat to La Porte, where they bought a small white frame house. In April, 1897, she took the train to Houston for a ceremony in which she was mustered into the

McClellan Post, Grand Army of the Republic, the only woman member of the GAR. To have been accepted must have been a balm to her twisted, solitary spirit.

Emma Seelye's neighbors heard her dog wailing the eerie, mournful cry of a dog in the presence of death. Emma, alias Frank Thompson, was found alone, dead. First buried in La Porte, her body later was moved to the cemetery on Washington Boulevard on Memorial Day in 1901.

———————————————

On April 9, 1865, General Robert E. Lee surrendered at Appomattox. On May 13th, the last battle of the Civil War was fought at Palmito Ranch near Brownsville, Texas. Colonel John S. Ford of the Confederate Army captured 800 Federal troops only to learn from them that the war was over. Houston felt the War between the States as much as any Confederate city, but it recovered with the resiliency of youth. Plantation families from Virginia, Kentucky, Tennessee and the Carolinas began to come to seek new fortunes in Texas.

"Magruder never really surrendered. In May of 1865, he called his army together and disbanded it with these words: 'Boys, the jig's up! Help yourself to any supplies you can carry home.'" ("Rebel Leader Discovered by Kin," Alice Murphy, *The Houston Post*, printed with permission.)

CHAPTER SIX

"'Mr. Panell,' an angry Federal officer stormed, 'they tell me you dislike to bury Union soldiers.' 'General, that is a damned lie. It's the pleasantest thing I've had to do in years and I can't get enough of it.'"

MAIN STREET, 1865, rumbled to the tune of Federal soldiers. The war was over. The soldiers stretched a rope high across Congress Avenue, to which they attached a large U.S. flag over the boardwalk. Women refused to pass under the flag. They simply lifted their skirts to their boot tops and traipsed through the mud. Bewildered, idle ex-slaves, in small groups, hung around the street corners, waiting their turn to see the Freedmen's Bureau with charges against their former masters.

General Gordon Granger was sent to Texas to maintain order and hope for the ultimate return of Texas to the Union. He arrived in Galveston and issued an order emancipating all slaves and declaring all former laws enacted during the secession illegal. On June 19, 1865,

General Granger, a compassionate man, read aloud the copy of the Emancipation Proclamation. That day, called Juneteenth, has been celebrated annually in Houston.

With their new status and cast adrift, slaves wandered from plantation to plantation, from bottomlands to rivers.

Many Houstonians were sympathetic with their plight. The *Tri-Weekly Telegraph* wrote:

> We cannot help but pity the poor freedmen and women that have left comfortable and happy homes in the country and come to the city in search of what they call freedom. Nearly all the old buildings that were not occupied . . . serve as homes for these people. Many of these buildings are not fit for stables.

However, some ex-slaves were able to find employment on a sharecropping basis for area planters. (Courtesy Harris County Heritage Society.)

Texas had not been the scene of major battles of the Civil War. The state was more a storehouse, furnishing the military with beef, farm products, leather goods and cotton cloth. But she sent her sons to fight, more than fifty thousand of them. One had been the heroic, devil-may-care Dick Dowling, who had returned to Houston after routing the Federal fleet at Sabine Pass. He was reopening his "Bank of Bacchus" on the corner of Main and Congress.

> R. W. Dowling, President and Cashier and Dealer
> in the following Exchange
> Brandy, Eau de Vie de Cognac
> Whiskey-A la Bourbon,
> Monongahela, Rye, Champagne,
> Of all the Brands of the Old or New World, Claret

and Port-de vintage 46 and a Variety of other liq-
uors. Drafts and Acceptances Cashed on Sight.
Liberal Discounts on Deposits. In Re-Opening the
Bank, the Proprietor tenders his congratulations to
his old customers and fellow citizens and begs them
not to forget the Bank of Bacchus.

Dick Dowling

As for Dowling, who died a young man in 1867, a
statue stands in his honor in Hermann Park. Each year
the Irish still commemorate his courage on St. Patrick's
Day.

The Yankees in Texas brought with them the new
game of baseball, a healer of deep wounds on both sides.
The Houston Bayou City Club team, made up of Un-
ionists and Confederates, clad in their military uniforms, played the Galveston team, yelling, "Oh, you
Sand Crabs—see us bury you!"

And the Galveston team hollered back, "Oh, you
Mud Cats—let us at you!"

By 1866, 25 brick buildings were rising downtown.
Houston, then as now, was a town of violent contrasts.
Side by side with rat pits and lynchings, was Miss
Brown's seminary, the "Vassar of the South," at 284
McKinney. She prepared young ladies for the finest
Eastern Colleges.

In addition, she taught proper social behavior at the
new ZZ Balls. The ZZ Club was formed one night when
Rufus Cage and Henry Sampson, Jr., well-known young
men about town, invited their friends and the prominent
older men to meet them in Sampson's Store, all lit up by
candle light. The idea was to form a new, exclusive
dance club where they could dance something besides
the square dance. The older men, naturally opposed to
any social change, finally agreed it couldn't do too much
harm to learn something new. They wouldn't dance it
anyhow. The ZZ Club was to dominate Houston Society

until the turn of the century, with dashing, imperious Spencer Hutchins, Houston's "King of Society," who also led the Cotillions. The ZZ Club was the outstanding social center of the time and brought out the debutantes each year. Social life was very gracious.

Houston dragged at low tide after the Civil War. Reconstruction's abusive laws made life intolerable for men and women, in business and in social life. Development of the Ship Channel came to a halt, just as it had won the support of the town's leading bankers, merchants, hotels and newspapers. As always, however, Houstonians carried on.

Every man out at night carried a lantern and a six shooter. The women had to scrape the bottom of their purses and secret hiding places to buy food necessities. The need for flour was great. It filled you up. But all they could buy was ". . . war time stuff, made mostly of ground peas and corn mixed with some wheat, the best on top of the barrel, the flour getting progressively worse as it neared the bottom." They learned from the Alabama-Coushatta Indians to dry the root stocks of the common cat-tail, remove the fibers, and pulverize them into a substitute flour. They even tried the Apache's way of basting the red clover, growing everywhere, with dandelion and poke berry leaves. It turned out to be a fairly savory, nutritional "mess o' greens."

East Lynne and *Camille* played to full houses. The first theatre—the old Market Square Theatre on Congress between Travis and Milam—provided the setting for some of the finest plays and actors of the period. Pillot's Opera House presented "The Jersey Lily" (Lillie Langtry) in 1882. John L. Sullivan appeared there in a sparring match in 1884, and a year later Edwin Booth trod the same stage as Hamlet.

Women, as never before, identified with tragic heroines. It gave them a chance to wear the latest thing in a bonnet called the "Gypsy," a sort of cross between a stove pipe and a soup plate. The 1866 *City Directory of Houston* listed improvements: "40 blocks to be shelled. A contract has been made for putting up sign boards at the corners of the streets and it is anticipated that the City Fathers will shortly cause different lots to be numbered and require the owners of the buildings to put numbers upon them accordingly!" And the first electric street light turned on at Main and Preston in 1880.

Thomas H. Scanlan bought the late Sam Houston's cabin and property on Main and tore the cabin down. He replaced it with a brick structure, the Scanlan Building, restored by Jack Cannata. Fannin House was advertising on its Bill of Fare: "Children at first table, Full Price; at second table, Half Price. For entertaining a drunken man per day $10!"

Along with this influx of civilization, 300-pound black "Auntie" was selling cocaine in "Tin Can Alley," just off Preston Avenue. "Queen Caroline" ruled this shanty area with "teeth, claws, six-shooters, and razors, devoutly assisted by Big Foot, Charley Johnson, Julia Baker, and Lillie Rivers. The area was later known as Vinegar Hill. When the "Queen" died in 1881, the area was sold at public auction for the site of Union Station." (*The Houston Daily Post*, 1887)

Like the red clover growing everywhere, the seed of Houston kept renewing itself in the darkness of the radical Republican rule. President Andrew Johnson, in 1866, wanted to pursue a less severe course in the South. But his moderate proposals for reconstruction of the South were defeated by the radicals in Congress. They wanted to keep the South under military rule until the Negro was enfranchised and elections held.

Voting became a humiliating experience for the white Houstonian. He often waited hours in line while Negroes, some of them his former slaves, were ushered ahead of him. When he reached the polls, he could be told they were closed for the day. Many Houstonians, unwilling to swear an oath of allegiance to the United States, were forbidden to vote, much less hold office.

In March, 1867, the United States Congress, over President Johnson's veto, passed the first radical Reconstruction Act: "No legal state governments will exist in any of the Southern States which have been organized under President Johnson. Any local government set up under the President's Reconstruction plan will be abolished by the Military ruling power!"

The Radicals demanded that all "rebels" be disenfranchised, all legislation passed on from 1861–65 be declared void, and that all former masters be responsible for payments to their Negroes from Lincoln's proclamation on January 1, 1863 until 1865. The "unpardoned rebel" who had held office under the Confederacy was to be denied citizenship without special dispensation from the President of the United States.

To add to the pall over the town came one of the worst yellow fever epidemics. Mayor Alexander McGowen ordered Main Street to be cleaned up and ". . . after the 31st day of December 1867, it shall not be lawful for hogs, sows, pigs or goats . . . to go at large in the limits of the city."

Dick Dowling, the courageous Irish Texan, was one of the fever's first victims. "He will be remembered throughout the country as the hero of the Battle of Sabine Pass, an achievement not only not equaled during the War, but hardly matched by the renowned affairs of Thermopylae." (*Daily Telegraph*, September 25, 1867)

Vats of tar burned on Houston streets day and night. Undertaker Pannell hired Negroes with drays, Negro grave diggers and extra carpenters to make coffins. But he couldn't keep up with the bodies.

Pannell was considered to be "unreconstructed." One day an angry Federal officer sent for him. "'Mr. Pannell, they tell me you dislike to bury my soldiers.'

'General,' said Pannell, 'whoever told you that told a damned lie. It's the pleasantest thing I've had to do in years and I can't get enough of it. I would like to bury every damned one of you!' The interview ended abruptly for the General ordered Pannell to jail. He did not stay long for his services were in too great demand and he was released and went back to work." (*True Stories of Old Houston and Houstonians*, Dr. S. O. Young.)

Out in Harrisburg, at 614 Broadway, a 13-year-old girl was nursing yellow fever victims around the clock. She was Maggie Tod, daughter of Captain and Mrs. John G. Tod.

Some families sent their children to Galveston or to Louisiana until the epidemic was over. But since Maggie had suffered the yellow fever and lived, it was considered only right that she remain and help with the overwhelming burden of nursing victims.

Maggie's father, Captain Tod, was Commodore of the Texas Navy. Mrs. Tod was said to have possessed the only fine needle in south Texas. With babies ever on the way in the new settlement, her prized needle was in demand for the tiny stitches necessary for long baby dresses, undershirts, and blankets. She made only one stipulation. She herself must bring the needle and return for it. The redoubtable Mrs. Tod was a familiar sight trotting off in her buggy to Houston, bearing her fine needle.

But one day in this year of the deadly epidemic, her needle was used for a grim purpose. Her young son, John, lay prostrate. Thirteen-year-old Maggie was the only member of the family who could take care of him. She placed her delirious little brother on a blanket. Carefully, she rolled it around him, wrapping his arms against his sides so that he couldn't scratch. With trembling fingers, she stitched him in his safe cocoon with the fine needle.

Unprepared for death at 13, she had to face it all around her. There were no funerals. Bodies were thrust into make-shift boxes. Some lay in the streets, shunned even by members of their own families. John recovered and one day, at last, the yellow fever scourge subsided. As always, Houston after floods—the town was new washed in the sun.

Maggie felt the sunshine, listened to the many bird songs, the steamboats whistling up the Bayou. Forgetting yesterday, she ran, jumped, cried aloud her joy in being alive. Maggie Tod went back to school to memorize Kerr's Geography.

> Galveston Island long and low,
> Ships can there for safety go,
> Pass Canals long and slim,
> Ships go there and can't get in.
> Ducks and geese come flying back,
> On the way to Anahuac.

Years ago, Rosa Tod Hamner showed me John Tod's worn little Geography book. In the margin, the small boy who was to become Secretary of State of Texas (1901–1903), wrote in the margin, "Oh Kerr! Oh Kerr! What did you write these verses fur!"

At eighteen, Maggie went on picnics in the moonlit square across from her house. But parties weren't enough for a young girl who had nursed the dying. She became a teacher in Halseys Private School in Harrisburg, where she had been a pupil. She met Charles Milby and forgot the books. They lived in her childhood home on Broadway in Harrisburg until she died in 1941. All but 13 years of her life were lived in this same house.

In 1954, Mary Ellen Shipnes and I paid a farewell visit to the old Milby house. It was about to be demolished. It had been offered to the newly-formed Harris County Heritage Society to restore. Unfortunately, the group had no funds and found few Houstonians were interested in preserving the past at that time.

The once-finely-wrought iron gates and walls of handmade bricks had rusted and crumbled. Coral vine twisted in the wind around the columns with paint peeling off the three-story brick house. The cypress shutters at each tall window creaked their forlorn farewell.

Pushing open the heavy, cypress front door, blackened by time and weather, we went silently through the big rooms with their fourteen-foot-high ceilings. Wide oak floor boards buckled here and there. Some of the walls hung with stained ribbons of once elegant wallpaper.

We left and drove to the Glendale Cemetery in Harrisburg. It had once been the private burial ground of the family of John Harris, founder of Harrisburg. Part of the 4,425 acres Harris received from the Mexican Government in 1824, the old cemetery lies at the foot of Magnolia Street on a bluff overlooking the intersection of Brays Bayou and the Ship Channel.

In the morning fog, we walked along the bluff where General Sidney Sherman's house stood until it burned in 1859.

We read from the aged tombstones: "Jane Birdsall Harris, died 1869." She was the wife of John R. Harris, founder of Harrisburg. He died of yellow fever on his boat, *The Rights of Man*, in New Orleans. His grave has never been found.

"Colonel John A. Williams, died 1867." He was the first surveyor of Harrisburg. His original map, still used, was owned by his descendant, the late Judge Wilmer B. Hunt of Austin.

"Judge John Birdsall, died 1839." He was Attorney General of the Republic of Texas, Chief Justice of the Supreme Court.

The Briscoes, Tods, Milbys, Allens; they were all there, the people who helped build Houston. (Author's column, *The Houston Post*. Used with permission.)

West of Houston are two other old cemeteries on Washington Boulevard: the German Cemetery, only recently cared for; and Glenwood, one of the loveliest retreats in the city. Here, the early citizens of Houston lie at peace within gentle rises, beneath aged oaks. As one prominent native once put it, "I know more people in Glenwood than I will ever know again in Houston!"

———————————⊳◁ ▷⊲———————————

In March of 1870 a bill was passed in the United States Congress offering readmission to Texas, but it depended upon all members of the Texas Legislature taking an oath to accept the 14th Amendment, "that the State Constitution should never be amended as to deprive the Negro of the right to vote or to hold office or to attend free school. . ."

Some former slaves were placed in high offices. One, Erastus Carter, was said to have been made Supervisor of Education in Harris County in 1870. The military under General Ulysses S. Grant supported the most radical Republicans, who in turn were supported by Negro voters and Yankees.

Living under the regime of the Texas Radical Republican Governor Edmund J. Davis meant living under a crank, a petty tyrant. He organized an 80-member Negro State police. It had all the powers of local police as well. "Special Charters were granted many towns and cities and the Governor saw to it that they gave him the power to appoint the mayors and in some instances the other city officials as well." (*Texas Under Many Flags*, Clarence Wharton)

On July 26, 1870, Davis appointed Thomas H. Scanlan as Mayor of Houston along with four Negroes as aldermen. White men of prominence began to band together to, "maintain white supremacy by *lawful* means." Thus, was the Ku Klux Klan, the ultra-secret, terrorist organization dedicated to southern sovereignty, born in Texas. Although it was more active in East Texas, the Klan in Houston was unable to muster much influence. There were 300 members in Houston and thousands over the State. No written record was kept of their meetings or activities.

"I belonged to the order from the day of its organization until it was dissolved and I never knew of an unlawful act done by it, nor of one done by some over-zealous or silly member that was not promptly rebuked." (*True Stories of Old Houston and Houstonians*, Dr. O. S. Young)

But in time, the Ku Klux Klan became as guilty as the evils it believed it was pursuing. It was revived after World War I. The 20th Century Klan had no connection of historical root in the old one. The early Klan was a political group formed to control the black vote. The revived Klan was much closer in spirit to the old Know-Nothing party, nativist, protestant and secret. It merely borrowed the hoods and mysterious trappings of the 19th Century Klan, which had been adopted to terrify superstitious Negroes. (*Lone Star*, T. R. Fehrenbach.) As late as 1921, more than 2,000 Houstonians would be inducted in the Ku Klux Klan on the prairie a short distance south of Bellaire.

The year 1873 saw the end of the Republican stranglehold on Houston and Texas. For the first time since the Civil War, the Democrats convened. They nominated ex-Confederate soldier Richard Coke as Governor to run against the renominated radical Governor E. J. Davis. "To everyone but Davis, the result was never in doubt. Stubbornly refusing to believe himself beaten, he carried the fight to the counties with a heavy black population where he had made himself hated by the white people. The whites were determined that Davis and the carpetbag regime must go. Davis' 'Niggers' were in many counties ordered to keep away from the polls, and minors voted." (*Texas Under Many Flags*, Clarence Wharton)

Richard Coke was elected by a majority of 85,549 to 42,633. Davis refused to recognize defeat or to surrender his office. He wrote for the President's help but Grant refused, advising him to accept facts.

Coke wired his good friend, a Federal Judge in Waco, George C. Clark, (my grandfather) to come to Austin at once and help him straighten out the political mess. Coke insisted on making him Secretary of State. Clark agreed, but only on a temporary basis. He hoped to be named the next Attorney General of Texas.

After a number of Gilbert and Sullivan scenes, Davis was ousted and Coke finally took office, according to *A Glance Backward,* by Judge George C. Clark.

Coke immediately removed Houston's Mayor Scanlan and his board of radical Republican aldermen. He appointed James T. D. Wilson Mayor. The town's Municipal Treasury was at its lowest level. In the summer of 1874, the City Hall, "Scanlan's Scandal," was completed . . . "a princely building . . . the debt is also princely." The structure had grown into a $470,000 fiasco, with leaking roof and problems in venting the lower floors, with expensive chandeliers and fluted columns "bespeaking a theatre" on the second floor. The City Market was on the ground floor, with vegetable and meat stalls on either side. This arrangement was to continue well into the 20th century.

With the radical Republican regime gone, W. D. Cleveland's General Merchandise Store on Main and Congress couldn't keep up with business. "At one time, 80% of the commerce of Texas went by this corner." (*Wave of the Gulf,* Jesse Ziegler) F. W. Heitmann's two-story brick hardware store was nearby, as was Carl Illig's furniture store with rocking chairs out front for his friends to watch the street's goings on.

Benjamin Shepherd's First National Bank gave an air of stability to the town. T. W. House's two story bank and wholesale grocery faced Franklin. Here, six or eight yokes of oxen waited daily to carry away bacon, groceries, bagging and rail ties. Latham's store was the only one south of the Masonic Temple. Beyond, "Beautiful gardens continued to Calhoun Ditch, and Calhoun River at times carried the storm waters off into Braes Bayou." (*Wave of the Gulf,* Jesse Ziegler.)

———————————⊃◄ ►⊂———————————

The history of cotton is the story of Houston; the story of cotton is the history of Houston; for since its early beginings, it had but one "money crop" and that, of course, was cotton.

The business developed in the export of this fiber to Liverpool, England, and other consuming centers. Houston became recognized as a warehousing and shipping center to all four quarters of the world.

One might stop here and pay tribute to the various elements in this picture—bankers, producers, merchants and others—whose vision gave impetus to this development. But the real history of this great industry, which was the mainstay of the early days, stems from May 15, 1874 when a group of men met in the Hutchins House to organize the first Houston Board of Trade and Cotton Exchange. Within modest walls, over bourbon and tobacco, they plotted the town's future in cotton, rice, lumber, cattle, banking, railroads and the development of a Ship Channel. There was born here "an iridescent dream"—the idea that Houston should become a major port city.

When the plan was made public there was a great deal of merriment on the part of West Gulf competitors. They could not conceive the narrow tortuous channel choked with logs, infested with alligators, and full of all kinds of debris, ever becoming a port-of-call for ocean-going vessels.

However from that day forward these men of great vision and indomitable energy persevered and with men who came after them lived to hear that Congress had approved the project for dredging to a depth of 25 feet from the foot of Main Street to Galveston Bay. This was later amended; and by then there were fifty cotton firms in Houston that handled more than a million and a half bales each season.

At this juncture Thomas W. House became an ardent spokesman for the proposed waterway. Membership committeeman, Colonel Henry M. Robert, better known as the author of *Robert's Rules of Order* estimated construction and maintenance costs, William Marsh Rice's nephew, Baldwin Rice, was one of Houston's mayors (1905–13) who also helped develop the channel and a leading Houston business man, Jesse H. Jones was influential in raising the $4.25 million to purchase the bonds thus guaranteeing the completion of the project.

Like all government projects there were delays. At last in 1910 Congress passed an appropriation to complete the 51-mile 25-foot channel, if the people of Harris County would pay half the cost. Hence, known to this day as "The Houston Plan" it was brought into being and fostered almost entirely on the basis of cotton exports.

The channel was completed in 1914 when the good ship *Merrymount* lifted more than 20,000 bales of cotton bound for Liverpool. Cotton men who had watched the ship's departure with their fingers crossed, heaved a tremendous sigh of relief after she passed Morgan's Point and headed for the open sea. At the dedication, a 21 gun salute was fired by the *USS Windom*. While the "Star-Spangled Banner" played from a barge, a wreath of white rose petals floated by. At last, the dream that was dreamed in 1874 by a handful of men, in a room at the Hutchins House, became a reality.

The Cotton Exchange building on Travis and Franklin, built in 1884, designed by Eugene Heiner and Jesse Edmondson, has been restored by David Hannah. Hannah, with astronaut Deke Slayton, recently built and fired successfully the first privately-built rocket designed to put payloads in earth orbit.

In the 1870s as now, streets were an eternal problem. J. V. Dealy, who had a book bindery and printing business, wrote: "The streets got so bad in a long rainy spell that it was almost impossible to navigate them with a vehicle. I have seen a two-horse wagon bogged down with a load of one barrel of flour on Court House Square. The butchers had to bring their meat to market on pack horses and the milk men likewise. I attended at least one funeral on the streetcars because the hacks could not make it to the cemetery. A young couple got married and wanted to go to New Orleans on their wedding trip. The best they could do to get from the house to the depot was in a high-wheeled ambulance pulled by four street mules!"

The City Directory in 1879 listed the Kennedy House, built by John Kennedy, the owner of the Indians' favorite trading post on Market Square. It was a three story hotel at Travis and Congress. The building is still in existence.

Kennedy House boasted 26 bedrooms. According to an 1879 inventory, most of the bedrooms had a "Chandelier with three gas burners, four beds, moss pillows, marble wash stand, cane bottom chairs, painted tin slop bucket, mosquito bars, chamber pot, china bowl and pitcher." Most of the beds were high posted, some with half canopies. A few were low posted or "cottage" bedsteads. Only three rooms offered the privacy of just one bed. Apparently, one could expect roommates.

The parlor boasted a piano and china spitoons. The bar was furnished with black, round back, wood chairs, glass lamps, cut glass decanters and surprisingly, a foot tub. The dining room was spacious with 53 cane bottom oak chairs, seven extension tables, 3 movable hat racks, 1 clock and 3 chandeliers with 4 burners each. In the kitchen copper stew pans, tin coffee pots, tin graters and strainers hung on the wall near the big cast iron wood burning stove. Iron cauldrons sat near by. Tin pudding moulds, coffee mills, pepper mills, flat irons, wash tub and wash board occupied corners and shelves. The sturdy pine meat block also got heavy use.

In front of Kennedy House, a Jersey spring wagon, carts and horses waited at their posts for guests. Nearby, Kennedy's son-in-law, W. L. Foley, operated a dry goods store in the 200 block of Travis. He advertised French Imports, Ladies Piece Goods, Notions.

Children would watch the wire baskets carrying the customer's purchase and money singing across Foley's high ceiling, clanging to a halt, then jingling back over the cable with package and change . . . would love the feel of the handsome wrought-iron elevator, one's skinny bottom sinking into its deep cushioned seat as it rose in slow dignity to the second floor.

Something was always happening on Main Street. A crowd might be watching Browne and Bolfrass receive a medal for the best stick candy made in town, a steamboat land, or over on Crawford watching the train come whistling and puffing into the new Union Station.

On March 29, 1880 more than 50,000 people turned out to welcome ex-President Ulysses S. Grant when he arrived on the first train to enter the new Union Station.

The bitter memories forgotten, the former Union Commander received a rousing reception. The large crowd followed Grant's party to the Hutchins House. Later the balcony where Grant was standing started swaying and cracking and almost collapsed under the weight of those who sought to shake his hand.

At a reception later that day, Grant was impressed by the good will of the guests. When asked his impression of Houston, Grant replied: "Next to each other are hovels and good buildings, business and private homes, stores with poor goods, worse taste, beside establishments whose windows will vie with any in New York, London, or Paris, churches beside saloons, Anglo Saxons and Latins. Underlying all, a love of Texas and an ambition that defies description."

It was a rapidly-moving quarter of a century for Houston. Free public schools opened in 1876. In 1891, William Marsh Rice gave the first $200,000 endowment to begin Rice Institute. That same year Houston saw its first street car, and Paderewski played in the Auditorium.

In this era, Houstonians were great picnickers. All Saints Day was a favorite picnic day. On November 1, 1886, from early morning on, more than 4,000 people of all ages came by buggy, trap, carriage, and streetcar, carrying baskets of sandwiches, cookies, and flowers to their family graves in Glenwood Cemetery.

Fifteen extra streetcars transported the crowd out Washington Avenue. Families spent the whole day, picnicking and visiting each other's plots beneath the moss-heavy oak trees. Not in a melancholy mood, but sharing warm, happy memories of their loved ones. Children's laughter and cries of delight on discovering family names were sounds as natural as the blue jays and mockingbirds.

Main Street sprouted an architectural wonder in 1895, Jacob S. Binz' six-story office building on Main and Texas. Designed by Ollie Lorehn, designer of many of the town's early buildings, it was of buff-colored brick and concrete. The outside steps were of gray granite from Burnet, Texas. The windows were arched and ornamental with carved limestone, the two-foot-tall cornice on top of the structure gave it the look of a European castle.

The building not only was tall, it had an elevator! People came for miles to ride it to the top floor and gaze out in wonder at the countryside! Binz was one of the many Germans who had come to Houston in the 1860s. His grandson, Norman, and his family, live in Houston today.

Every morning in his stable at 208 Caroline, W. L. Foley, the merchant, held a dress parade for his small, white delivery wagons. They had to be spotless, the brasses sparkling, the manes of the white Percherons brushed, the smartly-dressed drivers immaculate. Only then would Foley give the command to let the rubber-tired wagons roll.

But a new mode of transportation came to town in 1897. A newspaper reported: "Yesterday, an electric, horseless carriage was seen on the streets. This horseless carriage was built at a cost of $3,000. It is run by a set of storage batteries, 28 cells, the tires are solid rubber and the carriage weighs 2,000 pounds! Houston has the best-equipped electric streetcars in the South and a street railway system second to none in the world. In every part of the city, handsome cars of the latest, most approved de-

sign are constantly skimming over the rails. Less than
two years ago, the cars were drawn by mules!" (*The
Houston Post,* March 16, 1897.)

But many Houstonians kept their faith in the horse-
drawn carriage. When James E. McAshan, who organized the South Texas Commercial National Bank in
1890, died in 1917, his close friend Ed Settegast followed
his request. He combed the city until he found enough
horse-drawn vehicles for his friend's funeral.

CHAPTER SEVEN

"On weekends, Houstonians escaped to Clear Lake or Galveston Bay. The waters were fresh and sweet; gray and white pelicans rode the whitecaps. Frame houses shaded by oleanders faced the sandy beaches of the Gulf."

F OR SOCIAL Houston, the turn of the Century also dictated a finely equipped carriage with a matched team and properly dressed coachman to announce which family was "well turned out" and which wasn't. Victorias, phaetons, landaus, broughams, surreys, traps, and gigs once rolled down Main Street in the afternoon bearing ladies to leave calling cards. In the evening the carriages lined up in front of Sweeney and Coombs Opera House on Fannin for such stars as Sarah Bernhardt.

Carriages had various ratings. One early Houstonian, Mrs. E. A. Peden, complimented on her brougham, a four-wheeled closed carriage, snapped, "But not half so swank as the Clevelands' Victoria!" Mrs. W. D. Cleveland's shining black rig sported high-stepping horses and an impeccably attired coachman. Clad in a pale blue dress with matching parasol, she was thought to be the most fetching sight on Main.

On a certain afternoon every month, carriages rumbled over the brick and wood block streets carrying handsomely attired ladies to make their "at home" calls. A call lasted about fifteen minutes. The caller placed her card on the small silver tray in the front hall and sat, boned and straight, white gloved hands folded, pointy-toed shoes neatly side by side, until the polite exchanges were over and she departed. It was a graceful, brief ballet.

Now and then, the unexpected occurred. A carriage of ladies went to call on the lumber magnate's wife, Mrs. John Henry Kirby. The butler departed with their cards. He quickly returned, grinning in confusion. "Miz Kirby, she changin'. She say she ain't home!"

The wife of a founder of The Texas Company, Mrs. W. B. Sharp, in her fine Victoria, drew eyes when she rolled down Main Street. Forbiddingly erect in a silk dress with a high, boned, lace or velvet dog collar, she was driven by a coachman who flashed a diamond for a front tooth.

The carriages of two Houston friends were so similar that, after shopping at Foley's, one absentmindedly stepped into the other's and the coachman silently drove her home.

Banker S. F. Carter was noted for his pair of fine hackney horses. Hackneys were spirited trotting horses used only for carriages. J. S. Cullinan, another founder of The Texas Company, owned a pony cart, a surrey, a Victoria, a phaeton, and a station wagon, which later became an electric. They were still in the stables behind the mansion in Shadyside when it was sold to Governor William P. Hobby. The mansion has since been torn down and the carriage collection is in the possession of the Cullinan's granddaughter, Mrs. Anderson Todd, at her farm near Columbus, Texas.

Landaus, drawn by a pair of horses, were numerous on Houston streets. A landau was a four-wheeled, covered carriage with the top divided into two sections. The back section could be thrown back while the front part was left up or removed. When the weather was fine, the top went down and the ladies unfurled their lovely little parasols against the sun. It was the convertible of the 1890s.

The young men preferred a single-horse rig for speed. Spencer Hutchins, for years the town's "King of Society," never came home from New York in the Fall without the latest thing in a "drag" or "trap." For additional dash, he used brightly colored ribbon reins. A "trap" was a two- or four-wheeled carriage with the occupants sitting back to back.

But all wasn't grace and tranquility along Main Street. John and Henry Brashear, whose father came to Houston in the 1840s, staged some wild races out to McGowen Street. Beyond, only a dirt road stretched into the prairie. Chickens, hogs, and dogs flew, grunted and tore for safety. John Brashear's son, Sam, was to become Mayor of Houston in 1899 and set aside Sam Houston Park as a memorial to the Republic.

The most popular destination for young women on an afternoon's carriage drive was the Houston Light Guard Armory on Main and Franklin. This was an imposing structure with its flags, sentinel boxes and smartly uniformed young men high-stepping to and fro. These "World Beaters," as they were called, won all of the prizes at the volkfests, maifests and fairs. On parade, the gray-clad precisionists could march in quick time, 238 steps in 2 minutes and 35 seconds; in double time, in 1 minute and 27 seconds! The eyes of the young women strained especially for a glimpse of Spencer Hutchins.

A social era is distinguished by a leader who stamps his or her every word, act, attire with his own original signature. He or she has the imagination, daring and personality to carry others along in a lifestyle they would never attempt on their own.

Spencer Hutchins, "Indispensable Spencer" at the turn of the century, was such. He was the son of W. J. Hutchins, owner of Hutchins House, and a prominent Houston leader. His sister Ella married Lord Stuart of Scotland. She divorced him and later married Seabrook Sydnor for whom Seabrook, Texas was named. She became almost as compelling a figure in Houston society as her brother.

For the last twenty years of the 19th century, Spencer Hutchins was to dominate the social life of Houston. He was lean, elegant, dark-eyed, aquiline of face, hair totally black save for a striking white lick at the back of his head. Light as a ballet dancer on the ballroom floor, this sought-after bachelor held every young woman about to "come out," and her ambitious mother, in the palm of his hand.

He made out the list of Houston's "400." He was the sole arbiter of who would be presented at the ZZ Ball, deleting names at will. His final decision was left at the bachelors' social center downtown, Cockrell's Drug Store, on the southwest corner of Main and Texas. He also kept a secret list of his favorites which he allowed only his closest friends to see.

But when the night of the glamorous ZZ Ball arrived, all was forgotten. Ladies, young and old, hair in jewelled pompadours, a curl or two over bare shoulders, splendid in silks and brocades, in gowns of crystal beads with flowing trains, sparkled like fireflies around Spencer Hutchins.

To open the Ball, Hutchins, in frilled waistcoat, satin knee pants and silken hose, blew his silver whistle for the first cotillion. The ballroom darkened, the music swelled. The men wove in a long serpentine line, each carrying a lighted brass candlestick. At a command from Hutchins' whistle, they snuffed out the candles. The ladies, holding tiny lighted lamps, circled gracefully to the music each seeking the man of her choice.

In one cotillion, the ladies, with beribboned sticks, drove small balls about the ballroom. The men glided along behind, each trying to catch the ball of his lady love. All somehow done to music, and with grace!

Spencer Hutchins had the reputation of being a "devil with women." It was said he was not universally popular with men. But there was one who unreservedly idolized him—his Negro servant. This devoted valet, coachman, butler, chef, literally walked in Hutchins' footsteps. He wore the latter's castoff elegant clothes. He copied his mannerisms. He organized his own ZZ Club among the Negroes, making out *his* list of debutantes.

Spencer Hutchins wasn't all frilly waistcoat, waltzing patent-leather pumps, Saratoga and Palm Beach. He was a liberal spender, but he was also a great money raiser and a political power in Second Ward. He promoted Houston's first horse show. He helped to organize the Houston Light Guard, famous all over America for its parade and field performances.

And when the Spanish-American War came, Houston's "King of Society" and the other Light Guardsmen were the first to go. And when Spencer Hutchins left the life he found so splendidly gay in 1905, it was said that he had one of the largest funerals ever held in the city.

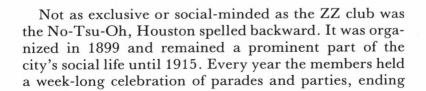

Not as exclusive or social-minded as the ZZ club was the No-Tsu-Oh, Houston spelled backward. It was organized in 1899 and remained a prominent part of the city's social life until 1915. Every year the members held a week-long celebration of parades and parties, ending in an extravagant ball where King Nottoc (cotton spelled backward) crowned his queen. The identity of the masked king was kept secret until that night. A handsome newcomer, Jesse Jones, was the king in 1902. Until his death in 1956, Jones would be regarded by many as Houston's "First Citizen."

H. Malcolm Lovett, son of Rice University's first president, Dr. Edgar Odell Lovett, told me of his boyhood memory of Houstonians crowding the San Jacinto bridge to watch the flotilla of decorated launches coming up the bayou. His father was King Nottoc that year. On the King's launch were Mayor H. Baldwin Rice and the Governor of Texas, O. B. Colquitt. Herb and Lewis' Military band, aboard the *Mabel,* was playing "Alexander's Ragtime Band."

Each year Main at Capitol was blocked off with a big arch and sentry boxes for King Nottoc's landing and spectacular parade down Main Street. In some years, the gentlemen of the Royal Court were said to have reveled overmuch on board the launches, and the King's parade ". . . exhibited more carnival spirit than was called for!"

One of the grander arrivals of King Nottoc featured a ". . . flying-swan throne for the King, in a carriage drawn by four spirited black horses, shod with gold and led by a quartet of costumed grooms!" ("Society Then & Now," Betty Ewing, *Houston Press,* May 9, 1961)

The Flower Parade of the Carnival Week drew everybody to Main Street. Flower-bedecked floats pulled by festooned horses had to be careful not to collide with the new electric autos blanketed with flowers and filled with men and their ladies in big garden party hats.

"A gorgeous illuminated night parade follows the triumphal entry of the Carnival King into the city and during the week fantastic pageants and other demonstrations of various and unusual character add interest and pleasure to the Festival. Upon the entry of the King, the whole population accepts it as a signal for enjoyment and for an entire week they revel in frolic and fun. Class lines are obliterated, the lawyer, doctor, teacher and sedate preacher, the butcher, baker, candlestick maker, all meet upon common ground of pleasure and good fellowship." (*The Standard Blue Book of Texas,* 1907–08)

Today, the Houston Festival attempts each Spring, to revive this old carnival spirit. But the lawyer and the butcher, the society leader and the maid, no longer frolic together. Pan long ago departed from Main Street.

———————————⇒◄ ►⇐———————————

In 1886 William Marsh Rice acquired the Capitol Hotel for back taxes and added a five story annex where the stables had been. When Rice Institute acquired the property, at his bequest, the name was changed to Rice Hotel. Of little interest to Houstonians was a quagmire way out Main Street. For thirty years, Houston garbage had been dumped there. That it was a no-man's-land, George Hermann could testify. In 1887, he was running a wood and saw mill on 284 acres across from the garbage dump.

George Hermann, the son of Swiss immigrants John and Fannie Hermann, lived where the City Hall reflection pool is now. On a trip to New York, Hermann became ill and collapsed unconscious on the sidewalk. On regaining consciousness, he found himself in a large charity hospital. The indifferent, even cruel treatment he received horrified him. He vowed that once he got well he would build a charity hospital in Houston. Hermann Hospital and Hermann Park are in Houston today, thanks to one of the most tightfisted men in Houston's history.

Hermann, a bachelor, was so close with his self-made millions he once threatened to take a man to court over $2.75. When the debtor found it would cost him $5 to hire a lawyer, he paid up. Hermann sailed to Europe several times, always second class. At the time of his death, he rented a room in a friend's house in Houston. Yet he left Hermann Hospital for the poor and 278 acres on Fannin for Hermann Park. He had paid 50 cents an acre for the land.

He traded two mules and a wagon for 30 acres of land near Humble. Oil was discovered on the land and he became a rich man. Loggers for his lumber business came to Houston on pay day. They landed in jail so often he bought a plot of land in the center of downtown where they could sleep it off. Today, City Hall faces that plot of land, now called Hermann Square.

Because he couldn't get the medical help he needed for his stomach cancer in Houston, he died in a Baltimore hospital. Apparently seeing himself as a cattleman to the end, he was buried in a cowboy suit and boots, holding a cowboy hat. Thousands crowded Main Street to see the mile-long line of carriages, a funeral cortege of men on foot, a horse-drawn hearse followed by an aged Negro man, "grown old in Mr. Hermann's service," leading "Leo," Hermann's beloved saddle horse.

When no hospital was built in 1914, the land reverted back to the Estate. In 1922 the Houston Zoo was started on Hermann's land gift. Hermann Hospital was finally built in 1925 for $1 million.

———————————————————————

By 1911, Houston had four theatres, six department stores, nine hotels, eight office buildings, nine banks and six schools. The First Methodist Church on Main was finished. The Beaconsfield Apartments at Main and Pease, the Savoy across the street and the McAshan Flats in the 1300 block of Main, were offering exclusive apartments. Beyond Eagle, Main Street was not paved. Today, the restored Beaconsfield is the only proud dowager left on Main.

Houston was such a potpourri of commerce and homes that leading Houstonians built their own small, private enclaves. They kept the restrictions high as to family background, lot size, architecture and above all, congeniality in philosophy and politics.

Courtlandt Place, built in the second decade of the 20th century, with its stone piers intended for gates against intruders, central esplanade of palm trees, and its big, galleried houses, was such a place. It maintains its exclusiveness today.

But only one of the original descendants of Courtlandt Place remains—Effie Hunt Heald. She lives with her daughter, Sarah Andersen, and her grandson, Jeffrey, in the red brick mansion of her parents, William and Irma Jones Hunt. The lumber, doors, handsome stairway, and fine paneling were all moved in 1919 from the home of her grandmother, Sarah Brashear Jones (Mrs. James W.), on Main Street where Sakowitz now stands. The house had been built in 1896.

Westmoreland Place was another enclave, if less exclusive. Some of the dignified homes with porte cocheres and big lawns have been restored, principally the Waldo mansion. It too was moved, brick by brick. Montrose Place, promoted by J. W. Link, was much larger, about 165 acres, and socially less restricted. The Link mansion, now seat of the University of St. Thomas, remains on Montrose Boulevard.

In 1916, J. S. Cullinan, founder of The Texas Company, bought a tract of land across Main Street from present Hermann Park. He formed the highly exclusive Shadyside enclave where he and his friends built some of Houston's finest early homes. And a new impetus was given to home architecture when Harry T. Lindeberg was brought to Houston from New York. The interiors housed in addition to fine furniture, sizeable collections of American art and French Impressionists.

Cullinan's neighbors certainly weren't ordinary. Among them were Robert Lee Blaffer, William S. Farish, Harry Wiess, and Hugo V. Neuhaus. Blaffer and Farish were founders of the Humble Oil and Refining Company. Sarah Campbell Blaffer's father, William T. Campbell, was one of the organizers of The Texas Company, later Texaco. Her marriage to Robert Lee Blaffer was called a wedding of the oil greats. But one European visitor, groping his way through the English country house filled with French Impressionist paintings lit only by candles, thought it was a pity this Texas family was without electricity! He didn't know that Sarah Campbell Blaffer, with her deep sense of aestheticism felt the special beauty that lives under candle glow.

Another Shadyside family was that of the affable, delightful Jim M. Lykes, head of Lykes Brothers Steamship Company. On the day the Lykes' moved from Galveston into the red brick mansion on Remington, their neighbor, Mrs. Hugo Neuhaus sent over a big wash tub of five dozen roses from her rose garden, with her card, "From one Mother of five to another!"

Lykes Steamship Company gave a big thrust to the development of the Port of Houston. Foreign vessels had been carrying the bulk of American commerce until Lykes Brothers bought the Daniel Ripley Steamship Company. It had cargo service between Texas and the North Atlantic ports, in addition to the Tampa Inter-Ocean Steamship Company, serving the South Atlantic—Spain, Portugal, North Africa, the Western Mediterranean.

J. M. Lykes Jr. and his wife, Jean, their children and Fredericka Lykes Thompson (Mrs. Ben), daughter, and her children live in Houston today.

Polished 18th century English and American pieces graced the rooms of the W. S. Farish house. As a young married woman at "Miss Libbie's" formal dinners, I often had the sensation of taking part in an elegant court play. But behind her aura of wealth and protocol, Libbie Rice Farish, like the few other genuine *grandes dames* of Houston, had a down-to-earth humor and a generous heart to match.

St. John's School on River Oaks Boulevard might well have remained a dream of Ellen Clayton Garwood (Mrs. St. John), James O. Winston, R. E. (Bob) Smith, Lewis White, Ardon Judd and Marie Lee Phelps (Mrs. Merrick) had it not been for Libbie Farish. She donated the money for immediate construction of West Farish Hall, in memory of her son, William S. Farish, Jr., who had been killed in a plane crash. The following year she gave the Arts and Science Building in memory of her husband.

Mrs. E. L. Neville gave the Elizabeth Neville Wood Memorial Cloister in memory of her beautiful young daughter. And today Louisa and Fayez Sarofim's Stude-Sarofim Learning Resource Building is nearing completion. It will house computer, chemistry and biology labs.

(I remember when Alan Chidsey, the school's first headmaster, came early each morning to study on our porch before a single stone was laid for the school.)

⸻

If Houston society has had a male leader since Spencer Hutchins' day, he was Hugo V. Neuhaus. The "Baron," as he was called, with his tall, Greek god handsomeness, looked every inch of it. Head of Neuhaus & Co. Stocks & Bonds, he carefully cultivated the aesthetics of life: proper dress, fine food and wine, beautiful people in his Shadyside house. Hugo Neuhaus, Stephen

D. Farish, John Garwood, and Maurice S. McAshan were founders of the Bayou Club, one of Houston's country clubs which maintains its exclusiveness. Baron Neuhaus' sons, architect Hugo V. Jr., stock brokers Joseph, Philip and Harry, live in Houston. W. S. Farish III lives in Versailles, Kentucky and has a Houston residence as well. The daughters of Olga and Harry Wiess are Caroline Law (Mrs. Theodore) and Margaret Elkins (Mrs. James, Jr.).

J. S. Cullinan's daughters, Margaret (Mrs. Andrew Jackson Wray) and Mary (Mrs. J. Rorick Cravens) still live in the compound, close by where their father's mansion and stables once stood. Craig Cullinan, Jr., grandson of J. S. Cullinan also lives in Houston.

It is said that when the William P. Hobbys bought the Cullinan house, Oveta Hobby hired architect John Staub to make some changes. He found that the partitions were load-bearing concrete and could not be moved. Mrs. Hobby then considered turning the house into a meeting place for the nearby Texas Medical Center. When her neighbors heard of this, they got a restraining order to stop any such violation of Shadyside regulations. The strong minded former Woman's Army Corps leader, owner and editor of *The Houston Post,* then tore the house down and gave the grounds to Rice University.

After the war, President Eisenhower appointed Oveta Culp Hobby America's first Secretary of Health, Education, and Welfare.

On weekends, Houstonians felt the need to escape to Clear Lake or Galveston Bay. The waters were fresh and sweet; grey and white pelicans rode the white caps. Only a few duck blinds, which children were led to believe were stork's nests, interrupted the long, blue horizon.

Frame houses buttressed by galleries, shaded by oleanders, faced sandy beaches, catching every breeze. Long,
planked piers that had to be rebuilt after each storm,
warmed children's racing bare feet. Bayridge, the bay's
"Riviera," was kept enclosed, inviolate, behind tall
gates and hedges of oleanders. It contained the bay's
most prestigious summer homes. Chief among them was
Governor R. S. Sterling's replica of the White House,
facing the bay, built in the early 1900s.

The Interurban ran from Houston to small stations
near Seabrook and Sylvan Beach. On San Jacinto Day,
filled with celebrants, it was beribboned from cow
catcher to caboose.

Houstonians, in this era, didn't lack fine dining. On
festive occasions, the Grand Central Hotel on Washington Avenue offered a 10-course dinner. This included
suckling pig or larded quail, goose with calve's foot jelly,
English Plum pudding and, in season, fresh strawberries. On the informal side, there was popular Mike and
Genora's place and Stude's Bakery and Coffee Saloon at
810 Preston.

Gus F. Sauter ran what many considered the leading
restaurant in town. It was in a two-story brick building
on Travis and Preston. Houstonians dined at sidewalk
tables beneath an awning or upstairs to the music of Belgian cellist Julien Blitz and his ensemble. Sauter's was
the first restaurant, it was said, to make a woman feel
she had any right to be there!

One evening as my parents were enjoying a dinner at
Sauter's during their honeymoon, a thief drove away in
their surrey, drawn by Red Jim. The surrey and horse
were wedding gifts from my mother's father. The sheriff
with my father jumped on a train and caught the thief in
Madisonville. On the train ride back to Houston, the
sheriff wanted to sleep so he manacled the thief to the
new bridegroom. Beautiful Red Jim, who had been rid-
den too hard, had to be put out to pasture.

Years ago, the late George Hamman, president of the Union National Bank, talked to me of this era. He made $25 a month in the bank. He bought his breakfast for 10¢ at Stude's Bakery and Coffee Saloon. He got a free lunch at the Big Casino on Congress and dined at night for 25¢ at Colby's! Colby's was famous for its game dinners of venison, partridge, snipe and ducks.

At home, some Houston families dined too well. Hot biscuits, regular as the dawn, appeared on the breakfast table, buttered with their cow's rich cream, churned on the back porch. There were likely to be platters of salt mackerel, fish roe or quail with grits, pancakes, blackberry jam, and oatmeal. From the smokehouse, during the day, came wild game, beef, and sides of bacon. Sweet potato pie, seasoned with a good half cup of bourbon; syllabub with its tumbler-full of Madeira, brown sugar, rich cream; Southern Spoonbread of eggs, cornmeal, butter, milk, and sugar, appeared on the white damask-covered tables of a generation that had never heard of cholesterol.

Big blue-clawed crabs and soft-shell crabs, boiled, fried or pungently stuffed; seafood gumbo with its dark rich roux made from bacon or sausage grease and flour; flounders gigged at night in nearby Galveston Bay by the whole family, broiled in lemon juice, butter, and white wine; buckets of sweet, fresh oysters from the un-polluted bay—all were as normal to the palates of the more fortunate as parma violets were to the other senses.

Main at Texas, Capitol Hotel and Stagecoach stop, 1857.

Steamship *St. Clair* loading on Buffalo Bayou, 1873. (Courtesy Texas History Room, Houston Public Library.)

John Kirby Allen, 1832. (Courtesy Houston Public Library.)

Augustus Chapman Allen, 1836. (Courtesy Houston Public Library.)

Main and Texas, 1876.

General Sam Houston. President of the Republic of Texas. (Courtesy J. Carrington Weems collection of antique Texas and Gulf Coast maps.)

Concert day at Sam Houston Park, 1890.

The pavillion at Magnolia Park, 1890.

Mammoth magnolia trees, as much as 24 feet in circumference, in Magnolia Park, 1893.

Main and Capitol in 1901. Before No-Tsu-Oh Parade.

James W. Jones' residence, where Sakowitz stands today, on Main Street.

Foley Bros., on Congress Avenue in 1893.

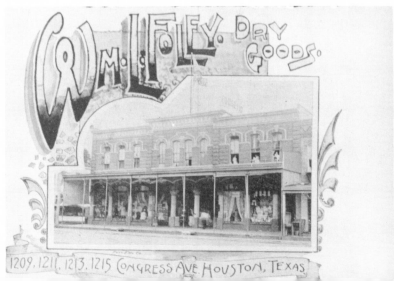

The Levy mansion, at 2016 Main. 1900s. Residence of Mr. & Mrs. Leopold Meyer in the 1950s.

George Hermann's funeral, 1914. (Courtesy Texas History Room, Houston Public Library.)

FIRST TEXIAN LOAN SCRIP.

No. 200.   ◄◄◄◈❈◈►►►   **640**
ACRES OF LAND.

CERTIFICATE OF TITLE TO SIX HUNDRED AND FORTY ACRES OF LAND.

Know all Men, That, in consideration of a Loan to the Government of Texas, negotiated by the Commissioners of said Government in New Orleans, on the eleventh day of January, 1836, *Thomas D. Carneal, of Cincinnatti, Ohio* is entitled to have and to hold, **SIX HUNDRED AND FORTY ACRES OF LAND,** of the Public Domain of Texas, according to the terms and conditions of a Contract of Compromise, made and executed on the first day of April 1836, between the Government ad interim of Texas, and the Stockholders in the aforesaid Loan; and of the Act of Congress for fulfilling and carrying into effect the said Contract of Compromise, approved the twenty-fourth day of May, 1838. This Certificate shall be authority for any duly appointed surveyor, to survey, at the expense of the holder hereof, any land, belonging to the Government of Texas, that may be selected by the said holder, at any time after the first Thursday in August next. And should the same be located on any land to which the government of Texas has not the prior right, it may be removed, and laid on other land. When the holder of this Certificate shall file the same, together with the boundaries, or field notes, of the land intended to be covered by it, in the General Land Office, a title or Patent, for the same, shall issue to the said *Thos. D. Carneal,* his heirs or assigns, in the usual form.

In Testimony Whereof, I, **SAM. HOUSTON,** President of the Republic of Texas, have hereunto set my hand, at the **CITY OF HOUSTON,** this *Twentieth* day of *June* in the year of our Lord eighteen hundred and thirty-eight, and of the Independence of Texas the third.

BY THE PRESIDENT

Henry Smith
Secretary of the Treasury.

Document signed by General Sam Houston. (Courtesy Henry David collection, Harris County Heritage Society.)

Stude's Bakery and Coffee Shop. (Courtesy Texas Research Room, Houston Public Library.)

The Rice Hotel, corner of Main and Texas, 1890.

Hutchins House, 1876. (Courtesy J. Carrington Weems collection of antique Texas and Gulf Coast maps.)

A romantic world gone by. On the Buffalo Bayou, 1895.

Wall and Stabe Undertakers, 1883. (Courtesy Texas Research Room, Houston Public Library.)

First mule-drawn trolley. (Courtesy Texas Research Room, Houston Public Library.)

City Hall and Market Square, 1900. (Courtesy Harris County Heritage Society.)

Sweeney Coombs Opera House, 1890, San Jacinto and Congress. (Courtesy Harris County Heritage Society.)

Electric streetcar, 1893. (Courtesy Harris County Heritage Society.)

Main Street, early 1900s. (Courtesy Texas History Room, Houston Public Library.)

Andrew Carnegie Library, 1898.

Westheimer Transfer Company founded by the Westheimer family whose farm was located where Lamar High School is now. The Horowitz family bought it in 1923. (Courtesy Harris County Heritage Society.)

Baseball Play Off, the Fats vs. the Leans, 1895. (Courtesy Houston Public Library.)

Harris County Courthouse. The Sweeney-Coombs Opera House is in the background, 1890s.

niel Denton Cooley's residence, lo-
ed in the Heights, boasted the first
ctric lights in Houston homes. (Cour-
y the Cooley Family.)

Major Benjamin Francis Weems on the
front porch of his home. (Courtesy J.
Carrington Weems.)

Interior of Major Benjamin F. Weems House at 1616 Rusk. Weems
was one of the developers of the ship channel. Interior designed by
Tiffany & Co., New York, in 1868. (Courtesy J. Carrington
Weems.)

San Jacinto Battlefield, April 21, 1910. (Courtesy Texas History Room,
Houston Public Library.)

Black groups of musicians and artists came to Houston early. (Courtesy Metropolitan Research Center, Houston Public Library.)

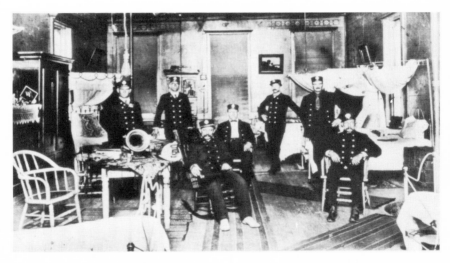

Fire Station No. 5, early 1900s. (Courtesy Harris County Heritage Society.)

Fire engine, "Protection No. 1," 1890. (Sketch by Mary Ellen Shipnes.)

The Brazos Hotel, early 1900s. Located on Washington across from what is now the main post office.

Houston's first service station. (Courtesy Harris County Heritage Society.)

The Thalian Club, 1880s. (Courtesy Harris County Heritage Society.)

The Samuel M. McAshan residence, 1300 Main Street, founder of the South Texas Commercial Bank.

Second Majestic Theatre, 1910. Site of present *Houston Chronicle*. (Courtesy Metropolitan Research Center, Houston Public Library.)

Houston's first aero industry, January 1903. The Wright brothers successfully flew their plane December 17, 1903. (Courtesy Harris County Heritage Society.)

Early gasoline delivery truck, 1910. (Courtesy Metropolitan Research Center, Houston Public Library.)

Cotton, Houston's "money crop," early 1900s. (Courtesy Rice University.)

William Marsh Rice.
(Courtesy Rice University.)

Cotton Exchange Building, early 1900s. (Courtesy Harris County Heritage Society.)

Jesse Jones, King of No-Tsu-Oh with court. Left to right: Mrs. Ogden Oden, Spencer Hutchins, Jesse Jones, Mrs. James Bute, and Mrs. Nell Lee. Child unknown.

Mrs. Baron (Katie) Neuhaus on her engagement day.

Daniel Denton Cooley, 1925. (Courtesy the Cooley Family.)

Sylvan Beach Amusement Park, 1921. (Courtesy Harris County Heritage Society.)

No-Tsu-Oh Parade float on Capital Avenue (site of present Civic Center); Misses Valena and Linda Gieseke in front seat. (Courtesy Mrs. James C. Boone.)

No-Tsu-Oh Parade in 1904. Bedecked Haynes-Apperson auto won second place. Driver, Mrs. F. B. King; left to right: Sadie Campbell Blaffer (Mrs. Robert Lee), Mamie Fisher, Mrs. W. Abbey. Dr. F. B. King in bowler hat. Tom Dunn house in background. (Courtesy Jane Blaffer Owen [Mrs. Kenneth].)

The Houston Country Club, 1908.

Sam Houston Park, about 1910. (Courtesy Harris County Heritage Society.)

Nichols-Rice-Cherry house after restoration. (Courtesy Harris County Heritage Society.)

Funeral in downtown Houston. (Courtesy Harris County Heritage Society.)

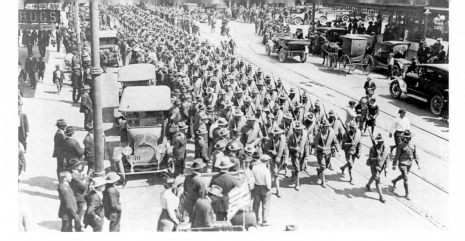

World War I Infantry Troop from Camp Logan (now Memorial Park). (Courtesy Harris County Heritage Society.)

Camp Logan, 1917. (Courtesy Metropolitan Research Center, Houston Public Library.)

Museum of Fine Arts when it opened April, 1924. (Courtesy Metropolitan Research Center, Houston Public Library.)

Texas Business Institute, 1920s. (Courtesy Harris County Heritage Society.)

Robert Lee Blaffer, co-founder with W. S. Farish of Humble Oil Company. (Courtesy Jane Blaffer Owen [Mrs. Kenneth].)

J. S. Cullinan, philanthropist, founder and president of The Texas Company (Texaco). (Courtesy Houston Public Library.)

Mrs. Robert Lee Blaffer (far right) with shipmates on her honeymoon trip. (Courtesy Jane Blaffer Owen [Mrs. Kenneth].)

Home of Joseph S. Cullinan in Shadyside, 1924. (Courtesy Metropolitan Research Center, Houston Public Library.)

Two black Confederate veterans who fought with their masters. (Courtesy Metropolitan Research Center, Houston Public Library.)

River Oaks, a Will Hogg project in the planning stage, looking down Kirby just west of Shepherd.

Rice Institute opened in 1912 on the old garbage dump. (Courtesy Metropolitan Research Center, Houston Public Library.)

Armistice Day Celebration. Main and Texas, December 17, 1918. (Courtesy Harris County Heritage Society.)

The Metropolitan Theatre, 1016 Main, featured a Greek interior, 1926.

Howard R. Hughes, Jr., waves to the crowd at the corner of Main and Texas following his round-the-world flight. (Courtesy Metropolitan Research Center, Houston Public Library.)

Gusher at Goose Creek, Texas, 1922. (Courtesy Harris County Heritage Society.)

San Jacinto Monument, begun in 1936 as a centennial project. (Courtesy Metropolitan Research Center, Houston Public Library.)

Herman Brown, Captain D. C. Redgrove and George Brown, September 28, 1943. (Courtesy Texas Research Room, Houston Public Library.)

Charter members of Suite 8-F in the Lamar Hotel: Jim Abercrombie, Jesse Jones, and Leopold Meyer. (Courtesy Rice University.)

Oscar Holcombe who served 11 terms as Mayor of Houston. (Courtesy Metropolitan Research Center, Houston Public Library.)

The First Lady of Texas, Miss Ima Hogg (seated) with Mrs. Lawton Deak. (Courtesy Houston Public Library.)

Mrs. J. S. Abercrombie (Miss Lillie) and Michel Halbouty in the Sponsors Club at Pin Oak Horse Show. (Courtesy Houston Public Library.)

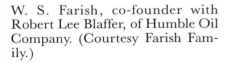

W. S. Farish, co-founder with Robert Lee Blaffer, of Humble Oil Company. (Courtesy Farish Family.)

W. S. Farish II as a young man. (Courtesy Farish Family.)

Houstonians let their hair down each year at the Rodeo. (Courtesy Metropolitan Research Center, Houston Public Library.)

John and Mary Elizabeth Mecom at opening of Warwick Hotel.

William S. Farish III and John Armstrong of the King Ranch following a polo match for the Texas Sports Hall of Fame.

Original seven astronauts.

Allen Parkway and downtown Houston, 1961. (Courtesy Metropolitan Research Center, Houston Public Library.)

CHAPTER EIGHT

*"On Sunday, September 23,
1900, Charles Jones was persuaded by Albert Patrick to make
preparations to murder William Marsh Rice."*

H OUSTONIANS were fascinated by two murders at the turn of the century. One was the famous murder case of William Marsh Rice; the other was the murder of Colonel Jared Kirby.

When Rice first landed in Houston in 1839 he went to work in a saloon for $3 a day. When he was murdered in New York in 1900 he left huge interests in railroads, banks, hotels, factories, 30,000 acres adjoining Houston where Bellaire now is, 40,000 acres in Beauregard Parish, Louisiana, and $10 million to incorporate Rice Institute, according to Historian Andrew Forest Muir.

The foundation of Rice's tremendous fortune was laid during the Civil War and the Federal blockade of Houston and Galveston. Like others, he engaged in the traffic through Mexico. Indeed, he moved to Mexico from his house adjoining the Post Office on the north side of Courthouse Square to better handle his affairs.

Julia Elizabeth Baldwin Rice, Rice's second wife, as the late Dr. Muir portrays her, had a dazzling, ambitious ego that led to her husband's murder. Beautiful and bright, she "lived for the best in Society and she wanted her place in it."

When the Baldwins moved to Houston, then still the capital of the Republic, the young woman hadn't received the social attention she had to have. The fact that her father became Mayor, in her eyes, didn't increase her social stature. She married John H. Brown, "an obscure politician" which hadn't helped her any either. The Browns soon left Houston for the California gold rush.

At the end of the Civil War, Julia Elizabeth Baldwin Brown returned to Houston, as a widow. She was childless and without any means. During the Reconstruction days she met William Marsh Rice. On June 26, 1867, they were married in Christ Church. That afternoon, the newlyweds left for New York. "Only in their old age were they to stay any length of time in Houston."

Soon after they moved to New York, the Rices bought a farm in Somerset County, New Jersey. Here he began to lay his plans and to draw up a will endowing Rice Institute, a School for poor boys of Somerset County, which he would operate on his farm.

Rice, "though uneducated and childless, determined to found an educational institution," wrote Dr. Muir. It is all the more interesting that Rice, according to Dr. Muir, possessed no general fund of knowledge, rarely if ever read a book, had no interest in any of the arts. He did enjoy newspapers and the theater. Dr. Muir believed the Reverend Charles Gillett, Christ Church Episcopal minister was the one who aroused Rice's interest in education, encouraging him to become a trustee of the Houston Educational Society, Houston Academy, Second Ward School, and Texas Medical College.

All of this was quite fine and philanthropic to everyone but Julia Rice. Like most women of her era, though married to a rich man, she suffered a "humiliating lack of ready cash." Rice paid all household bills but the flow of money stopped when it came to change in her purse and helping her poor relatives.

It grew to be an intolerable situation for her. There she was, born, she felt, to dazzle society, buried on a farm in New Jersey with no money! She at last persuaded Rice to move back to New York. Once back in her element, the handsome Mrs. Rice tackled the job of crashing New York society—volunteering time and lavish funds to social and philanthropic organizations. Soon Lord & Taylor named her the best dressed woman in New York. She became a member of the "Drawing-Room," an ultra elite society.

Rice didn't object to all of her strenuous social activities, but he refused to become involved. Meanwhile, he had written a new will endowing Rice Institute which now was to be in New York City.

"Mrs. Rice was left pretty much to her own devices while her husband stacked dollar atop dollar," wrote Dr. Muir.

She began to grow irrational. She claimed that her husband was a monster; that he threw a cup of coffee in her face. Her relatives kept her stirred up. Although she gave lavish gifts to the right people, her social rise was not meteoric.

On a visit to Houston in 1891 Rice decided to establish Rice Institute in Houston. He appointed six old friends as Trustees of the William M. Rice Institute for the Advancement of Literature, Science and Art. He gave them a $200,000 note and got a Texas Charter. The six Trustees were Cesar Lombardi, Emmanuel Raphael, Frederick A. Rice, James A. Baker, Alfred S. Richardson, and James E. McAshan.

While Rice was making this philanthropic gesture, his wife was talking to her Attorney cousin about a divorce. He told her that since she and Rice were still residents of New York she couldn't file suit in Texas. In New York, the only grounds for divorce was adultery.

Momentarily at a loss, she went to another lawyer, Orren Thaddeus Holt, "a society lawyer and later Mayor of Houston." Holt told Mrs. Rice that as her husband had never voted anywhere since he left Houston, it could be hard to prove where their permanent residence was. He advised her to get him permanently back to Houston and stay married to him. Only then could she divorce him and claim half of his estate under the Texas community property law.

On their return to New York in 1895, Julia Elizabeth Baldwin Rice's "frustrated and troubled spirit" was given a momentary lift. The Rices were admitted to the New York Social Register. Mrs. Rice, remembering her lawyer's advice, insisted on an East Side address where she must have all new furniture. At this time Rice, building an annex to his hotel in Houston, was planning an apartment in it for the two of them.

At his wife's unusual demand for all new furniture, he shipped all of the pieces from their old New York apartment along with some paintings he had bought for Rice Institute, to their Houston apartment. From that moment on, Mrs. Rice began to tell everyone that their permanent address was in Houston.

A short time later, she became quite ill, apparently from a stroke. Rice took her to Houston's warmer climate. She didn't recuperate and often drifted into a coma. In the summer, he arranged passage for her to Waukesha, Wisconsin, where he hired a sometime superintendent of the Wisconsin Lunatic Asylum to arrange for her care.

The aging Rice, still sharp in handling his vast fortune, apparently couldn't conceive that his wife and her lawyer had already conspired against him. But before she was taken to Wisconsin, Mrs. Rice had ordered Attorney Holt to draw up a new will for her, which she signed. It was witnessed by two of Holt's relatives. In this new will she claimed the Rices resided permanently in Houston. She gave away half of what she thought to be their communal property. According to Historian Muir, she greatly underestimated the extent of the estate. She made personal bequeaths to her relatives, big endowments to Houston churches, philanthropies, and even founded a park to be called Elizabeth Baldwin Park, which today is located at 1718 Elgin.

At her death, "As Holt had anticipated, her philanthropy created in Houston a favorable climate of opinion for the probating of the will."

Rice's attorney argued that Mrs. Rice was a resident of New York and because of unsound mind, was incapable of making a will. However, the county court of Harris County admitted her will to probate.

Rice then filed suit against Holt, stating that he, Rice, was a New York resident, and probating of his wife's will would cloud the title to his extensive Texas properties.

Rice, now 81, came to Houston in 1897 for the last time. When he left to return to New York, he took with him Charles F. Jones, 22. This would later prove to be a fatal decision.

Jones became his houseboy in his apartment at 500 Madison Avenue on the corner of East 52nd Street. Dr. Muir described it as "a strangely arid place, with no pictures, no books, only a set of encyclopedias . . . "

But there was nothing arid about the mind of the aged Rice who continued to handle every facet of his empire and to nourish his dream of a great institute of learning.

On some days Rice took Jones with him to Wall Street to the counting room of S. M. Swenson & Sons where he let the thrilled houseboy help him clip coupons. According to Dr. Muir, Rice liked Jones but apparently not well enough to put him in his latest will in which he had made Rice Institute his sole heir.

Meanwhile, in Houston and in New York the case of Rice versus Holt was coming up for trial. Holt hired Albert T. Patrick, native Texan living in New York, to represent him. Dr. Muir thought that Patrick seemed a curious selection for the honorable Holt, considering that Patrick had moved to New York just as the Harris County Bar Association was about to disbar him for unethical practice in a divorce suit!

Patrick, 33, was scarcely a legal success in Texas and even less in New York. Apparently, however, he decided that stealing Rice's fortune was his only hope of getting rich.

He began to cultivate young Jones' friendship, slowly flattering him into a state of hypnosis. The young man obeyed his every request. Patrick got Jones to show him a copy of Rice's will. The attorney had no trouble convincing the brainwashed young man that the will, leaving everything to a mythical institute, was unfair. He, Albert T. Patrick, would make a new will and no one would be the wiser.

He made out a four page will forging Rice's signature on each page. Jones' part in the deal was supplying witnesses. These were a New York Notary Public and a Texas Commissioner of Deeds, who were used by Rice whenever he needed an instrument acknowledged.

In this bogus will, Albert T. Patrick was named sole heir. Since Rice's health didn't deteriorate fast enough for Patrick, he convinced Jones to give the old man some mercury pellets "for his health." All they did was to give him diarrhea. When he recovered, he appeared livelier than before.

When the 1900 hurricane damaged some of his Houston properties and his cotton seed mill burned, Rice decided to send the balance of his checking accounts, a quarter of a million dollars, to Houston to help re-build it. This was a terrible blow to Patrick, who had counted on this bank balance to pay for the legal fees necessary to probate the forged will. He had to act at once.

On Sunday, September 23, 1900, Jones was persuaded by Patrick to make preparations to murder William Marsh Rice. When the latter's nap time came, he helped the old man into bed. At the sound of Rice's irregular snoring, Jones took a towel he had saturated with chloroform and silenced him forever.

Jones called Patrick, who called an elderly doctor friend. "This decrepit physician pronounced Rice dead from natural causes even while the odor from the towel, which Jones had burned over the kitchen range, still filled the apartment," Dr. Muir recorded.

The next day one of Patrick's associates went to S. M. Swenson & Son's with a check signed by what appeared to be Rice's signature. A Swenson partner, instinctively suspicious, called Rice's apartment and asked to speak to him.

The terrified Jones told him that Mr. Rice had died the night before. S. M. Swenson & Sons sent a wire to James Addison Baker, Rice's attorney in Houston, that they were suspicious as to the cause of his death. Baker, who had received a telegram earlier from Jones informing him of his client's death, wired Swenson & Sons to do nothing until his arrival.

He and Rice's brother, Frederick, left for New York. At each train stop, newspapers were announcing Albert T. Patrick the wealthy Rice's sole heir. In New York Baker hired Pinkerton detectives to cover Patrick's every move. He told the District Attorney of New York that he personally would pay for all costs of proving Patrick guilty of forgery and murder.

Albert T. Patrick and Charles F. Jones were arrested. A Grand Jury indicted Patrick on a charge of murder in the first degree. After a nine-week trial, a jury found him guilty and sentenced him to die in the electric chair at Sing Sing.

Rice's will as drawn by James A. Baker was admitted to probate in New York County. In 1906, Governor Higgins of New York committed Patrick's sentence to life imprisonment. In 1912, Governor Dix pardoned him. He moved to Tulsa, Oklahoma, where his prominent family lived. He died in 1940 at the age of 74.

"Jones was never even indicted for his complicity. In the course of a long life spent dodging newspaper reporters, he inherited a few small oil wells in the Goose Creek field. Toward the end of 1954, at the age of seventy-nine, he put a bullet in his head near the site of his birthplace in Baytown, Texas." (Preceding based on "Murder on Madison Avenue—the Rice Case Revisited," Andrew Forest Muir, *Southwest Review*, 1959, Southern Methodist University Press. Reprinted with permission.)

One of the town's most spectacular murders—the climax of a long-standing feud—occurred directly after the Civil War. The victim was Colonel Jared Ellison Kirby, descended on his mother's side from the pioneer Groce family of Waller County (which I described earlier in this book). He was a man of wealth and influence in the Hempstead area, and his killing created state-wide attention.

Kirby was in Houston to see the commander of the Union occupation forces on the second floor of the Wilson Building on Congress Avenue near Main Street.

Also in the building was Captain John Steel, a veteran of San Jacinto. He was calling on his attorney, W. P. Hamblen, to arrange the sale of some Waller County land he had farmed for years before vacating it.

The two men emerged simultaneously from the separate offices they were visiting. They saw each other. Neither spoke. The next moment Steel drew his revolver and shot Kirby through the heart. He refused to make any kind of statement when he was lodged in jail.

Over at the Rusk House, working as a night clerk to keep body and soul together, was a young Confederate veteran who, before the war, was a budding lawyer with a bright future. He bore the improbable name of Decimus et Ultimus (tenth and last) Barziza. On the night of his birth his father, in the traditional manner, went to his favorite tavern in Virginia to celebrate with friends. He told them he had run out of names for his offspring; this son was his tenth child.

"Then, damn it all," one said, "name him Decimus et Ultimus—and have no more!"

He would be called Deci.

Barziza left his desk at Rusk House and went to see Steel in the jailhouse. He talked of his past as a Confederate soldier, and asked questions of Steel. He won Steel's confidence. Steel told him of a long feud between himself and Kirby. The feud came to a head. Kirby, with the friends that wealth and power can bring, told Steel to get out of the county within 24 hours or be shot on sight.

Steel left, giving up the life he loved on his land. He had started all over as a laborer in Houston. He had tried to forget the past. But he told Barziza that he shot in fear of his life when he unexpectedly bumped into Kirby in the Wilson Building.

Barziza believed him. And in a brilliant *tour de force*, he pictured the nagging fear of a man, who thought every moment he might be killed, reacting with an animal's instinct to live when faced with a man who had sworn to slay him. Steel walked out of the court a free man.

But that was not the end. Kirby had a son who was four years old when Steel shot his father. Eighteen years

later, as Steel was walking out of church in Waller
County with his wife, young Kirby stepped from behind
a grove of trees and killed him with a rifle. He fled the
County and that murder, like many others, became only
a good tale.

Decimus et Ultimus Barziza went on to become a successful lawyer, politician and a founder of Houston Land
& Trust Company, the first trust institution in the State
of Texas.

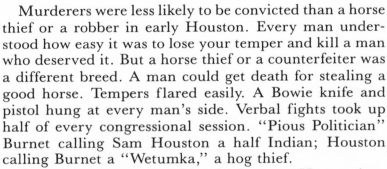

Murderers were less likely to be convicted than a horse
thief or a robber in early Houston. Every man understood how easy it was to lose your temper and kill a man
who deserved it. But a horse thief or a counterfeiter was
a different breed. A man could get death for stealing a
good horse. Tempers flared easily. A Bowie knife and
pistol hung at every man's side. Verbal fights took up
half of every congressional session. "Pious Politician"
Burnet calling Sam Houston a half Indian; Houston
calling Burnet a "Wetumka," a hog thief.

One of the most unusual battles between Houstonians
was on Christmas Day in 1871. In front of the Capitol
Hotel there was a fierce fight between Captain J. Waldo,
Dr. Louis A. Bryan and Dr. S. O. Young, all prominent
citizens. Their weapons—hard to believe—blazing roman candles. They ran down Main Street, throwing the
torches at each other until more than a hundred "leading citizens" got in the act. Battle casualties were ". . .
loss of hair, mustaches and beards!"

Duels were at their peak in Houston, 1837–38. There
was a special dueling grounds. On June 25, 1837, Dr.
Chauncey Goodrich of Mississippi and Levi Laurens, a
young reporter sent by a New York publisher to cover
the Texas Republic House of Representatives, were

sharing a room at the Mansion House. A young traveler, Marcus Cicero Stanley, was the other roommate. The next morning, Dr. Goodrich discovered a $1,000 bill was gone from his pouch. He accused Laurens. Laurens demanded he take back the accusation. Goodrich refused. Laurens challenged him to a duel. Stanley agreed to be Laurens' second.

The men met at the dueling grounds after agreeing upon rifles as weapons. At 20 paces each man turned and fired at the other. Laurens fell, shot in both thighs. He died later. As for Marcus Cicero Stanley, the second, it was later proved he was the one who had stolen the $1,000 bill!

In 1840, the Congress of the Republic of Texas passed a law against dueling. "Dueling, gambling and intemperance were three of the most pernicious vices that ever befell the human family, the great springs from which all other vices flow. Texas knew all three!" (*Austin City Gazette*, January 29, 1840.)

CHAPTER NINE

"Oil, shale, and rocks were raining down and pipe leapt like activated spaghetti over the top of the derrick. A six-inch stream of oil blew in waving a black plume 190 feet into the air. Almost to himself, Lucas whispered, with rising emotion, 'A geyser of oil! A geyser of oil!'"

HOUSTON gustily celebrated New Year's Eve—welcoming in the new 20th Century. Little did they dream that one Act of God, and one Act of Man would change Houston's destiny forever, within a year.

Not even Reconstruction and pestilences could halt Houston's steady but not spectacular growth. At the turn of the century the population stood at 44,633, and the city held more than 200 manufacturing plants. The downtown streets were paved with stone; Main Street boasted some electric lighting. And the Buffalo Bayou Ship Channel Company was busy clearing snags and maintaining the bayou at a nine-foot depth.

The town's ambitious entrepreneurs talked and talked and talked about enlarging the bayou to accommodate major shipping vessels instead of the small steam packets, but it took a great tragedy to make such a channel a reality.

On September 8, 1900 a terrible storm struck Galveston. The island was completely inundated, and an estimated 6,000 to 8,000 dead were left in the ruins. Not a single structure went undamaged. Immediately there was a cry for a "storm-free deepwater port."

Four months after the disaster, the great Spindletop Gusher roared in. It began at 10:30 a.m., January 10, 1901, when from 1,139 feet, in a large mound of salt, 85 miles from Houston and named "Spindletop" a six-inch stream of oil blew in waving a black plume 190 feet into the air. The world's first gusher had arrived. This well produced half as much oil in one day as all of the other wells in the United States combined. Houston would become the prime recipient of the wealth the subsequent boom produced. Just north of town the Humble field was discovered in 1904, and during the next three decades 13 major oil fields would be found within a 50-mile radius of Market Square.

The Spindletop boom reinforced the cries for a safe deepwater port, and work began on the bayou that would lead to a great ship channel and set Houston off on a boom that would continue into the 1980s.

Houston wasn't prepared for the events that were to come. A district attorney, who had been recently elected would start a war on gambling. A diamond discovery was reported from Capitan near El Paso. Tom Sharkey was crying for a crack at Kid McCoy and Dr. Walter Reed announced his discovery of the carrier of yellow fever. William Jennings Bryan was due to visit Houston and John Phillip Sousa's band had been booked for the Opera House.

Simultaneously, as the new century dawned, Houston was reminded none too gently by articles in national publications, that it was culturally immature. Houston children at school were growing up ignorant of the world's great art. These articles inspired four Houston women, Mrs. John McClellan, Mrs. W. G. Smiley, Mrs. R. W. Knox and artist Emma Richardson Cherry to meet in Robert Lovett's big colonial home on Main. Also attending was James Chillman, later first director of the Museum of Fine Arts.

The group of workers was small but enthusiasm and determination were great. An authority of art for children, Jean Sherwood of Chicago, delivered a stirring indictment of Houston's school system. With little or no funds, that first organizational effort to secure public recognition of the arts in our social structure was made in Houston. Their efforts resulted in the formation of the Houston Public School Art League; later the Houston Art League, and finally the incorporation of the Museum of Fine Arts of Houston.

The Houston Public School Art League commissioned fiery little Emma Richardson Cherry to paint reproductions of the world's great artists. Cramming these paintings into her buggy, she saw that every school in town had at least one painting.

She organized Houston's first Art Class, daring to use the first female nude model. Proper Houstonians were scandalized.

The new Art League's next step was to purchase a full-sized cast of Venus de Milo made in Paris to give to Central High School. It was refused admittance by City authorities on the grounds of indecent exposure. The cast was finally given shelter in the recently built Public Library, a handsome Italian Renaissance building on McKinny and Smith. Julia Ideson, head librarian, took a deep breath and accepted it. She invited the City Council and Houston School Board to the dedication ceremony. Not one official showed up!

Jesse Jones' aunt, Mrs. M. T. Jones, gave a bronze bust of Sappho to the Library. It is fascinating to think of the City Fathers' reaction when they learned that Sappho was a lesbian.

Within 25 years of this occurrence, however, the first unit of a museum of art was open to the public with these words inscribed over its doors:

"Erected by the people for the use of the people."

The inscription is a true one. The museum was built by the people with voluntary gifts. If in some future day the metal box within the museum's cornerstone is opened, there will be found beside the names of those who gave thousands, the names of those who gave their thousands in dimes and quarters.

When this first phase of the museum was being built, two names stand out—William C. Hogg and Florence B. Fall, who singlehandedly enlisted the financial support to complete it to its size, and she who ensured the successful completion of twenty-five years of work by the Houston Arts League. The museum opened April 12, 1924.

Emma Richardson Cherry painted the murals of early Texas homes on the walls of the Julia Ideson building of the Houston Public Library. In 1914, George Hermann and J. S. Cullinan gave a triangular plot on the intersection of Main and Montrose to the Art League for a permanent Museum of Fine Arts.

Houston's interest in art in the early days was about on a par with its interest in sanitary streets. One day Mrs. Harris Masterson, watching a push-cart boy spill all of the freshly baked loaves of bread on the horse dung filled street, was horrified to see him calmly replace them on his cart. She marched straight to the Mayor's office and demanded he enact a law forbidding push carts without tops and sides. She got her law.

Later, she and a few of her friends decided there were too many young women coming to town looking for jobs without any place to turn for help. They rented a room over Sweeney's Pawn Shop. All too soon it was over-crowded with girls seeking jobs and help.

One day in 1907 one of the girls knocked over a pitcher of milk. The milk seeped through the floor cracks down on men's suits in Sweeney's Pawn Shop. Sweeney, understandably agitated, told Mrs. Masterson and her friends they would have to move elsewhere with their grandiose plan to help young women who should have stayed home anyhow! Mrs. Masterson and the ladies marched over to Houston leader-philanthropist Will Hogg's office. They poured out their story of homeless females with no place to go for advice and help.

Surrounded by the town's leading ladies, impressed with their zeal but sympathetic with Sweeney, Hogg bel-lowed, "This has got to stop!" He wrote the group a fat check to start them on a building of their own. *The YWCA was founded!*

Mrs. W. A. McDowell was the first President of the Board, followed by Mrs. Masterson in 1909. The first YWCA was at 805 Main Street in a house with six rooms and a barn which they turned into a gymnasium.

Mrs. Masterson was a tall, commanding woman. She lived in her big colonial, red brick house with white col-umns on Burlington and West Alabama. Her garden was famous for its large, intricate maze of hedge where neighborhood children enjoyed getting lost. *The Houston Post* Poet Mortimer Lewis delighted in leading children through the maze pretending to be lost, too.

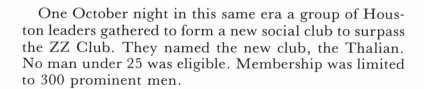

One October night in this same era a group of Hous-ton leaders gathered to form a new social club to surpass the ZZ Club. They named the new club, the Thalian. No man under 25 was eligible. Membership was limited to 300 prominent men.

Organized in 1901, the Thalian Club erected its own building on the corner of San Jacinto and Rusk for $40,000 in 1907. It contained a barber shop, wine cellar and ice room in the basement, smoking room, reading room, parlor, dining room on the second floor; on the third, was a ballroom called the most beautiful in the city.

The Thalian Club gave two Balls each season and announced it would "support a Literary Club, maintain a library, promote painting, music, other fine arts." Rules for proper conduct at the Balls were rigid!

The late Houbert Roussel of the *Houston Post*, gave his view in his column on the elitism of the Thalian Club Balls: "The era of big business was just starting. Girls with rich fathers were finding it possible to open doors which heretofore had yielded only to the presence of ancestors." A new era had dawned.

On January 10, 1901, at 10:30 a.m., 90 miles from Houston and six miles from Beaumont, a crew of three—brothers Al and Curt Hamill along with Peck Byrd—had just put a new fishtail bit on a well they were drilling. That done, the drill stem was lowered back into the hole. With the pipe down about 700 feet and Curt Hamill steering it from the double boards forty feet above the derrick floor, something began to happen.

Mud started to bubble up over the rotary table. Al Hamill and Peck Byrd backed away when suddenly the force increased and mud spurted high up the derrick. Curt, drenched with mud and gumbo, grabbed for the ladder and slid down it to safety. All three scampered in different directions. This was a new experience for these old hands of the Corsicana field. As they ran, six tons of four-inch pipe came shooting up through the derrick, knocking off the crown block. Then the pipe leapt, like activated spaghetti, on over the top of the derrick and broke off in sections, falling around the camp like giant spikes driven into the earth.

Then everything was quiet. The Hamills and Peck Byrd cautiously returned to the derrick floor. It was a shambles, with mud, muck and water standing a foot deep. The disgusted crew looked over the situation, started cleaning up the debris, and expressed themselves in a manner of eloquence reserved for men of the oil fields.

"What the hell are we going to do with the damn thing now?" Peck Byrd asked Al as he shut off the boiler fires.

"Well, Peck," Al was saying, "I guess we'll just have to shovel this mud away and see if . . ."

His words were interrupted by a roar like the shot of a heavy cannon. Then again the flow of mud started up through the hole, followed by a terrific column of gas. The startled crew scattered again. Peck missed his footing and tumbled headlong into the slush pit. Within seconds, the gas was followed by a solid flow of oil—green and heavy.

"Peck, run to the house and get the Captain," Al shouted, "while Curt and me try to figure this thing out. It looks like oil! Hurry! Hurry!"

The mud-soaked Peck Byrd ran to the Lucas home. When he got there he was out of breath and sat holding his side, panting a few minutes, before he could deliver the message to Mrs. Lucas.

"Get the Captain! Tell him to come right now!" Peck shouted in excitement.

"Hurry, Anthony, something awful has happened. The well is spouting," she shouted into the telephone.

The Captain turned and fled from the store without explanation. He mounted his gig, as Louie Mayer watched in astonishment, and stood on the floor-boards whipping his horse as he raced out Park Street, past the

O'Brien and Carroll homes, out Highland Avenue and past his own home without even looking toward his wife, who was trying to attract his attention by waving from the porch.

The phenomenon was in full view now. It was frightening to the Captain. His eyes had never beheld such a sight before. Could it be oil?

"Al, Al," he was shouting, "what is it? What is it?"

"Oil, Captain! Oil, every drop of it," the jubilant Al replied.

Grabbing Al Hamill by the waist and swinging him around, Lucas looked up toward the gray skies and said, "Thank God. Thank God, you've done it! You've done it!"

"It came in at ten-thirty, almost an hour ago, and it has been shooting a steady six-inch stream of oil more than a hundred feet above the top of the derrick, just like it is now. I can't understand it," Al said. "But I don't think we are going to pay George Carroll for that derrick."

Captain Lucas was exultant. He stood under the shower of green oil, felt it, smelled it and tasted it to make certain he wasn't dreaming.

Then he backed off and looked up to the top of the great plume. Oil, shale, and rocks were raining down. Almost to himself he whispered hoarsely, with a rising emotion, "A geyser of oil! A geyser of oil!" (*Spindletop*, James A. Clark, Michel T. Halbouty.)

There wasn't a man on the streets of Houston in cotton or lumber any longer. All were prospectors for oil. Cars were bumper to bumper from Houston to Beaumont, less than 85 miles away. Instant oil companies were formed with nothing more than a handshake.

Spindletop was to break the oil monopoly of Russia and Standard of New Jersey. It was to change men and the economy. It was to change Houston permanently.

Only one man in Beaumont that morning was not surprised—real estater Patillo Higgins. Since the 80's he had been convinced there was big oil in the Spindletop mound. He said it would be found at 1,000 feet. He bought up land. He had hired Walter B. Sharp "a young but experienced well man," and told him just where to drill on the mound. But at 418 feet, Higgins ordered the drilling stopped. He knew Sharp's light, rotary equipment would never make it 1,000 feet! This was to happen twice more. He lost the support of his Beaumont investors. He put a last, desperate ad in the paper for a driller with heavy equipment. He got one reply. The letter was signed, "Captain F. Lucas."

J. S. Cullinan (Buckskin Joe), referred to as "the most important oil man in Texas, was the first to call on Captain Lucas. A former Standard Oil of New Jersey man, he had been asked by Corsicana city officials to help develop the industry there. But the morning he saw the Lucas gusher, he knew Corsicana's day was over." Cullinan organized The Texas Fuel Company. He came to Houston in 1905. Ex-Governor James Hogg, Walter Sharp, and William Thomas Campbell banded with Cullinan to create one of the two most important oil companies in the world, the mighty Texas Company (Texaco).

Spindletop gave birth to Houston's "big rich." After the Lucas well blew in, two young future Houstonians, then in their twenties, were staying in the same boarding house in Beaumont. They were Robert Lee Blaffer and an attorney from Natchez, Mississippi, William S. Farish. It didn't take them long to decide to be partners in the oil business. Across the street lived a wealthy lumberman, Captain Wiess. He had a bright teenage son, Harry, who quickly became friends with Blaffer and Farish. None of the three young men dreamed of the conglomerate power they would one day possess. In the same boarding house were Ed Simms and Ed Prather.

"Ed Prather arrived in Beaumont with Walter Sharp the morning after the Lucas gusher came in. They leased everything they could get between Spindletop and Sour Lake." Jesse Jones, a rising young businessman from Houston, frequently visited with Blaffer and Farish, as did Ross Sterling.

Another young Houstonian was Walter W. Fondren. "He had built a drilling company from nothing and was a genius at the application of new techniques. He was drilling a crater well a few miles from Beaumont when Spindletop blew in. His job as a driller got him a rig of his own. He soon worked with Blaffer and Farish on oil deals. Blaffer and Farish moved to Humble, 30 miles from Houston. On March 1, 1917, the Humble Oil and Refinery Company was formed and applied for its charter. It included the partnership of Blaffer and Farish. The Shultz Oil Company owned by Blaffer, Farish, Prather, Carlton and Bert Brodoy; the Globe Oil and Refining Company, which was owned by Blaffer, William and Steve Farish, and which was the first oil company to sell products at a service station; the partnership of Farish and Ireland, which included Bill Farish, Frank Ireland, Jesse Jones, Carlton and Prather; W. W. Fondren's drilling company . . . properties owned by J. Cooke Wilson and C. B. Goddard and important properties out of three companies in the Wiess Estate . . ."

The Secretary of State refused to issue a charter when it was learned that the group was going to "produce, transport, refine, purchase and market oil." It is remarkable that the owners of all these invaluable properties stayed together with only a verbal understanding between them. It took four months for the legislature to change Texas laws to allow the company to operate. The Charter was granted on June 21, 1917. Ross Sterling was the first president, Farish, vice president, and Blaffer, treasurer. Farish succeeded Sterling as president in 1921. In 1932, he left Humble and became president of Standard Oil of New Jersey, majority owner of Humble. Blaffer then became president of Humble. In 1936, Harry Wiess was named president of the Humble Oil Company.

On the same day the Houston Oil Company was formed under Houstonians Joe Eagle and H. F. Bonner, the $10 million Kirby Lumber Company was organized. John Henry Kirby's life story was paralleled many times in early Houston. Kirby came from deep in the piney woods of East Texas. He earned a law degree at Southwestern University at Georgetown and, at nineteen, became the "lumber king of the Southwest." These early men were big in stature, vision, and independence. When the stockholders of The Texas Company voted to move its headquarters to New York, J. S. Cullinan resigned. He then formed the American Republic Corporation.

Spindletop and the discoveries of the men that followed built the Gulf Building, the Esperson Building, the Petroleum Building, the Shell Building, the Exxon Building, the Pennzoil Building, the Tenneco Building, the Shamrock-Hilton Hotel, the University of Houston, the Texas Medical Center, the Fondren Library, Rice University, the University of St. Thomas, churches, hospitals, public schools and highways. Today it still supports art galleries, museums, the symphony, opera, theatre groups, and philanthropies. Oil is the sun that shines down on Houston.

CHAPTER TEN

"I believe that love of art is closely associated with love of God. It has been true all through history. Man's art is God's gift to him. It is His signature across the Face of Creation."—Sarah Campbell Blaffer

O VER a century ago a young district attorney in Mineola, Texas wrote to his brother "Our cup of joy is now complete! We have a daughter and her name is Ima." That day—July 10, 1882—also marked the beginning of a legacy to the people of Texas.

The father was James Stephen Hogg, a man of integrity and high ideals who was to become Texas' first native-born governor. He instilled in his children his concern for the citizens of Texas and throughout his lifetime encouraged rising generations to honor the "home" where he felt the pivot of constitutional government was rooted.

Ima Hogg grew up in the shadow of the State Capitol. As a young girl her home was the governor's mansion, a home filled with political figures and famous people. At nine, Ima and her older brother, Will, were among the guests of honor at her father's inauguration as Governor; and later were often included at State dinners, discovering early to listen and learn from knowledgeable people in a variety of fields.

The lives of Ima and her brothers were changed drastically after the move from the governor's mansion to another home in Austin, with the early death of their mother, Sallie Stinson Hogg.

After this, Jim Hogg played an increasingly important role in Ima's life. He wrote, "My ambition is to raise my children after her (mother's) model. If I succeed, the world will be made better for it."

A few years later Ima enrolled at the University of Texas. "No freshman," she recalled, "could have been more unprepared or more frightened than I." Music, however, became Ima's primary interest. So after two years at the University, she left for New York to attend the National Conservatory of Music. With the family divided, they remained close in spite of the distance. All were prolific letter writers.

Jim Hogg saw to it that the family always had a home to return to. He had said:

> "Home! The center of civilization. Home! The pivot of constitutional government. Home! The ark of safety to happiness, virtue, and Christianity. Home! The haven of rest in old age, where the higher elements of manhood can be taught rising generations by splendid example. Every man should have a home!"

So, after moving his family from rented houses to the governor's mansion, to rented houses (his purse was lean), he finally was able to acquire a special home, outside of West Columbia, Texas. It was here that the family could gather and entertain. It was also here that the Hogg family fortune began. The land was an 1824 grant from Mexico and had functioned as a sugar plantation. The first cabin on the property became the kitchen of Hogg's big galleried house, which he named the Varner Plantation. Here he began to raise cattle, goats and vegetables. He also became deeply interested in developing the agricultural and water preservation possibilities; in teaching the newest improved methods of farming.

One morning Jim Hogg walked down to his artesian well to get a bottle of fresh drinking water. The elderly honey bee tender, who had his cabin near the well, told him: "See that brown stuff on the ground there around the well? Strike a match to it and it burns!" Many times later, the visionary Hogg was to say to his daughter Ima, "Missy, there's oil on this place sure as I live. The place may get to be a burden to keep, but don't ever let your brothers sell it!" He had stipulated in his will, in an almost clairvoyant way that the Varner Plantation could not be sold for fifteen years.

His prediction came true in 1914. The first well the Hoggs drilled on the plantation flowed 100,000 barrels per day. Two years later, the West Columbia oilfield was producing 12 million barrels a year. However, James Hogg would never live to see it.

At the Varner-Hogg Plantation "Miss Ima" kept house for her father and later for her brothers, Will, Mike and Tom. She encountered problems she hadn't dreamed of with the older Negroes, who had been on the plantation when the Patton family owned it.

The Negroes refused to enter the house after dark. They told stories of often hearing at night the relentless hoof beats of the filly young Patton was riding to death on the race track he built near the house. They could hear the crack of his whip, could feel it cut across their own bodies.

One evening as dusk was settling down on the plantation Miss Ima's young house girl, reaching for a pitcher pulled a tall highboy down on herself. In spite of Miss

Ima's frantic cries for help, no Negro would enter the
house. She somehow managed to extricate the terrified
girl.

Ghosts are not easy to exorcise, but Miss Ima found a
way. When a young Negro couple on the plantation told
her they wanted to get married at Christmas, she invited
them to have the wedding in the big house. She made a
beautiful wedding veil for the bride out of fine lace curtains. On the wedding day, seated at her grand piano,
Miss Ima played Lohengrin's *Wedding March* for the
overwhelmed couple. And, from that day on, the ghosts
were forever laid to rest.

When the Lucas gusher came in at Spindletop, Hogg
went to Beaumont. He saw many old friends there; John
H. Kirby who owned hundreds of acres of pine timber-
land and Walter Sharp. He talked to Patillo Higgins, no
longer considered the pathetic local dreamer. The Hogg-
Swayne Syndicate was formed (Hogg never liked the
connotation of the word corporation). Andrew Mellon of
Pittsburgh who was in oil and pipeline competition with
John Rockefeller knew that Standard Oil faced legal
problems in Texas. He recounted, "Northern men were
not very well respected in Texas in those days. Governor
Hogg was a respected power down there and I wanted
him on my side because I was going to spend a lot of
money." Jim Hogg was brought into the oil business.

Hogg's oil interests and law firm with Edgar Watkins
and Frank Jones kept him busy in Houston.

On March 2, 1906 James Hogg was visiting Frank
Jones in Houston. He mentioned to his friend that at his
death he wanted no monument but instead:

> Let my children plant at the head of my grave a pe-
> can tree and at my feet an old fashioned walnut
> tree. And when these trees shall bear, let the har-
> vest be given to the plain people so that they may
> plant them and make Texas a land of trees.

That night he died, unexpectedly, in his sleep.

James Stephen Hogg was known for his unselfish de-
votion to the people of Texas. His hopes that his children
would become concerned, sensitive and productive citizens would be realized. From orphanage in boyhood to
becoming the most beloved man in the State, the people
of Texas respected him for his uncompromising honesty.
He rests in Austin in Oakwood Cemetery. (*James Stephen
Hogg, A Biography*, Robert C. Conter.)

The example set by James Hogg of acting for the bet-
terment of the people of Texas became the lifelong ambition of his sons Will, and Mike and of Miss Ima.

Education, particularly The University of Texas, was
of foremost importance to the Hogg family. Will Hogg
continued the tradition. He was instrumental in forming
the Ex-Student Association and he helped provide the
funds for educating the needy. He gave financially to
Memorial Stadium, the Student Union and the campus
YMCA. He gave anonymously saying, "Relieve the dis-
tress, and investigate afterwards. If he is a student at the
University, that is all I want to know."

There can never be a full accounting of the Hogg
Foundation gifts. However, after the deaths of her brothers Miss Ima Hogg continued in the tradition and carried out the ambition of her father with modesty and
charm. Out of this great financial reservoir came the
Houston Civic Center, River Oaks Corporation, The
Houston Club, Houston Country Club, Forum of Civ-
ics, Houston Symphony, The Museum of Fine Arts and
The Foundation for Mental Hygiene.

Bayou Bend, built by John Staub, became Miss Ima's
home for many years. While living there with her brothers Will and Mike, she planned how to convey the collection and home to the Museum of Fine Arts and how to

present the many pieces she had carefully collected. Her unerring taste and sense of what was best, as well as her great knowledge and color sense, became legendary. But as she explained to the docents, "When you love something enough it's easy to give it up in order to see it go on."

Ima Hogg wanted nothing for herself. Her wants were for the people of Texas. When praised for her help she merely said, "I only open doors." Miss Ima firmly believed in giving young people a start, if they were willing to help themselves. She was mentally young and in fact more "in tune" with younger generations.

Firm in her opinions Miss Hogg was more than concerned when she learned that the oak trees on the site of Saks Fifth Avenue were to be bulldozed down. She wrote to the directors in New York. That is why the beautiful oak trees on Post Oak Boulevard grace the entrance of Saks Fifth Avenue.

Her abiding love for balance in architecture was exhibited when her close friend Roger Rasbach, architectural designer, built his home in Raintree on Post Oak. It was a large, elegant contemporary house in terra cotta designed in what she felt should be reflected geographically in Texas—*Latin Colonial.* Miss Ima marched to the River Oaks Garden Club and exerted her influence to place the house on tour. It is the only house owned by a bachelor that has ever been shown on the River Oaks Garden Tour.

Miss Ima demanded perfection in herself and in others. Quite a taskmaster, she had that facility for getting people to work for her. When she formed the Houston Symphony Society, it was she who pounded the pavements, getting ads for the Symphony programs. Miss Ima served as president of the Symphony for many years. Betty Ewing, *Houston Chronicle,* reported "Remember how all eyes would be on Mrs. Cornelius Vanderbilt at the Metropolitan? Well, for decades Miss

Ima's settling in her seat at the Symphony had the same effect."

In 1966 Miss Ima, called First Lady of Texas, donated to the Museum of Fine Arts her beloved Bayou Bend which contains a cherished collection of early American heritage. It stands on 14 acres along the bend of Buffalo Bayou. David Warren is the Director.

She had restored and furnished the Varner-Hogg Plantation in 1956 for the people of Texas in memory of her parents. It is a state park and museum containing documents of early leaders of Texas.

Her attention remained focused on Texas and she was still busy with her many interests until she left for England after her 93rd birthday in 1975. After a fall as she was stepping into a taxi in London, Miss Hogg was taken to a hospital with a broken hip. She hastened to reassure the cab driver and friends that whatever happens, it is the way it was meant to be. She never returned from that trip. Miss Ima did become a legend in her own time.

The State of Texas recognizes three men who have contributed the most to the people as statesmen. They are: Stephen F. Austin, Sam Houston and James Stephen Hogg.

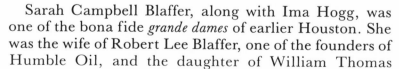

Sarah Campbell Blaffer, along with Ima Hogg, was one of the bona fide *grande dames* of earlier Houston. She was the wife of Robert Lee Blaffer, one of the founders of Humble Oil, and the daughter of William Thomas Campbell of the Scottish Clan of Argyle.

Sarah Campbell (called Sadie) was raised in Lampasas, Texas in a beautiful white colonial mansion, surrounded by high walls complete with guard house and gate-keeper.

Possessing startling beauty, intelligence and salty earthiness, she had swarms of suitors including Howard Hughes, Sr. However, Mr. Campbell kept a keen eye on the husband-to-be for his poetic daughter who attended a convent school in Houston.

One of the brightest suitors, Robert Lee Blaffer, whose fortune and destiny would be cast at Spindletop when he met his life long partner, William S. Farish, won the admiration and approval for marriage to Mr. Campbell's daughter, Sarah. Since Mr. Campbell had been one of the original signers of the charter of The Texas Company (Texaco), the Blaffer-Campbell marriage was what most Houstonians proclaimed "the conglomerate of the century."

A Lone Star cast attended the ceremony held in a small church in Lampasas in 1909. A private railroad car brought Houston's society to the ceremony including Will and Mike Hogg, W. S. Farish, the J. S. Cullinans, W. B. Sharps and Miss Ima Hogg, who was maid of honor. Will Hogg, famed for his wedding gifts, promptly presented the new bride and groom with a fine, fat milk cow. The young Blaffers named her "Wedding Bells." Later, when they moved into the beautiful house that they built in Shadyside, one of Wedding Bells' descendants went along. She produced enough milk for all of the Blaffer's neighbors.

Sarah Blaffer was to begin her life-long interest in collecting art, while on her wedding trip. The three month European honeymoon took her to the Louvre in Paris and it was here that she had her first mature contact with the greatness of art. It changed her life. Fortunately, it also altered the destiny of Houston.

Art became her passion, and this genteel, cultured lady wanted to share it with her fellow Texans. The new Museum of Fine Arts was off to a fine start when she donated paintings by Renoir, Cezanne, Soutine and

Vlaminck. In 1971, she donated 12 paintings to the University of Houston valued at $900,000.

She originated a traveling art exhibit. Rather than hang them on her mansion's walls, Sarah Blaffer answered the hunger of intelligent people who live in small towns for beautiful things.

Fortunately for Texas, she had the expertise, the urge and the money to collect and share truly fine art. The paintings were loaned free to Texas schools, colleges and museums that did not have the funds to buy or to house large collections.

The Robert Lee Blaffers had four children. John, the only son is deceased, but Sarah Blaffer's three daughters consciously carry on the tradition and the legacy of beauty in art that their mother bequeathed to them.

Jane Blaffer Owen (Mrs. Kenneth) has and is restoring an entire community in New Harmony, Indiana, one of the most unique undertakings in the United States today. A second daughter, Cecil (Titi) is married to Prince Tassilo von Furstenberg and with her father's intuitive business sense, keeps the Sarah Campbell Blaffer Foundation a growing living monument to her mother and her love for her fellow man.

Joyce Blaffer is married to Dietrich von Bothmer who is the curator of Greek and Roman art at the Metropolitan Museum in New York.

Before her death at age ninety-one, Mrs. Blaffer told one of the trustees, Mr. Gilbert M. Denman, "I believe that love of art is closely associated with love of God. It has been true all through history. Man's art is God's gift to him. It is His signature across the Face of Creation. Every experience of man's art . . . in the creation of art we are fellow workers of God, whether we recognize it or not."

CHAPTER ELEVEN

"For the Houston woman of this era, the philosophy of sweeping unhappy realities under the rug prevailed. There was much bragging among the ladies that Houston had no divorces. They were all in Dallas!"

"AUTOMOBILES have come to Houston," reported the *Houston Chronicle,* Christmas, 1901. "For more than a month now, the agile, swift moving steam engines have been dashing back and forth over the downtown streets." The ladies excitedly shopped for the revolutionary style of dress for motoring, "Motor millinery for ladies is a soft felt, like a cowboy hat, with a veil at least three yards long and three yards wide." Founder of Houston Heights O. M. Carter, in this year, prophetically predicted, "A traffic almost too vast for contemplation will pass unceasingly up and down the city's thoroughfares!"

Two years later, A. T. Brady was fined $10 for speeding down Main. He not only exceeded the speed limit of six miles an hour, he incited a carriage and horses to a dangerous run away!

The new City Hall and Market buildings rose in the ashes of the old in Market Square. Built of stone and buff brick, the building had fancy stone trim, gables, twin towers. One had a big chiming clock with four faces; "1903" carved in its pediment. The City Hall and Market, later to become the City Bus Station, thronged with families shopping and coming to Market Square to dine.

Will Hogg and Joseph S. Cullinan hired Edward Teas to plant hundreds of live oaks in the new River Oaks, Shadyside, on North and South Boulevards, Main Street at Rice University, and in Harrisburg. In the older neighborhoods, Teas set out elms, pecans, magnolias, and crape myrtles. Houston is said to have been treeless except for the lush banks of Buffalo Bayou. Mr. Teas' Scanlan oak on Main grew to such size it was looked on as a state treasure. Teas Nursery still thrives on Bellaire Boulevard.

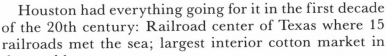

Houston had everything going for it in the first decade of the 20th century: Railroad center of Texas where 15 railroads met the sea; largest interior cotton market in the world.

Main Street had other marvels in this new century. Houstonians called Samuel F. Carter's 16-floor bank building "Carter's Folly." The foolhardiness of laying bricks so high in the air! When Jesse Jones, owner of the Rice Hotel proposed to Carter that ten stories was the best height for Houston buildings, Carter said, "You build your building, I'll build mine." Jones promptly increased his Rice Hotel to 17 stories.

The Majestic made her glittering debut. Also built by Jesse Jones on part of the block now occupied by the *Houston Chronicle,* it was the town's first vaudeville house. "Curtained silk and plus, columned in gilt and gold and over-arched with streams of incandescent extravagance. The effect was dazzling and indescribable!"

Monday was "Society night." Houston's social leaders held season tickets for Will Rogers, Sophie Tucker, Mae West, Eddie Foy, Guy Bates Post and Al Jolson. The Majestic later became the Palace, home of the Palace Players stock company. In later years, with spine-tingling expectancy, young girls watched the curtain rise on Clark Gable, Gene Lewis and Olga Worth! A second Majestic was later built on Rusk near Travis.

The City Auditorium, built by Jesse Jones for $500,000, was a grand temple of cultural and civic activity in the first quarter of this century. Through the years, the big barn resounded with the outpourings of great singers and musicians of the day such as Caruso, Lily Pon and Paderewski; the flamboyant oratory of politicians; the groans and bumps of wrestlers, and boxers such as Jim Corbett. Over a half-century later, Jones Hall would rise on the site in Jesse Jones' honor.

With the world coming to Houston, could sin be far behind? Mayor Baldwin Rice and the City Council decided not. They issued an ordinance forbidding men to make Goo-Goo-Eyes at women on the streets.

The Baptists doubled their crusade against liquor and its sins. Carry Nation felt the town needed her help. Some wag on the Northside had named his saloon after her, so she came to town and wrecked it.

She marched in one night with a full house on hand, smashed every mirror in sight with rocks out of a stout handbag, and was going after the bartender with a hatchet when finally subdued.

From the 1880s until World War I, Howard Street, where the present San Felipe Housing project is now, was called Sin Alley. This red-light district had houses of "chandeliered magnificence," (George Fuermann, *Houston: Land of the Big Rich*). The girls could come to town only at certain hours of the day. By World War I, Howard

Street was such a scandal, the police closed it down. In the 1930s it vanished under the San Felipe Housing project, now itself condemned, but not for the same reasons.

A Madame Sasser is said to have owned the most prosperous whorehouse in town. She ran it in an antebellum house, white frame with striped awnings, on Bastrop. It looked like so many of our houses, comfortable and proper. Sasser had a big garage at the rear, well out of sight, where customers parked their cars.

Whether she was one of Madame Sasser's "spectacular girls" or a woman of her own social class, the Houston woman of this era kept any knowledge of her husband's mistress (if he had one) locked in the back closet of her mind. The philosophy of sweeping unhappy realities under the rug; that everything turns out for the best, prevailed. It still does. The wife and mother was the matriarch of her family and her household. But beyond the locked front gate, the man made the rules. For some time she was to live by this system. There was much bragging among the ladies that Houston had no divorces. They were all in Dallas!

One society leader in 1910 even bemoaned the passing of a New Year's Day custom that gave men unrestricted freedom. "In former times, it was the custom of every married woman to be at home on New Year's Day, while her husband went the rounds of other homes with men . . . it was said that often too much wine was drunk as wine was served at every house. But a gentleman can usually be trusted to remember that he is a gentleman . . . there is little to be feared of the men in Houston!"

In the first decade of the 20th century, the *Standard Blue Book of Texas,* published in 1896, was the criterion of manners, dress, even vocabulary.

"A lady is known by her boots and her gloves."

"A lady does not stop to chat with a friend in the middle of a sidewalk."

"Avoid 'I say,' 'You know,' 'Dear.'"

"A lady does not take the arms of two gentlemen, nor should two ladies take one arm of a gentleman, sandwiching him in as it were!"

Handshaking had its perils. "A young lady gives her hand but does not shake a gentleman's hand unless she is his friend. A man has no right to take a lady's hand until it is offered. He has even less right to pinch or retain it! It is the privilege of a superior to offer or withhold his or her hand, so that a younger or less important person should never put his forward first."

How could you tell who was less important? "You just *know!*" children were told.

It must have been of some comfort to one who might have felt inferior to read the *Blue Book's* next words: "Every human being should feel that he is *at least for the time* upon a social equality with every guest present! In a ballroom where the introduction is to dancing, *not* to friendship, you never shake hands. An introduction is not followed by shaking hands, only by a bow. Persons born and reared in the best society never make a hasty presentation or introduction."

That is, one had better not barge into the group beside the potted palms simply because he spies a vaguely familiar face.

"It perhaps may be laid down that the more public the place of introduction, the less handshaking takes place. But if the introduction be particular, if it be accompanied by personal recommendation such as, 'I want you to know my friend Jones,' or if Jones comes with a letter of presentation, then you give Jones your hand and *warmly* too."

The *Blue Book* put up with no nonsense about a man's smoking or dress. "A man is permitted to smoke only when walking or driving alone."

"The fancy colored shirts with cuffs attached or detached is quite the thing for business wear, collar being white."

"For automobiling, wear double breasted coat and buttoned across." When entertaining in his summer bay home, he should wear a "white tuxedo suit."

If a man owned a yacht, and many did, "The regulation dinner coat aboard is a blue broadcloth tuxedo finished with braid on edges and the Yacht Club emblem embroidered in the corner of the collar."

Mayor Baldwin Rice often entertained on his luxurious yacht *Zeeland.* He delighted in taking visitors on a tour of the ship channel. The Camille Pillots sailed the *Augusta* on Sunday afternoons, the men appropriately dressed, the ladies in long linen skirts and starched shirtwaists.

The *Blue Book* listed the "At Home Days" of prominent social leaders. "A newcomer is to call between 2 and 3 o'clock, send in her cards with those of her husband, father or brother and a cordial interview follows. This call should be returned within a week or an explanation sent." If the call is simply returned by a card, this implies that ". . . the stranger prefers solitude!"

Fifteen minutes was the limit of a first call. "The wife who calls on her married friend leaves *two* of her husband's cards and *one* of her own." Men were given an ambiguous warning: "A man never carries or leaves the card of any other man."

The calling card, monogrammed, pristine white, was the "host" the "best people" in Houston offered to each other in a weekly socio-religious ritual. The calling card conveyed its message in a language subtle but unmistakable as the smoke signal of the Indian.

"Turn down the upper left corner, it said 'congratulations.' Turn down the lower right corner, it said 'adieu.' Turn down the lower left corner, it murmured 'condolences.' "

I can see the calling cards of my mother's visitors lying chastely on the small silver tray on the marble-top table beneath the gold-leafed mirror in our living room. The soft murmur of their voices drifted through the open French doors, mingling with the fragrance of lemon blossoms, camphor trees and cape jasmine. They may have known or suspected each other's problems and griefs, but the facade of calling cards, the self-discipline of good manners, were their shield and fortress.

———————————◄ ►————————————

There were women in Houston who didn't "care a pig's hind tooth" about the *Blue Book*. One was Keziah Payne. She came with her family from Funchal, Madeira Island, to Galveston in 1837, when she was nine years old. She survived a yellow fever epidemic in which she lost her mother and other members of her family. She learned early, as girl children did, to nurse the ill and dying.

When she was 13, she moved to Houston with her stepmother. Taking care of other children who had lost their parents through the Civil War or an epidemic had fired her with a dream of a home for orphans and for children with working mothers.

Born in the luxuriant hills and green valley of Madeira, how did this impressionable young girl adjust to the mud and flat ugliness of the raw town of Houston? One guesses through her love of music. It wasn't long before she was playing the organ at Christ Church.

An early marriage to Belgian musician Adolph de Pelchin didn't last long. Through more years of nursing yellow fever victims she never gave up her dream. When Baylands Orphan Home for children moved from San Jacinto Bay to Houston, she became the matron.

Finally, in 1892, Keziah Payne de Pelchin at last had her own small orphans' home on Center Street. She called it Faith Home because that was all she had to put in it. But she got help from women of the town like Mrs. T. W. House and Harriet Levy. Still, to help pay the bills, she kept her job at Baylands Orphan Home. In her mid-sixties, she walked to and from Baylands instead of taking a mule car—and it wasn't for the exercise!

When this wonderful woman died she could not have foreseen the Faith Home that today sprawls over 12 acres at Shepherd and Memorial Drives.

In 1904 Lionel Hohenthal, a businessman representing the English Steamship Line, suggested a new idea to a few friends at the Thalian Club. The friends were Will Hogg, A. W. Pollard, B. A. Baldwin and Will M. Rice (nephew of William Marsh Rice). The little group succeeded in obtaining $25 from 100 men to launch the First Houston Golf Club, and put up a club house, "a cozy artistic cottage," on land leased from Rice Institute (where Jefferson Davis Hospital now stands). The game caught on at once!

It quickly became too cozy. So, in 1908 the group set about creating a real country club.

They bought beautiful, pine forested acres along the Houston and Harrisburg Interurban on the east side of town. Here, they built a sprawling, gracious club house, shaded by towering pines, its broad verandahs filled with high backed rocking chairs overlooking the rolling, hilly golf course. The membership was limited to 500 with Will Rice as President, F. B. Parker, Vice President.

Glenn Owen Sneed, the gentlemanly Negro maitre d'hotel of the large, bay-windowed dining room, was known only as Sneed. He knew parents and grandparents. When children came along, he embraced them as his own in his kind, wise heart, making them feel a link with Houston's past, black as well as white.

Shorty McDade, known only as Shorty, the little, hunchbacked gnome, the jolly ruler of the swimming pool, lived only for his special world of obstreperous small children and wet towels. His black face, held in its tragic vise between his hunched shoulders, was eternally wrinkled with laughter. When he sorrowed or angered, he never let anyone know. He taught compassion, without words.

The present Houston Country Club opened its doors in 1956 after a committee headed by Thomas W. Moore relocated to its new location on Potomac. Robert Trent Jones laid out the new course. The committee included David Gordon, Edward Rotan, John Wimberly, William Farrington and Gus Wortham who quickly set the wheels in motion for its completion. However, late in 1956 as moving day grew near, most felt a deep sadness at saying goodbye to the lovely old club and golf course and their forty-eight years of memories.

The Houston Country Club is handsome but the intimate spirit of that pine-sighing, galleried, open-windowed old Houston Country Club can never be duplicated.

The year 1912 would be remembered for years for the great Fifth Ward fire and the opening of Rice Institute, one a great loss, the other a great gain.

The fire broke out on the freezing night of February 21 when a northwest wind raced across the city. It originated in an abandoned two-story shanty called the Madhouse, once a saloon and rooming house. Five derelicts, warmed by whiskey and an old oil stove, were shooting craps by the light of a kerosene lamp. A fight ensued; the oil stove crashed on its side and exploded.

A strong northeast wind, blowing 70 to 80 miles an hour, quickly spread the fiery holocaust over 40 blocks. Ninety houses went up like kindling. People fled, dragging possessions only to drop them and run for their lives. The fire spread to the Cleveland Compress at the Hill Street Bridge, destroying 35,000 bales of cotton. Other plants were engulfed.

The dawn rose. Houstonians viewed the smoldering remains of 119 houses, 116 boxcars, 9 oil tanks, 13 plants, and St. Patrick's Catholic School and Church.

Hundreds of people had lost everything they owned.

―――――――――――――――――――――――――

In 1907, Oscar Holcombe came from San Antonio to Houston to work for his uncle in the lumber business. When he ran for mayor in 1920, he was little known. But he was to quickly change that. "Politically for more than 30 years, Houston had only two schools of thought; the Holcombe School and the anti-Holcombe School." (*Land of the Big Rich,* George Fuermann.)

Holcombe dominated the town politically for so many years that he won the appellation "The Old Gray Fox." Many wealthy Houstonians were anti-Holcombe until a labor leader ran against him in one of his many re-elections.

Holcombe claimed to have built every underpass in the city and every major street, among them Buffalo Drive, now Allen Parkway, curving along the south bend of Buffalo Bayou and River Oaks. He also built Holcombe Boulevard at the end of Main to run in front of his home. Will Hogg, whom Holcombe had appointed to head the City Planning Commission, submitted a well-thought-out plan for Houston's future growth. Holcombe permanently shelved it. In 1928, Hogg concluded: "I have seen him violate the best ideals of city welfare and construction by paving, bottle-necked street widening, destruction of tree life." ("Winter 1980," *Texas Review,* Vol. II, No. 1 from *The Houston Post,* Nov. 27, 1928, p. 1)

Nevertheless, Houstonians continued to elect Oscar Holcombe Mayor 1921–29, 1933–37, 1939–41, 1947–53, 1956–57!

I best remember Mayor Holcombe as the member of the City Council who voted first to give the condemned Kellum-Noble House to the newly-formed Harris County Heritage Society to restore in Sam Houston Park. In the 1950s only a handful of Houstonians thought the town's past worth preserving. Even historic Sam Houston Park was about to be cut through the middle by the proposed Allen Parkway. Fortunately, the oldest house on its original site in Houston was preserved, and Allen Parkway was diverted through Holcombe's intervention.

His daughter, Elizabeth Holcombe Crosswell (Mrs. Markley), lives in Houston and is as active in the cultural life of the city as her father was in politics.

CHAPTER TWELVE

"Mrs. Kinkaid was a rigid disciplinarian and Christian Scientist. Let a student misbehave and he had to apologize to his class every morning for a week—in Latin!"

I HAVE written about strong and generous women in these pages, women from Pamela Mann to Keziah Payne de Pelchin. But a woman I'll always remember was a redhead with a will of iron, Margaret Hunter Kinkaid. In 1906, she decided that Houston needed a private, non-parochial school. There were Roman Catholic schools and schools in private homes, but none like she envisioned.

She had a husband and two small sons when she began her school in her cottage home at Elgin and San Jacinto for neighborhood children, first through the third grades. Seven small boys and girls climbed the cottage steps that first morning.

From then on there were so many applicants from the children of Houston's financially privileged families that Mrs. Kinkaid raised her cottage to two stories and extended the grades. Early on, she had the powerful leaders of Houston behind her—Robert Lee Blaffer, W. L. Clayton, Harry C. Wiess, E. L. Neville, Burke Baker; in later years, J. W. Hershey, H. M. Crosswell, Jr., and Isaac Arnold. John and Camilla Blaffer built the auditorium.

Kinkaid School moved to Richmond and Graustark in the 20s and in 1957 to its present 40 wooded acres on Memorial Drive. Today, it is light years away from the frame, two-story school house on San Jacinto Street.

In those early days, boys and girls formed two lines in the small schoolyard beneath the big magnolia tree. Solemnly, they pledged allegiance to the American flag, said the prayer, "Our Father Who Art in Heaven," and were given a Bible reading. The older group marched upstairs. The younger students remained downstairs. The older boys had fire duty which meant bringing in the wood every morning for the big pot-bellied stove. Mrs. Kinkaid was a strict teacher not only of books but of learning the responsibility of duties.

Mrs. Kinkaid was a rigid disciplinarian and Christian Scientist. Let a student misbehave and he had to apologize to his class every morning for a week—in *Latin!* When an eight-year-old boy, at recess, had fun splashing his milk on his little sister's high button shoes, the next day he was shining the black shoes of three of his classmates. Children were expected to be able to sit at their desks for long periods without a break. The only time Mrs. Kinkaid relented was before exams. Then, she led them in deep breathing exercises. (*Kinkaid and Houston's 75 Years,* by Susan Hillebrandt Santangelo.)

Memory is a capricious hoarder when it comes to one's childhood past. The most vivid memory of Kinkaid on Elgin is of the morning Mrs. Kinkaid marched into the class, her mien matching her red hair, and gave a lecture on cheating that brought the quaking boys and girls back to the straight and narrow! The cheating occurred during exam time. Students studied at tables set close together. Underneath the tables there were open slots so that notes, letters, or jokes could be passed from one table to another. Mrs. Lee, the teacher, had never caught onto this subterranean activity. At exam time, on this morning, it had become a serious line of communication. It was also the morning Mrs. Kinkaid chose to inspect the room, and not one student was ever quite the same again.

⸻

In June of 1913, Miss Ima Hogg ran an ad in *The Houston Post* inviting everybody to come to the first concert of the newly-formed Houston Symphony Orchestra at 5 p.m., June 21, in the Majestic Theatre at 807 Texas Avenue. Tickets were 25¢ to $1. Five o'clock was the only hour when the theatre was available, and the musicians, who played in the pit of the silent movies and in the cafes in town, were free.

"Those twilight concerts were lovely," Miss Ima later recalled. The men would come from their offices and the ladies would come down in hats and gloves. After the concert, most of them would go out to dinner downtown before going home.

Rosetta Hirsch, sister of General Maurice Hirsch, was first instrumental soloist with the orchestra, and Bessie Foley, whose beautiful mezzo-soprano voice had been trained in Europe, was another early soloist. (*"The Symphony was Born,"* Marguerite Johnston, *The Houston Post,* May 8, 1969.)

Courtly General Hirsch with the ever-present sweetheart rose in his lapel, four decades later was to be the inspiring President of the Houston Symphony for 14 years (1956–70).

But war broke out in Europe a year after the Symphony was formed, on November 10, 1914. The U.S. was drawn into the war in 1917 and the new Symphony Orchestra had hardly drawn a breath before its musicians put on military uniforms.

In Houston, the opening of the port to world shipping was more momentous than a war in Europe in 1914.

"I christen thee Port Houston; hither the boats of all nations may come and receive hearty welcome!" So did schoolgirl Sue Campbell, daughter of Mayor Ben Campbell, christen the new harbor, scattering white rose petals on the "new-born deep water" of the Ship Channel.

At the Turning Basin, then only a small, widened area in the bayou, crowds of people on yachts watched the ceremony. Among Houston's leaders were William P. Hobby, Camille G. Pillot, John T. Scott, Joe Rice, Jesse H. Jones, R. M. Farrar, Charles Dillingham, R. S. Sterling, and Joseph W. Evans.

"At precisely 11 a.m., President Wilson, interrupting a cabinet meeting, pressed a pearl-topped button at the White House which was connected by a telegraph wire to the firing apparatus of a cannon at the Turning Basin. As the Mayor's daughter tossed the beautiful white rose petals on the waters of the Ship Channel, bells rang, whistles shrilled, the cannon roared, and the band played 'The Star Spangled Banner,'" (*The Houston Post,* Nov. 9, 1964.)

Seventy-eight years had passed since Augustus Allen stepped ashore at what would become known as Allen's Landing to found a city that would in such a short period present a challenge to the great ports of the world.

Did Allen dream it would happen? He boasted of a great future for Sam Houston's town, but he was a promoter wanting to sell town lots and get rich, and he left town in 1843, long before the metropolis-to-be began taking shape. The town did not grow toward greatness until after 1900 and Galveston's devastation and the Spindletop gusher at Beaumont. But dreams or not,

Augustus believed he was at the start of something big when he stepped off that boat at Allen's Landing.

———————————◣ ◗———————————

According to George Fuermann in *Houston: Land of the Big Rich,* George Brown only thought big when it came to Brown & Root or to Rice. Chairman of Rice's $33 million capital fund campaign that he was to spread over the whole country over three years, he led off with a pledge of $4.5 million. In less than three years, the $33 million had been over-subscribed. George and Alice Brown gave more than $8 million to help make Rice University one of the country's important centers of learning.

Their daughter Isabel Wilson (Mrs. Wallace) is an art leader in Houston. Masonda O'Connor (Mrs. Ralph) also lives in Houston and a sister, Nancy Nagley, resides in San Antonio. Herman Brown's daughter Louisa (Mrs. Fayez Sarofim) is active in Houston art circles. Her brother, Micajah Brown also lives in Houston.

———————————◣ ◗———————————

In 1915 a second hurricane hit Galveston. Tobias Sakowitz had had it! He put his family in his Reo and set out for Houston to join his brother Simon, who had left after the 1900 hurricane. Tobias and Simon Sakowitz started early in Galveston on the road that would lead them to the big, handsome store on Main Street and four large suburban stores in Houston. At 19, Tobias was the young manager of Hausen & Kline Notima store in Galveston. Seventeen-year-old Simon sold clothes on the wharves to shrimpers and seamen. When they arrived in Houston, the brothers put up a small shop named Men's Furnishings on Main Street. It contained 1800 square feet, and was the first step toward building a 224,000-square-foot Sakowitz on Main Street. Robert Sakowitz, third generation, is Chief Executive Officer of the stores today, and also serves as Chairman of Houston's Sesquicentennial Committee for the year 1986.

———————————————>◄ ►<———————————————

In the early 1900s Will Vinson had a flourishing law firm on Main Street. But a day came when he lost his partner. Overwhelmed with work he had been looking for another. He mentioned the fact over lunch where he had just met the son of a Texas sheriff in Huntsville, Texas. James A. Elkins, always quick on the uptake, asked, "What's the matter with me? I'd like to move to Houston." Thus one of the most powerful law firms of the United States and the Southwest was born—Vinson-Elkins. These were quite dissimilar men. Vinson was a strict, moral, lawyer's lawyer. Judge Elkins (as he was later called) was a political power mover. "No Houstonian except Jesse Jones had Jim Elkins' bone crushing influence." (George Fuermann, *Land of the Big Rich.*) The First City National Bank and the building he built for it were his babies. Today, James A. Elkins, Jr., is Chairman of the Board of First City and lives in Houston. He married Margaret Wiess, daughter of Olga and Harry Wiess. The Vinson daughters live in Houston today—Virginia (Mrs. Griffith Lawhon), Martha (Mrs. Dean Emerson), and Julia (Mrs. Charles Dabney).

———————————————>◄ ►<———————————————

I have written earlier of M. D. Anderson, one of the founders of Anderson Clayton & Company, and his contributions to Houston. The Clayton was William Lockhart Clayton, born on a Mississippi cotton farm. They were partners in an enterprise that would grow worldwide. As Author George Fuermann wrote of their accomplishment, "It is to cotton merchandising what

Shakespeare is to literature. It is practically the whole works!"

Clayton was a chief supporter of the Marshall Plan to economically aid Europe after World War II. He believed ". . . that the welfare of our country is internally related to that of other free nations, and that world peace is dependent both on this welfare and in the radiation of its benefits throughout the world by an unhampered flow of trade." (*Will Clayton, A Short Biography*, Ellen Clayton Garwood.)

In August 1940, Clayton had resigned from Anderson Clayton to become a Director and Vice President of the Export-Import Bank. In October, Jesse Jones, then head of the Reconstruction Finance Corporation, appointed Clayton Deputy of the Federal Loan Administration and gave him authority to buy critical defense materials for the United States. After the United States entered the War, President Roosevelt dissolved the Federal Loan Administration, placing the duties under then Secretary of Commerce Jesse Jones. In February, 1942, Clayton became Assistant Secretary of Commerce.

When he resigned two years later, Mrs. Susan V. Clayton received this masterpiece of cajolery from the President of the United States:

January 20, 1944

Dear Mrs. Clayton:

Recently Will told me of his desire to leave Washington. I am sure that he was influenced by the very natural desire to comply with your wishes.

He has been doing a grand job and I want to draft him to remain here and take over some new duties. However, I know that so far as he is concerned, you are the real commander-in-chief and I am writing to ask you to order him to remain here and undertake the task for which I am drafting him.

Please let me know when you have issued the orders.

Sincerely yours,

Franklin D. Roosevelt

Don't relinquish your authority over him!

(*Will Clayton, A Short Biography,* Ellen Clayton Garwood)

A short time later, Clayton took on the job of Surplus War Property Administrator, a position he also resigned from later, believing the "plan for the surplus property disposal unworkable."

Clayton was the ". . . voice of America at the sixteen-nation conference on the Marshall Plan . . . he *was* the Marshall Plan . . . he is probably the only man who ever created a $75 million business and lived to hear himself denounced as an impractical dreamer!" (Michael Hoffman, *New York Times Magazine,* September 21, 1947.)

Clayton and his wife, diminutive Sue Vaughn, gave a $290,000 site for Houston's first public housing project in 1952. Today, the handsome mansion on Caroline where the Clayton daughters Ellen, Susan, Burdine and Julia were raised is the Clayton Genealogical Library. Susan and Maurice McAshan built and endowed the 154-acre Aline McAshan Botanical Gardens on Memorial Drive.

———————————⇒◄ ►⇐———————————

Houstonians also were talking about James E. Ferguson, who had been elected governor of the state in 1915, and would be impeached and thrown out of office on August 25, 1917. And the price of cotton had tumbled.

Two days before Ferguson's ouster, however, an incident occurred in Houston that would leave the city shaken for years to come. It was called the Camp Logan Riot.

It was August 23, 1917, a moonlit night over Houston. A watermelon feast had been planned for the soldiers who had arrived at Camp Logan, in what is now Memorial Park. It turned into the bloodiest night in Houston history.

Camp Logan was a new 2,000-acre military base set up to house 30,000 men of the Illinois National Guard. An all-black troop, 650 men of the Third Battalion of the 24th Infantry Regiment, Illinois Guard was sent to guard construction of the camp. They were encamped on Washington and Reineman, near downtown. They were not familiar with the Jim Crow Law. They couldn't eat in the same cafes, shop in the same stores as the whites, nor play baseball in the same fields.

Houston merchants were excited over the prospect of all of the new business. They built shops along Washington. Young girls bought out the stores of summer hats and cotton party dresses to wear to the camp dances. But, in the minds of the men who had lobbied in Washington to get the camp for Houston, the black soldier parading along Main Street as if he had rights equal to his own, was beginning to ferment. They began to see him as dangerous.

The causes of the terrible night of bloodshed have never been fully explained. Reports lay it on police mistreatment and the Jim Crow Law. Most accounts lay it on a rumor that spread through the black unit the night of August 23 that black Corporal Charles Baltimore had been killed by city police. On San Felipe, the soldiers reacted like the fuse of a time bomb. Commander Major K. S. Snow hurried downtown to investigate. He found Baltimore in jail with only a head wound. Immediately, Snow brought him back to camp, saying the policeman who hit him had been suspended.

But neither words nor the sight of Baltimore alive could stop the long pent-up hostility the black unit felt against insults, real or imagined, from Houstonians.

Major Snow, alarmed, ordered all rifles turned in and put under guard, he reported to the Houston court, later investigating the tragedy of the riot. But the court was to indict him as the man responsible. He was accused of lack of discipline of the black unit, of letting the men drink and entertain the town's prostitutes in camp until dawn. Above all, he was accused of knowing about the men stealing rifles and ammunition on the fateful night, but doing nothing to stop the shouts, "Let's go!", nor their march toward town with guns firing.

About 150 black soldiers marched down Washington, crossed to the south side of the bayou on Shepherd's Dam Road (Shepherd Drive), turned up San Felipe Road (now West Dallas) and headed for town. They began shooting everything in sight—a jitney with two men, killing the driver, wounding the other so that his arm had to be amputated; four policemen putting a wounded man in a car. One of the wounded officers was T. A. Binford, later Sheriff of Houston. A young boy putting out the light on the front porch never made it to the front door.

A mob of white Houstonians broke into hardware stores seizing guns and ammunition. A large band of prominent Houstonians waited for the black soldiers with shotguns and pistols.

The night was filled with gunfire, the dark streets a bedlam of screams and terror. Five Houston policemen died that night. So did four white civilians, one Mexican, two white soldiers and four black soldiers. Eighteen were wounded.

The Houston Civilian Court of Inquiry placed the blame for the terrible night on Major Snow. But when Snow received word from his superiors to testify, he was in San Antonio getting ready to join his troops in New Mexico. The United States Army Court charged 63 members of the Third Battalion of the 24th Infantry Regiment with aggravated assault, mutiny and murder.

Forty-one got life imprisonment, 4 dishonorable discharge, confined to hard labor for 2 years; five were acquitted, 13 sentenced to be hanged.

At 9 a.m. on December 11, 1917, the United States Army hanged 13 of the black soldiers at dawn at Camp Travis. Only the Sheriff of Bexar County and a few Army officers gathered around the scaffold, built the night before. Nearby, thirteen graves lay open, waiting. The bodies of the men were taken to the coffins and without ceremony, buried, with only the nametag number, name and date.

Later 55 more were court martialed. Of these, 16 were sentenced to death and 12 to life in prison. President Wilson eventually commuted 10 of the 16 death sentences to life in prison. Most of the soldiers in prison were freed by Presidents Harding and Coolidge. (*Southwest Historical Quarterly*, Vol. 76.)

On November 12, 1918, at 4 a.m., *The Houston Post* hit the streets with the news:

"Greatest Celebration Ever Held in Houston"

"The city was slumbering calmly when the *Post* at 1:45 a.m. Monday received over the Associated Press wire the flash, Armistice Signed! . . . The *Post* could have had the paper on the street at 2 a.m. and aroused the town, but it was deemed better to let the people sleep . . . at 4:15 the *Post* was on the street . . . first the cry of the newsboys, then the honking of automobile horns, then far out in the city came the rattle of the city's private arsenal of light pocket artillery. The locomotives then got into action and gradually all the factory whistles and sirens for miles aroused . . . Lights gleamed in every dwelling . . . There was no doubt about it this time . . . the end of the War had come . . . the great story of November 11 . . .

the greatest in all history of mankind excepting Christmas and Easter, came to Houston!"

The streets filled with thousands, shouting, singing, and crying for joy. A parade of military bands, army battalions, Rice cadets who had hiked to town, and two Veterans of the Civil War, marched down Main Street. Banners flew: "Huns Are Out of Gas!" Two thousand ship builders put on their own parade.

I remember as a child lying on a front porch on Main Street and staring through the railings at the khaki-clad legs flying by. My insides quivered from the marching music, and the hysterical joy of adults shouting "God Bless America" and singing "Yankee Doodle Dandy."

———————————————

Rice Institute seniors were among the First Officer Training Camp (FOTC) graduates who would return home after the Armistice. Houstonians in the FOTC which would later become the "Old Boys" network included: James A. Baker, Jr., Rex G. Baker, Lewis Bryan, Jr., W. T. Campbell, Jr., Francis Coates, Sam H. Davis, John K. Dorrance, Raymond P. Elledge, David Frame, Gillette Hill, Mike Hogg, George Journeay, Aldon B. Judd, Frank A. Liddell, Edmond R. Lorehn, Perry Moore, John E. Price, George E. B. Peddy, John T. Scott, Robert A. Shepherd, Micajah Stude, Howard S. Warner, Ewing Werlein, and Colonel William B. Bates.

FOTC graduates who later held high political offices in Texas were Governor Beauford Jester; Adjutant-General Ike S. Ashburn; Robert Lee Bobbitt, Speaker of the House of Representatives; and Ernest O. Thompson, Railroad Commissioner.

Most were headquartered at Ft. Sill, Oklahoma or Ft. Belvoir, Virginia, before they were sent overseas.

After the war, Houstonians returned to old traditions. The city grew and began to attract industry, and the people began to lay the foundation for new growth.

CHAPTER THIRTEEN

*"The giants of early Houston
came with qualities in common. Most had little formal education,
but all were potent self-starters, had daring imaginations and were
unflagging optimists."*

T
HE PURPOSE of a uni-
versity is to make pro-
vision for the higher needs of a community. The needs
are many. The university, too, like the Church and the
State, must defend and foster the free flowing of the
spirit. To undertake this staggering task; how to build a
university, was in the minds of the original Trustees of
the Rice Institute as they undertook to fulfill the duties
committed to them by their personal friend William
Marsh Rice. They were given wide discretionary powers. Whether by accident or destiny, Rice Institute was
to stand in the very heartland of the great Southwest.

In 1907, Dr. Edgar Odell Lovett came to Houston to
be the first President of Rice Institute. Professor of As-
tronomy, head of the Mathematics Department at
Princeton University where his career was flourishing,
this unusual, erudite man gave all up for the creative

challenge of presiding over a seat of learning whose only
visible sign of life was an excavation hole out Main
Street.

While the mules were excavating the former garbage
dump, the President of the Institute-to-be travelled all
over the world, to various Universities, searching out es-
teemed members for his faculty. He asked the advice of
Woodrow Wilson, President of Princeton, Charles W.
Elliott at Harvard, David Starr Jordan at Stanford. He
wanted Rice Institute to be more than a technical school.
He wanted a University of high scholarly standards. Dr.
Lovett recruited an impressive faculty.

———————————————————

True tradition is not a dead stream but a vital current.
Who can think of Oxford without its quadrangles or of
Harvard without the Yard? Under a brilliant Houston
sky, one hot August day in 1910, William Ward Watkin
arrived with the plans for Rice Institute, that he had
worked on in the Boston offices of Ralph Cram,
Goodhue and Ferguson for over a year.

Lovett and Watkin got in Lovett's buggy and rode to
inspect the property on Main where the Institute would
be built. The site couldn't have been bleaker. The deep
Harris gully had eroded the land, since it flooded at every rain. For 32 years, the area had been used as the
town's garbage dump. The property had been offered
for $600 with no takers. But Lovett and Watkin didn't
see gullies and erosions. They saw buildings of Italian
Renaissance beauty rising.

On October 10, 1912, famed scholars from around the
world were in Houston for the opening of Rice Institute.
Among the speakers were Senator Benedeto Croce of
Naples; Professor Hugo de Vries of Amsterdam; Profes-
sor Emile Borel of Paris; Professor Rafael Altamania y
Crevia of Madrid; Minister of Education of Tokyo,

Privy Councilor Baron Kikuchi; Professor Henri Poincaré of Paris; Professor Sir William Ramsay of London.

Rice's first faculty dazzled the mind: Harold A. Wilson, Physics; Julian Huxley, Biology; Stockton Axson, English; and Albert Guerand, French.

At his Inaugural address, President Lovett expressed the future of Houston with poetical prophesy:

> "I have felt the spirit of greatness brooding over the city. I have heard her step at midnight. I have seen her face at dawn. I have lived under the spell of the building of the city—and under the spell of the building of the city I have come to believe in the larger life ahead of us . . ."

In 1912, a large segment of Houston didn't know the word "prosper." Common laborers worked for $1.25–$2.00 a day. Women were paid $1.25 a day, children 50¢ to $1.00. Brick masons who belonged to the Union got $6 a day, non-Union masons, $3–$4. Tailors worked ten hours a day for $2–$3. Plumbers, well organized, worked eight hours a day for $6.

Little more than 20 years later, the situation was to change tragically little. Seven dollars a week was considered fair wage for the black woman who showed up starched and smiling in your kitchen every morning at 7 a.m. and didn't leave until the last dish was washed at night.

The "larger life" that President Lovett envisioned in 1912 would grow out of a modernized ship channel and a burgeoning oil industry—and from the varying contributions of some remarkable men and women to the Bayou City.

Two men who came were tight with their money. They were also eccentric, anti-social bachelors. One was Monroe Dunaway Anderson. The other was Robert Alonzo Welch. They lived simply and frugally. Anderson's story has been ably limned in *Monroe D. Anderson,*

His Life and Legacy by Colonel William B. Bates. James A. Clark, the late noted oil historian, and Nathan Brock, wrote *A Biography of Robert Alonzo Welch*. I have borrowed from these two sources to illustrate the lives and generosity peculiar to Anderson and Welch.

Anderson, born in Jackson, Tennessee, came to Houston in 1916 to open the first office of Anderson-Clayton which would become the leading cotton concern in the world. He had invested his $3,000 savings to go into business with his brother Frank, William L. Clayton and his brother Benjamin. When the ship channel began to show its vast potential, Anderson Clayton & Company came to tie its future with the town.

Colonel Bates wrote of Anderson: "To him the spending of money except for a useful purpose was distasteful, a clear evidence of lack of breeding. His philosophy was that happiness and success could be attained only through hard work and self-denial. He did not believe in personal charity for the individual except for the handicapped and afflicted. In his opinion, an individual sound in body and mind, who sought or accepted charity was not worthy of it. . . ."

However, when Anderson died on August 6, 1939 he had given his entire fortune of $19 million to establish the M. D. Anderson Foundation, which helped to create the city's great Texas Medical Center! Contained in the Medical Center today are M. D. Anderson Cancer Hospital, Baylor College of Medicine, University of Texas Dental & Cancer Studies, Texas Children's Hospital, Methodist Hospital, St. Luke's Episcopal Hospital, and the Jesse H. Jones Library for medical research which houses the central book collection for the entire Medical Center. Each of which has received large contributions from the M. D. Anderson Foundation.

The Foundation also spread its help to the Boy Scouts, Rice University, and gave $1.5 million to the University of Houston for the M. D. Anderson Memorial Library.

Robert Alonzo Welch, the other loner to leave Houston the richer, landed in town penniless, six-foot-one-inch and 14 years old. He had left his hometown, Newberry, South Carolina in 1896. Reconstruction had so impoverished his once-wealthy family that his father could not give him $50 for his train fare to Houston. He had to borrow it from a kinsman. He never forgot that fact, and he lived from that moment on as if he wasn't sure of his next meal. This poverty-stricken young boy was to amass a fortune estimated at his death at $55 million.

Young Welch made it to Houston by train, wagon, buggy and on foot. He went straight to the house of his cousin, Professor C. A. Welch who lived on the corner of Caroline and Hadley. Young Welch couldn't have picked a worse time to start his career. Houston was being devastated by another yellow fever epidemic.

Professor Welch told him to leave town until the epidemic was over. Young Welch, along with a lot of other frightened Houstonians, took a northbound train. They didn't care where it was going just as long as it left Houston. But to their shock, they were not allowed to get off the train anywhere.

"At every station for hundreds of miles the train from Houston was met by mounted posses armed with long frontier rifles and pistols threatening death to any who dismounted to contaminate their towns or villages with the yellow peril."

When he finally could return to Houston, this well-born teenager saw Houston's wild frontier ways, streets of mud, no sewage, the only drinking water caught in cisterns. The exact place for him to cast his lot in life!

Welch's first job was at Gaines and Conklin's Drug Store. Out of his first $35-a-month paycheck, he opened a savings account and paid something on his $50 debt to his cousin in South Carolina. In the next few years, he worked in the bookkeeping department of a bank and lived along with other soon-to-be-prominent young men who lived at "The Old Mother Allen House," a boarding house at Main and Rusk. He then went to work for James Bute Co. and ended up running it.

Spindletop oil field blew in 1901. Welch bought one acre in the middle of it. One week later he sold it for $15,000. Then he commenced a serious study of geology, slowly accumulating a vast reservoir of knowledge of oil and its sources.

One day he and L. P. Garrett, later to be head of the Land Department of the Gulf Oil Company, were fishing in Black Duck Bay near Goose Creek (called the Ashbel Smith Tract) when Welch saw a large circle of bubbles. Gas bubbles, Welch thought, and where there was gas there was likely to be oil. The Goose Creek Production Company was at that moment born. Welch would team with Garrett, E. F. Simms and William S. Farish to make big money at Goose Creek and elsewhere. E. F. Simms had come to Houston in 1903 from Paris, Kentucky.

William S. Farish, a young lawyer from Mississippi, had gone to Beaumont at the height of the Spindletop boom to see about a client's interest. He caught oil fever and stayed. He would become a founder and president of Humble Oil and Refining Company in Houston, along with Robert Lee Blaffer, who had been sent by Southern Pacific from New Orleans to Beaumont to buy oil for the railroad and had not gone back.

"The Farish-Welch combination was just as intriguing as the closer Farish-Blaffer association. Farish, early in his career, was considered quite a plunger, exactly the reverse of Blaffer and Welch," historian Clark wrote.

While Farish and Blaffer were "making a bundle out of Humble," Welch was also buying Humble stock at $4 a share. He invested in big tracts of land in Bellaire. He also bought property on which the Hughes Tool Company would be built, and formed the Fidelity Oil & Royalty Company, hiring his own geologist, petroleum engineer, and drilling superintendent.

Welch moved to Mrs. Bryan's boarding house, then to the Beaconsfield on Main. The tall, bearded redhead made friends of prominent men in Houston, yet he remained a loner. He was rarely seen with women.

According to historians Clark and Brock, Welch took his friend E. A. Peden to eat lunch at Colby's where he could get a meat dish and a vegetable dish, served separately, for 10 cents. He would order both, and divide the dishes between himself and his guest.

In later years he lunched often at the Houston Club's "round table" with Hugh Roy Cullen. Cullen, in his early days, was just as poor as Welch. He told the latter about his $5 check to the Salvation Army bouncing. He hadn't realized his bank account was so low. But Cullen, who was to give away more than $160 million, didn't get any sympathy from Welch. In later years, when Cullen wrote to him asking for a donation of $576,000 for the Baptist Memorial Hospital, Welch answered that he was highly flattered but if he had that much he'd run away and hide. But he did send $10 to the National Recreation Association.

Welch, Clark wrote, had a ". . . life-long love affair with money. After a lengthy correspondence, he finally got back from the Southern Pacific twenty-six cents on a ticket he didn't use!"

Throughout his life, he never varied the tip he gave his barber—a dime. He never learned to drive a car. Owning one only for a short time, he gave it up as a waste of time and money. "All that gas, all that oil, all those tires that wear out!"

Shortly before his death, Welch was walking along Main Street with a friend of Clark. As they passed a newsstand, Welch said he would like a paper. After they

had walked a block or so, Welch took a look at the date
line on the newspaper. It was yesterday's! The terrible
consternation on his face was enough to send the friend
racing back to the newsstand. When he returned with
the day's paper, Welch was as moved as if his life had
been saved. The friend told Clark that for many months,
every time he and Welch met in the elevator or on the
street, the old man thanked him profusely for not having
let him waste a dime.

Yet on his death bed, he could say to his old friend,
Attorney Jesse Andrews, "I've done my part now."

Indeed he had! Out of his $55 million estate, he left
15% to his 29 employees. The remainder went to the
Welch Foundation Trust Fund for research and support
of Texas institutions such as Rice University and Texas
A & M in organic and colloidal chemical research and to
the University of Texas in bio-chemistry. "He had been
building for those who would come after him."

———————————=◄ ►=———————————

Hugh Roy Cullen came to Houston in 1911. Born on
a Texas ranch in Denton County on July 3, 1881, this
soft spoken until aroused to blasphemic heights man,
had little formal education. Yet, he was to build and en-
dow a great university, the University of Houston.

As a young boy, his first job was with a candy company for $3 per week. At fifteen, he worked for a cotton
company. When he came to Houston, like many young
newcomers, he was fascinated by a future in real estate.
When the oil fever hit town, he plunged into buying and
selling leases. He drilled his first well in 1915—a dry
hole. He was to be forty years old before he struck his
first oil well. Successful from 1918 on, he was one of the
undisputed kings of the Wildcatters. He had a gambler's
instinct about oil. His wife, Lily, a comfortable, perenni-
ally good natured woman, cooked delicious German

dishes and did all of the housework in their simple, frame house on West Alabama. Who would dream that she would one day preside over a magnolia-shaded, camellia-blossoming mansion on River Oaks Boulevard or that they would donate $160 million to Houston?

In 1927, Cullen and prosperous oil man J. M. West, Sr., formed the West Production Company on an equal share basis, each putting up $5,000. They brought in the Big Thompson Field and sold out to Humble Oil and Refining Company for $20,000,000. Later, in 1934, the Tom O'Connor Oil Field near Refugio would make Cullen one of the world's wealthiest men when he formed the Quintana Petroleum Corporation.

Cullen's only son Roy was tragically killed in an oil field accident leaving a young wife and three small children. Cullen's daughter, Agnes Arnold (Mrs. Isaac), is deceased. Their other daughters, Mrs. Corbin Robertson, Mrs. Douglas Marshall, his grandsons Isaac Arnold, Jr., Hugh Roy Cullen III, and Harry Cullen live in Houston today. A grandson, Enrique de Portanova, lives most of the year in his lavish villa in Acapulco, Mexico. Mr. Corbin Robertson, Jr., heads Quintana today.

Herman and George Brown came from Belton. Herman started a road-building business with scraper and mules in 1914. Four years later, he founded Brown & Root with his brother-in-law, Dan Root. George Brown joined in 1923. The company has become one of the world's largest builders of dams, pipe lines, offshore rigs, plants, and highways. Rice University's huge developmental fund was due to George Brown's insistence that the University buy a half interest in the famous Rincon Oil Field in Starr County, Texas, part of the tangled estate of Shanghai Pierce. Rice didn't have the down payment of one million and the Trustees didn't want any part of owning an oil field. George Brown, not easily dissuaded, "lit fires" under his friends W. S. Farish,

Harry Hanszen, Harry C. Wiess, S. P. Farish, and Roy Hofheinz. The M. D. Anderson Foundation contributed $300,000. When all of the contributions, plus a large donation from the Browns, were totaled, George Brown was able to hand over to the lawyers a check for one million. Oil lands with an estimated worth at the time of $30 million were acquired by Rice University.

Houston's future was limitless. It drew men to its throbbing promise of fulfilled dreams. It was here that a modern Horace Greeley could direct, "Go Southwest, young men."

And they came.

The giants of early Houston came with qualities in common. Most had little formal education, but all were potent self-starters, had daring imaginations and were unflagging optimists.

John Fanz Staub, architect, came from Knoxville, Tennessee and designed nearly every early home in River Oaks.

Michel Halbouty was only a water boy at Spindletop, but after his experience there he enrolled at Texas A&M earning a master's degree and marched out into the world to drill new well after new well. Millions of dollars later he wrote two early oil industry history books, *Spindletop* and *The Last Boom,* plus the definitive work on salt dome technology, *Salt Domes, Gulf Region, U.S. and Mexico.*

Eddy Scurlock was reared in the piney woods of East Texas. His was a modest background. He moved to Houston and got a job in the retail side of the oil business. He was promoted. With new confidence he saved his money and purchased his own service station on Louisiana and Webster.

As a retailer he also learned the wholesale end of the oil business. After selling his service station for a profit, he and his new bride Elizabeth Belschner moved to Austin where Scurlock enrolled in night school at the University of Texas. He managed an Humble Oil station as interim employment. He studied Business Psychology and Salesmanship and, as he recalls, it taught him to "know your product better than the person you are selling it to."

As most success stories of all of these early self-starters go, Eddy Scurlock, with $1900 of savings and $5000 borrowed from his Uncle Eddy Clark, formed Scurlock Oil Company. Today, forty-eight years later, the conservative company and its founder could later record a successful string of 55 out of 67 wells that came in.

Eddy Scurlock belongs to that exclusive club of Houston philanthropists, Jones, Anderson, Rice, Cullen, Fondren, Brown, and others who made fortunes and gave away fortunes. The main thrust of the Scurlock Foundation has been toward Methodist schools, churches and hospitals. From the day he started, he always gave 5% of pre-tax revenue for good works. Eddy Scurlock has given nearly half of his personal income away to benefit his fellow man for 48 years of his lifetime. His son-in-law Jack Blanton now serves as Chief Executive officer of the company.

To make many fortunes in a lifetime, to be in the right place at the right time, to win friends and will uncountable dollars and acres to heirs or a cause—is one thing! But to do all of these things, day by day, enduring hardship and hard work with unselfish dedication to a large family in bad times—to remember them all during the good years and with quiet thoughtfulness—to remember your fellow man along the way—is quite another thing. Such a man was Houston's James Smithers Abercrombie. Jim Abercrombie moved from Huntsville, Texas to Richmond (near Houston) when he was twelve. One of ten children, the Scottish Abercrombies had migrated from Alabama to Huntsville, Texas where they distinguished themselves in cotton and tobacco farming and law (Senator Leonard Abercrombie). J. B. Abercrombie

(Jim's father), however, was caught in the economic panic of 1903 and decided to launch himself and his young sons into the dairy business.

Jim was enrolled in school in the little ante-bellum town of Richmond, Texas in 1906, but was quickly out seeking a job in order to help out at home. Soon Jim was the new "soda jerk" at Cranston's Drug Store. The barefoot soda jerk would never forget his first job and remembered it over the years to friends. Also, he would forever love ice cream.

With his father's health failing, he had to leave school after three years to work full time, to help support nine brothers and sisters and his little grandmother Josephine (Josie) Wood. It was this tiny but powerful lady that left a strong life-long impact on Jim Abercrombie's abiding inclination to always keep the family together.

His brother Bob had bought "Old Gracie," a young gray mare, to pull the dairy wagon. Two other brothers, Milo and John, worked long hours to try to make the business prosper. Jim was the deliveryman, leaving before dawn to deliver cream to Stude's Bakery and Coffee Shop in Houston. Soon, he felt he had learned as much about the dairy business as he wanted to know. Then opportunity struck! The oil in Beaumont had become a boom. Probably his little grandmother had given him sound advice, because he took off for the Heights in Houston to look up a cousin Charles and to seek employment from him. He reported to work on Monday at Cypress. Jim soon learned what the term "roustabout" meant. It involved doing all the unskilled jobs around a drilling rig while you climbed the occupational ladder to roughneck. When he put his foot into the rung of that ladder, Houston and the world would one day be the recipients of that decision.

While he could have stayed with his cousin, Jim was grateful but felt it was an imposition and refused. He could have had room and board for $3.50 a week but this

was too much for his budget. He had lost both parents
(which was a source of deep and lasting grief) so he
rented a tiny room with fewer meals, so that he could
head for Houston Saturday noon with his paycheck for
the family. His sisters Annie and Vinnie became surro-
gate mothers to the younger children; cooking and keeping house. Above all, together they maintained a strong
central family home.

The rest is history as oil journals report. The brothers, Jim, Bob, Milo, John and Joe Rice formed
Abercrombie Drilling and Mineral Production Company. Then, late one night Jim sketched an idea on an
envelope for a new device to prevent well blowouts due
to high gas pressure. Early the next morning he was
waiting outside a machine shop for Harry Cameron to
arrive. They had met at Cypress and respected each
other on sight.

Jim Abercrombie and Harry Cameron signed their in-
corporating papers on Jim's 29th birthday, July 9, 1920.
Harry wanted to name the new enterprise Abercrombie
Iron Works. Jim's reply was typical: "Aw, I already have
an outfit named for me; you take this one." So Cameron
Iron Works, Inc. was official with Annie, Vinnie and
Bob Abercrombie included as stockholders.

When Jim Abercrombie met and married the beautiful Lillie Frank from Lake Charles, Louisiana, it was the
beginning of a life-long love affair. Their only daughter
Josephine was riding horses by the time she was four and
Mr. Jim, as he was later called, took great pride in her
skill. He felt it would give her development in life, self-
confidence and self-reliance. "When the gate shuts," he
told his daughter, "you're on your own." Miss Lillie,
however, said not to look for her in the box during Josephine's events; she'd be in the ladies room praying!
(*Mr. Jim*, Patrick J. Nicholson.) However, out of this interest in horses grew the launching of the Pin Oak Horse
Show.

Today Josephine Abercrombie lives in Houston. Her hard work and support of the Houston Boxing Association is becoming world class and her life-long interest in thoroughbred horses has not waned. Josephine serves as a trustee on the Board of Governors of Rice University and has accepted the responsibilities of Chairman of the Buildings and Grounds committee at Rice. With her two sons, George and Jim, Josephine Abercrombie functions as Chief Executive Officer of the vast industrial empire that Mr. Jim left her.

In the famous Suite 8-F in the Lamar Hotel many deals were struck with those charter members as they liked to be remembered. Some of those included Herman and George Brown, Jesse Jones, Gus Wortham, Bill Smith, Leopold Meyer, Eddy Scurlock and others. So Lep Meyer told Abercrombie up in Suite 8-F that he saw real possibilities in expanding the Horse show *IF* it could be the best horse show in the country and *IF* it could be the funding vehicle for David Greer's dream of a hospital for children. "All right" Jim replied. "See Ralph McCullough about drawing up some papers. We'll need a charter, but keep it simple."

Thus Texas Children's Foundation was incorporated in 1947 with these charter members: Drs. Lane Mitchell, John K. Glenn, George Salmon, H. J. Ehlers, Raymond Cohen and David Greer; and Miss Nina Cullinan, Mrs. H. Malcolm Lovett, George A. Butler and Leopold Meyer who served as Chairman of the Board. Proceeds of the Pin Oak Horse Show were now transferred to this foundation and The Junior League contributed its invaluable services to Texas Children's by transferring its Outpatient Department from Hermann after TCH opened.

Jim Abercrombie knew that the hospital would never be self-supporting; this was particularly true since he had insisted that no child be denied admittance regardless of "race, creed, color or ability to pay." Realist that

he was, he simply wrote out a check for the deficit at
year-end, but was already seeking a long-range answer
to the escalating needs of the young patients.

The 1950s and 1960s were stirring days in politics,
with Mr. Jim often involved in marathon sessions in
Suite 8-F. It was also in those years that with reluctance
born of his innate modesty, Mr. Jim was named Houston's Man of the Year for his contributions to Houston
Pediatric Society, Baylor College of Medicine, Sons of
the American Revolution, The National Conference of
Christian and Jews, the Houston Fat Stock Show, and
Texas Mid-Continent Oil & Gas Association.

The financial plight of Texas Children's Hospital had
continued to be a growing concern to Mr. Jim and Lillie
Abercrombie. The situation became acute because of a
decision to undertake the necessary expansion of the
combined Texas Children's Hospital and Texas Heart
Institute of St. Luke's Hospital from 400 to 1063 at an
estimated cost of $33.5 million—which upon completion
was $55 million.

Mr. Jim and Miss Lillie announced:

> "In furtherance of our desire to ensure the suc-
> cess of the current fund drive and to support over a
> number of years the Texas Children's Hospital,
> we have given to a trust all of the stock in the J. S.
> Abercrombie Securities Corporation, which com-
> pany is the owner of a substantial block of the stock
> of the Cameron Iron Works. Substantially all of the
> income from this trust is to be paid to the hospital
> for a period of forty years."

Every Christmas night the Abercrombies held open
house. It was one of Houston's truly elegant parties.
Once invited you were evermore expected. The big
rooms of the colonial mansion of River Oaks Boulevard
glittered with unjaded camaraderie. The Sheraton banquet table was laden with every conceivable nourish-

ment for body and spirit. More importantly, everybody knew everybody.

But, like everything that should be preserved, sheer numbers finally killed its special Christmas night magic. Even one of the maids had lost her ordinarily sensible outlook. At one of the final huge parties, she couldn't find a guest's fur stole. When at last the guest retrieved her squirrel cape, the maid apologized: "I guess I don't understand anything but mink!"

But Lillie Abercrombie understood a great deal more than mink. A wealthy friend asked her to use her influence to get a certain hotel reservation in New York. "Tell them who we are!" she said. Lillie asked calmly, "Who are we?"

On January 7, 1975 James Smithers Abercrombie died at home. Another of Houston's giants was gone. Six months later Lillie Frank Abercrombie was buried next to the husband she loved so well. Ten years have gone by but they are still well remembered by all who loved and respected these two whose one rule for living was not money, or position, or travel or success. Service to others was the secret.

Thus do acorns shade the world.

CHAPTER FOURTEEN

*"Houston roared into the 1920s
with Woman's Suffrage, bathtub gin, William Jennings Bryan
orating at the City Auditorium, and River Oaks lots selling for
$1000 each."*

I n Houston in the 1920s
there was a settlement on
the northeast side of town, in the Fifth Ward, whose soft,
beguiling tongue was rarely if ever heard on Main
Street. "Comment, ça va?" It was the voice of the Bayou
Teche Country of South Louisiana. "How you?" Black
eyes rolled mischeviously. "You come on to my house?
Pliz scuse!"

I was in Frenchtown on Deschaumes Street. The air
was heavy and sweet with a tropical abundance of pink
oleanders, the sense-tingling smell of Creole gumbo. It
was really only a stone's throw from that roaring artery
of the city, Jensen Drive. I felt as far away from Jensen
Drive as the Evangeline country is from Houston.

Frenchtown is one of the least known facets of Houston's multiple personality. It came into existence near
Liberty Road on the northeast side of the city in 1922.

About four blocks square, the heart of the settlement lay between streets with the poetical names of Lelia and Roland.

Here in an atmosphere as foreign as French pie and rub-bo'd music, lived approximately 500 people of French and Spanish descent. They came from Louisiana—Saint Martinsville, Lafayette, and Le Beau parishes. They called themselves creoles. They had lustrous, expressive eyes and beautiful black hair.

What brought these people from the Bayou Teche Country to Houston where they stayed together as a single family clan, yet ever apart from the city? Father Cornelius Sullivan, their priest, said they came when jobs were scarce in Louisiana. The Southern Pacific Railroad in Houston offered many job opportunities in the 1920s. When I first visited Frenchtown most of the men still worked for the railroad or in factories.

One of the first to build a house on this land that was once a dismal swamp was Albert Chevalier, carpenter, of Anoville, Louisiana. He convinced his brothers, sisters and cousins to follow him. Word spread through the Bayou Teche country. They came, helped one another build homes, kept their own language, put out their own newspaper, to preserve the old French customs and traditions.

On the day I visited Frenchtown, Madame Laura Dupree (known affectionately as Mama Dupree), joined by Madame Provost, Madame Prejean, Maurice Chevalier, Frenchtown's barber-tailor, welcomed me into their spotless homes. Now and then their broken English slipped merrily into a torrent of French. It was charming. But beneath the bubbling French gaiety, the easy warmth, I sensed that the real story of Frenchtown was one I would never get. I lived outside.

Young girls then rarely married out of Frenchtown. One young girl refused to marry a boy from Lafayette unless he agreed to be married by a Frenchtown priest.

On the other hand, there was Madam Prejean's granddaughter, a beautiful 16-year-old with a drawl as langorous as a slow moving pirogue on a lazy bayou. She planned to marry an Air Force cadet that summer and move away from Frenchtown. "But you'll never get the Frenchtown out of her!," so they all said.

Maurice Chevalier had just built his gay little shop on Deschaumes Street. In the front room of the building he and his two partners barbered. In the rear they turned into tailors! Maurice, the oldest of 14 children, put it this way: "Frenchtown people, they love each other. They stick together. You take me. They all come to my shop, not maybe because I'm so good barber, but more because I'm their friend. You see?"

On Saturday night, someone always held a "zottico" in his home. Out came the accordion, banjo and rubbo'd. The latter was an oldtime washing board. The musician played it with a thimble on his finger. Off the dancers whirled in a folk dance similar to the square dance.

Poverty and anonymity, like a gray burial shroud, have obliterated the once-sparkling French settlement. Preservationists talk today of saving Houston's ethnic areas. But for Frenchtown, it is too late. (Author's column. *The Houston Post*. Reprinted with permission.)

———————————— ➤◀ ▶———————————————

Houston roared into the 1920s with women shearing off hair so long that they could sit on it. Women's Suffrage, bathtub gin in obscure neighborhoods, William Jennings Bryan at the City Auditorium shouting against Darwin's Theory of Evolution.

I remember the sensuous aroma from the hot tamale man's stand on Main, swimming at Heights Natatorium in a Jensen suit that drooped to the middle of my kneecaps. Bands were playing "I'll See you in My Dreams" on the Rice Roof, "Jada!" at Sylvan Beach. Gaylord Johnson's "Gables" on Main was where ice cream sodas were consumed as fast as the stools whirled.

Houses had sleeping porches where the family slept together on hot summer nights; the moon full in their faces. They took drives together after supper. One Sunday, a rainbow made a perfect arc from downtown Houston to the middle of a nearby open pasture. There were no fences then. My father, quick to seize on adventure, gunned the Model T Ford straight across the prairie, my mother held on to her veiled hat in loud protest; the three children on the back seat screamed with excitement. We were off to get the pot of gold at the end of the rainbow!

Many Houstonians in this period had country places near Houston. Judge E. E. Townes who wrote the charter for the Humble Oil Company, had a farm 18 miles away on the Humble Road. Among Palmettoes and Yanquipin, small Negro girls sang spirituals for the guests:

> My Lawd is so high you can't get over Him,
> So low you can't get under Him,
> So wide you can't get 'round Him.
> You jus got to come in at the do'!

His daughter, Elsie Townes Pressler (Mrs. Herman), lives in Houston today. Her husband, Herman Pressler, was president of the Texas Medical Center. Grandsons Judge Paul Pressler and Townes Herman Pressler live in Houston today.

———————————⊃⊂———————————

The war was over. This was the time of optimism and graciously-lived days. Houston was never to be so Southern again. Children walked to school, and to music lessons. Entire families sang and played the piano at night.

The Renaissance Society was formed by Judge H. M. Garwood to bring together the artistic forces in town, few as they were. Dr. Edgar Odell Lovett and Mrs. W. Bedford Sharp were in the group. At their first banquet at the Rice Hotel, the guest of honor, a Belgian, delivered his entire speech in French! However, all agreed it was a fine banquet.

In the 1920s Gene Angelus was the bartender at every party worth attending. Once the manager of the 83-foot-long Rice Hotel Bar, he liked to talk about the days the Rice served free olives, crackers, cheese all day along with every glass of beer. From 4 to 6 p.m. you could get baked ham or roast beef between hot French rolls and a glass of beer for 10¢. After Prohibition, no more free lunches!

Children in this era were close to the sights, smells and sounds of their city. The organ grinder and his monkey, the clippety-clop of Mr. Rosenzweig's horse and wagon filled with fresh vegetables and fruit, his bell tinkling, coming down the street to stop at the kitchen door.

Mr. Rosenzweig was a great music lover, so he said. He would stop beneath the window, rolling his eyes heavenward when I ploughed through Minuet in G.

Thoughts of Mr. Rosenzweig's produce wagon bring back memories of an aromatic oasis, the old Farmers' Market near the bayou. The other senses also were served—the sweet, rich taste of an orange grown near town which Jim Jamail cut in half for children waiting like hungry young birds before his stall which was redolent with fresh earth clinging to roots of carrots and strawberries. Jim Jamail came to Houston from Beirut, Lebanon in 1904. Today his descendants run fine food stores, Clarence Jamail on Shepherd and Jim Jamail on Kirby. In 1984, the latter won the award of Finest Food Market in the United States.

The 1920s was an era of runaway population growth. River Oaks Country Club settled in elite comfort at the end of River Oaks Boulevard in 1923. River Oaks lots were selling for $1,000. Miss Ima Hogg assisted new home owners with their landscaping plans. Jesse Jones was busy erecting about 30 buildings. In 1926 he bought the controlling interest of Marcellus Foster in *The Houston Chronicle*. The following year "Mefo," as Foster was called, became Editor of *The Houston Press*.

Jones was busy persuading the Democratic party to hold the 1928 Convention in Houston by promising to build a Convention Hall. He did just that, in double quick time, erecting a big frame building where the Music Hall and Coliseum now stand. It was that Convention when Franklin D. Roosevelt nominated Al Smith, the "Happy Warrior," for the Presidency.

The petroleum industry was responsible for building many different types of companies. In 1916, a young newspaperman got the idea that the petroleum industry needed and would support a specialized petroleum publication. Thus, did Ray L. Dudley leave the newspaper business and found Gulf Publishing Company with its first publication, *Gulf Coast Oil News*. Today Gulf Publishing resides in the stately Spanish building on Allen Parkway where it has been since the early 1920s.

On August 1, 1924, Ross Sterling, oil man and former governor, owned the *Dispatch* newspaper which was dismally unprofitable. Roy Watson, president of *The Houston Post* 1917–1924, continually turned Sterling down when he offered to buy the *Post*. A representative of the Hearst chain came to Houston and asked Watson to name his price for his paper. Watson called Sterling to inform him in order to keep the *Post* locally owned. Ross Sterling bought it for a high figure. William Pettus

Hobby, who was Governor of Texas from 1917–21 was named President of the paper. It brought many friends together. Ray L. Dudley, dean of Texas oil editors, returned to the *Post* as General Manager, as a favor to Sterling (The Story of *The Houston Post,* April 5, 1945).

Sterling erected their newspaper building on Polk and Dowling in 1925. Today, *The Houston Post's* white pristine fortress on the Southwest Freeway is one of the city's visual pleasures.

Hobby married young Oveta Culp, who was to become World War II Commander of the Women's Army Corps and work with the Hoover Commission and the United Nations. This handsome, lively intellectual and her husband were to run the conservative *Houston Post* after buying it from Sterling, along with radio station KPRC and KPRC-TV. Until Hobby's death their teamwork was what Author George Fuermann called "softly potent." Their son, William Pettus Hobby, Jr., became Lieutenant Governor of Texas. The Hobby family sold the *Post* in 1984 to Toronto Sun Publishers Corporation.

———————————————▷◁ ▷◁◁———————————————

In the 1920s and 1930s Houston was the polo capital of the Southwest. French author Andre Maurois wrote that from time to time man had needed extreme exertion, coupled with danger, to satiate his needs. Since the 6th century polo apparently has satisfied man on both counts.

Will Cochran, vice president of the First National Bank, and George Dow, in the 1920s acquired pasture land at Post Oak and Westheimer where Weingarten's Supermarket stands today. The price, $550 per acre, was thought to be outrageous. Here the newly organized Houston Polo Club built their first club house and field. Bob Farish, Steve Farish, and Deke Randolph along with Will Cochran were the leading organizers.

In 1930 the Farish brothers formed the Huisache Polo Club. It was moved adjacent to the Bayou Club in 1939.

With the advent of World War II the Houston Polo Club ceased to function. After 25 years of absence, the game was welcomed back to the scene and it made its debut in the then new Astrodome.

In 1965 Texas Children's Hospital was beginning the task of raising the much needed funds for expansion. Phase I was $15 million. Mary Jo Hutchins Bell, formerly of St. Louis, saw the need for the sport that had always been so popular in St. Louis. She didn't know of the illustrious history of polo in Houston, when the team had won the U.S. Open in Madison Square Garden in 1936 and had made national news winning the famous East-West Match in Chicago in 1933. As announcer Will Rogers said, "It was a great day when the cowboys beat the dudes!"

Encouraged by Vinnie and Miss Lillie Abercrombie Mary Jo Bell went to Mr. Jim Abercrombie's office to suggest her idea of a polo benefit in the Astrodome with all proceeds going to Texas Children's. He advised her to make an appointment with Mr. Leopold Meyer, then Board Chairman of Texas Children's Hospital. Meanwhile Mr. Malcolm Lovett's daughter Mary Hale (McLean) suggested to Mary Jo that she talk with Will Farish III whose family had sponsored polo in Houston for a half century.

The meetings were fruitful. Will Farish was enthusiastic and supportive. The original committee included Mr. and Mrs. Jim Abercrombie, Mr. and Mrs. Will Farish III, Mr. and Mrs. John Mecom Jr., Mr. Ted Law, Mr. and Mrs. Ralph O'Connor, Mr. Leopold Meyer, Mary Jo Bell, Mrs. Milo (Grace) Abercrombie and Mr. Robert Gerry.

To publicize polo in 1964–65 was almost as interesting as the match itself. The first television press release was held at the Houston Polo Club. Ron Stone, Chris

Chandler, Sid Lasher and six photographers for the Houston media attended. There was one small problem. The goal posts had long ago rotted away and had been thrown away. So to improvise, Neiman Marcus hat boxes were stacked end on end at each end of the field to simulate goal posts.

Demonstration "polo" began with mounted players Juan Rodriguez, Will Farish, Laury Marcus, and Charles Armstrong. English saddles? What is that ball made of? Not really up on his homework, Ron Stone was told that the ball was either a bamboo ball from a whipple tree or the whipple wood from a bamboo tree.

Also, it wasn't unusual to hear radio's Hudson and Harrigan comment, "Well, I hear now they're going to play croquet on horses in the Astrodome!"

The first match drew only 15,342 fans on the coldest night in Houston in 25 years. Still $55,000 was contributed to the hospital.

Setting a precedent for following years, the Houston Astrodome, Mecca and mosque of indoor sports, drew an all-time attendance record crowd of 32,811 screaming fans when the United States scrambled to win over Mexico. Red Smith, sports writer for the *New York Times,* wrote, "The team from Mexico shouted as they crossed the border, 'Remember the Astrodome.'" A Texas-type victory for polo and for Texas Children's Hospital.

In 1977 when the Prince of Wales visited the ranch of Tobin and Ann Armstrong, former U.S. Ambassador to England, the guests enjoyed a royal polo match. The players were:

H.R.H. The Prince of Wales
Tobin Armstrong, Armstrong Ranch
John Armstrong, King Ranch
Charles Armstrong, King Ranch
Bobby Beveridge, Retama Polo Club, San Antonio
Norman Brinker, Willow Bend Polo Club, Dallas

Will Farish, Houston Polo Club
Steve Gose, Retama Polo Club, San Antonio
The Houston Polo Club today draws crowds and high
goal players from all over the continent. It is located at
Memorial Drive and I-10.

On April 12, 1924, the first art museum in Texas, the
Houston Museum of Fine Arts, opened its doors. When
the point of land between Main and Montrose was
bought with a check from J. S. Cullinan, it was deeded
to the Houston Art League for whom Emma Richardson
Cherry had traveled miles in her horse and buggy. Dr.
Henry Barnston, rabbi of Temple Beth Israel, said of
her: "Often we may apply the words of the Book of
Proverbs, 'Many daughters have done valiantly but
thou exaltest them all.'" (*Houston Chronicle,* "Texas
Magazine," February 11, 1968)

General Hirsch and Winifred endowed the Hirsch Library at the Museum. It has more than 15,000 volumes
and has become an important art history research center.

I remember each spring when the General would give
his friends a two-year-old sweetheart rose bush he grew
from cuttings from the 40-year-old bush once belonging
to his father. By the start of World War II, he had over
800 bushes. When a friend was ill or had a new baby, he
sent one of his miniature bud vases with a sweetheart
rose. He had collected 4,000 bud vases from all over the
world which he and Winifred circumnavigated 25 times.

Donors to the Houston Museum of Fine Arts were
Ima Hogg, John and Audrey Beck, Alice and George R.
Brown, the Brown Foundation, Edith and Percy Straus,
The Blaffer Foundation, and Samuel H. Kress.

Other leading donors are the H. R. Cullen Foundation, Mrs. Harry C. Wiess, Susan and Maurice

McAshan, Carroll and Harris Masterson III, Oveta Culp Hobby, Dominique and Jean de Menil, Clare and Alfred Glassell, Jr., Mrs. Edward H. Andrews, General Maurice Hirsch and Winifred, Alvin Romansky, Jesse H. Jones, and Charles and Faith Bybee. Nina Cullinan donated an entire wing designed by the renowned architect Mies Van der Rohe.

Cullinan Hall, the Brown Pavilion, Alfred Glassell School of Art, the Cullen Sculpture Garden, speak out as centers for education and enjoyment of art in Houston.

On March 17, 1926, 45 socially prominent women and a few daring men entered a sidewalk entrance to a basement room in a downtown building. A few windows looked out on the sidewalk and passing feet. The people sat down at freshly-painted black tables, lit by candles. Young women in yellow with crisp, white organdy aprons, scurried about taking orders to the small, cavern-like kitchen. The Houston Junior League Tea Room had formally opened. Its purpose was to support a Well Baby Clinic at Hermann Hospital. The Junior League of Houston had been granted its charter June 24, 1925 with the late Adelaide Browne Baker as president. Through the years the Junior League Tea Room moved from the building basement to the University Club, to the building on Louisiana and Smith today occupied by Brennan's. Today it is located at 1626 Post Oak Park. The Houston Junior League is planning another move to a new building under construction at 1811 Briar Oaks Drive.

The Tea Room supports the outpatient clinic of Texas Childrens' Hospital, Retina Research Foundation, Texas Heart Institute, Museum of Fine Arts Docents Program, Zoomobile for the Houston Zoo, and other projects too many to list.

In 1927, 27 women living in River Oaks organized the River Oaks Garden Club with Mrs. L. A. Stevenson as president. Seven years later they opened to the public a few of their choice gardens, with tickets at 25 cents each. Today, almost 60 years later, the Azalea Trail has become the city's biggest Spring attraction, drawing thousands to the brilliantly flowering gardens.

The River Oaks Garden Club also made possible the planting, seasonally in bloom, along Allen Parkway; 300 oleanders at De Pelchin Faith Home; the annual White Elephant sale, care of Bayou Bend Gardens, and publication of the *Garden Book for Houston,* indispensable to gardeners.

The Houston Garden Club Bulb Mart started small. Mrs. J. W. Slaughter conceived the idea of members growing plants which they would sell on the steps of the Museum of Fine Arts. Mrs. Herbert Roberts was the first president in 1924. Today the annual Bulb Mart raises $70,000.

The Houston Garden Club maintains the grounds and patios of the Museum and provides a greenhouse at the School for Retarded Children on Allen Parkway. There, children and adults learn to raise flowers and herbs which they sell at the Bulb Mart.

The first ball ever held in Houston for the zoo was sponsored by Zoo Friends in 1968 to raise funds to buy a pair of baby gorillas. Zoo Friends needed City Council support and Mayor Welch and the City Council not only gave their unanimous support but attended the festivities as well.

Zoo Friends was a small committee that included Mrs. Ford Hubbard, Mrs. Henry Hamman, Mrs. Jane Mosbacher, Mrs. T. W. Blake, Mrs. Jane Blaffer Owen, Mrs. Richard Jack, Mrs. James W. Baker, Mrs. Dudley Sharp, Jr., Mrs. Bernard Sakowitz, Mrs. Wade Wilden, Mrs. Tom Martin Davis, Mrs. R. H. Wilden, Mrs. Curtis Hankamer, and Marie Lee McAshan.

The committee planned an animal garden party held in the English garden of Jane Blaffer Owen. An English designer, Edward Gilbert, who was a house guest, erected an elaborate 20-foot wire aviary. This aviary was filled with white-ring-necked doves. John Werler, director of the Houston Zoo, brought small animals and two llamas that were in enclosures built by the husbands of the committee women. Hostesses, dressed in black and white zebra shifts, led the llamas through the gardens of roses for small children to pet.

Helium-filled balloons drifted through the tree-tops like huge peonies. Hundreds attended and children walked up the wooded drive to buy their tickets.

Every year in Houston, Zoo Friends sponsor a Ball donating the proceeds for maintenance and continuing upkeep of the Houston Zoo. Zoo Friends have contributed more than $1 million to the Houston Zoological Gardens.

———————————◄ ►————————————

Following World War II, some of the Negroes in Houston began their rise to positions of prominence, particularly in law and education. In 1919, Negro businessmen, led by C. F. Richardson, began publishing a weekly newspaper, the *Houston Observer.* Three years later, Richardson withdrew to found *The Informer* which still exists today. Texas State University for Negroes began in 1947. In 1951, the name was changed to Texas Southern University.

Houston, which is known more for its towering spires and metropolitan qualities than for its Western atmosphere, goes Western at the beginning of each year in late February. For twelve days, Houston is transformed into a maze of ten-gallon hats, bootheels that echo on the pavement, colorful shirts, fringed doeskin leather jackets; all in celebration of the Houston Livestock Show and Rodeo held originally in the Coliseum but moved to the Astrodome and Astro-Arena in 1964.

From throughout the United States and Latin America, thousands throng to exhibit prize livestock and to attend the action-packed rodeo and horse show. Thousands more look forward to the event year round. For youths especially, it can mean dollars in their jeans resulting from months of work spent grooming their animals for entry into the championship circle. The comprehensive purpose behind the show is that of helping Texas' youth to become better farmers and ranchers.

From the day that the trail riders arrive in Memorial Park (The Salt Grass Trail ride begins in Brenham, Texas) Houstonians turn back the pages in time and for some they once again catch a glimpse of the frontier town that struggled to survive beside Buffalo Bayou. It's covered wagons, bowls of hot chili, and rollicking fun at the chicken auction where businessmen forget themselves and spend thousands of dollars for a dozen chickens or $150,000 for a prize bull. Houston can still let its hair down!

CHAPTER FIFTEEN

"Salvador Dali arrived on a steaming September afternoon. He was wrapped in a great fur coat up to his drooping moustache. The auditorium was packed. With dramatic and fascinating flourish he delivered his one-hour lecture—entirely in Spanish."

G REAT EVENTS and golden names were a prelude to Houston's emergence on the universal consciousness. On March 17, 1949 the focal point of Houston life moved from the corner of Main and Texas. On that St. Patrick's Day, Oilman Glenn McCarthy opened his Shamrock Hotel in a burst of international publicity that put Houston on every tourist map and McCarthy on the cover of *Time* magazine.

Hollywood's movie colony and New York's Broadway flew in to launch the opening in true Texas-McCarthy style. A dramatic national radio broadcast from the Shamrock brought thousands of thronging sightseers that jammed all roads and the acres of open prairie to the extent that Mayor Oscar Holcomb, even with his police squad could not reach any entrance of the Hotel. An epic night, it would be credited as the debut of Houston's international reputation as "a great party town."

McCarthy, a daring and resourceful man whose lifestyle was as flamboyant as his gushers, had built his $21 million hotel far out in the boondocks at Main and Bellaire Boulevard in defiance of conventional wisdom. But the business district began creeping slowly southward as travelers swarmed the hotel's lobby and oilmen flocked to its watering holes and dining rooms.

Wildcatter Glenn McCarthy built his hotel on a 15-acre plot that he had purchased for $175,000. He decorated his hotel in three shades of green, provoking Frank Lloyd Wright's famous remark, "Why?" Nevertheless, the Shamrock became "Houston's Welcome to the World."

———————————————————————————

A year before the Shamrock opening the Contemporary Art Museum opened in a small, prefabricated hut next to the Kellum-Noble House in Sam Houston Park. Many Houstonians laughed at the Museum and the modern art it displayed. During an exhibit of rare Swedish ceramics the Museum got a prank call from the Houston Chamber of Commerce: "Are you having an exhibit of stoneware?"

"Yes, ancient and modern."

"Fine! We've got a company that just moved here and they want to put some of their sewer pipes in the show."

The little experimental Museum was a challenge to Houstonians unfamiliar with Max Ernst, Alexander Calder, and Rufino Tamayo. In the 1950s, anything experimental in any of the Arts was suspect. It was in this atmosphere that Diego Rivera's mural for the new Prudential Building was rejected as socialistic; John Dos Passos' great trilogy, *USA,* was banned from the required reading list at the University of Texas; famed psychologist-author Mortimer Adler was not granted permission, until the last moment, to speak at Sidney Lanier High School because of his equal-rights philosophy; Marian Anderson, the great black singer, was refused a room at the Rice Hotel.

But Houston had the philanthropists. Jean de Menil and his wife, Dominique (of the Schlumberger fortune), whose innate sense of the enduring in Art, collected and exhibited in a Museum that they had endowed at the University of St. Thomas, and later at the Rice University Museum. After Jean de Menil's death, Dominique built the Rothko Chapel on Yupon Street, designed by Phillip Johnson, to contain the artist's last murals. Today, she is building a $30 million museum in the same area. Designed by Renzo Piano, architect of the Beauborg Museum in Paris, it will house "one of the five most important privately-held collections of 20th century Art in this country."

The latest home of the Contemporary Art Museum is a large, modular structure on Bissonnet and Montrose.

The Houston Museum of Fine Arts, with its exhibits of Picasso, Rodin, 6,000 years of Chinese Art, its Fresh Paint exhibit of the "Houston School," has moved light years away from Emma Richardson Cherry and her buggy filled with canvases.

Today the Museum is part of the lives of thousands of Houston families and their children.

In 1953, the Robert Lee Blaffer memorial wing was built, a gift of John and Camilla Blaffer. In the same year, Carroll Sterling Masterson (Mrs. Harris) endowed the Frank Sterling Gallery. Carroll and Harry Masterson gave the Junior Gallery which opened in 1958. In the same year, Olga Wiess (Mrs. Harry C.) and Mr. and Mrs. Jesse Jones remodeled and air conditioned the other parts of the building.

Art directors have come and gone. Among the more distinguished and controversial was James Johnson Sweeney. Peter Marzio is the present director.

The new Alfred Glassell School of Art is directly across from the museum. Isaac Arnold, Jr., grandson of H. R. Cullen, is board president. His wife Antoinette serves on the advisory board.

The Humanities Lecture Series was started in the 1950s by Dothe LaCour Olsen and myself. With neither money nor experience we persuaded Will Durant, Salvador Dali, Carl Sandburg, and James Michener that Houston and Sidney Lanier Auditorium was just the place for them. (The committee didn't realize that these men expected to be paid.)

Salvador Dali arrived on a steaming September afternoon. He was wrapped in a great fur coat up to his drooping mustache. He cried for wax for his mustachio. Walgreen's came through. The auditorium was jammed to capacity. With dramatic and fascinating flourishing, he delivered his one-hour lecture—entirely in *Spanish!* Later, the committee solemnly placed the $1000 it had collected in ticket sales, into the be-ringed hand of the great Dali, whom nobody had understood.

Houstonians were not Symphony-goers. The men went to sleep in their tuxedoes. Enjoyment of the Houston Ballet and Houston Grand Opera, of all the arts, didn't come naturally to most Houstonians. Many years went by before the Metropolitan Opera Company ceased to by-pass Houston.

Then the great impresario, Edna B. Saunders, left her everlasting imprint on the city. The arts began to bring glamorous balls, raising big money, at the same time giving women a chance to show off glamorous designer gowns, fabulous jewels and talents as social leaders.

The Alley Theatre has not always been on Texas Avenue with its professional cast. It is so named because the small theatre's entrance was originally from an alley off of South Main with Houston amateurs playing the leading parts. Nina Vance, speech teacher, was the director. The Little Theatre, on Berry Street, featured local talent. Lottie Rice Farish (Mrs. Stephen P. Farish), with her throaty, genteel voice, swept across the stage in black velvet captivating the audience in the small, crowded theatre.

Oveta Culp Hobby appeared in George Bernard Shaw's "You Never Can Tell." Unfortunate fledglings John Mecom and myself, enjoyed a brief career on the "stage." In a play blessedly forgotten, Mecom perched on a garden wall, jumped down to grab the ingenue star (me) to kiss her. He jumped all right! All six foot three of him, landing at my feet. And since I didn't know much about kissing, it didn't take long to replace us.

Today the Wortham Theatre Center is taking shape in granite and rose brick grandeur adjacent to the Albert Thomas Convention Center, in Buffalo Bayou Park. The 110-foot-high building with an 85-foot high entrance arch, named for the late Gus S. Wortham, philanthropist, builder of American General Empire, will cost $75 million. The theatre, a gift to the city from Houston foundations and gifts, will serve the Houston Grand Opera and Houston Ballet. The Wortham Foundation donated $15 million toward its construction. The Brown Foundation and the Cullen Foundation were also large contributors. Former Governor John Connally was chairman of the fund raising committee. The total funding raised in one year was $69 million. That is Houston's style!

Like a tale out of *Arabian Nights* the Warwick Hotel gracefully opened its doors one soft-balmy night in 1964 to greet the rich and the famous from all over the world who gathered to toast her incredible beauty. Originally purchased in 1952 by John Mecom, he and his wife Mary Elizabeth, scoured the great cities of Europe collecting the most rare and indescribable works of art, bronzes, tapestries, authentic antique French and English furniture, all to be housed in one grand building called the Warwick, which they had renovated.

The walls of the entire first level are the original panels from the chateau owned by Napoleon's sister. The Presidential Suite with rich topaz and amethyst crystal chandeliers, have walls of hand carved walnut brought from the walls of the Hall of Justice in Versailles.

No one could choreograph such an evening in duplicity again. Five hundred people were on the stand-by waiting list. Cary Grant and others of equal importance could not get in. The finale is well remembered by all who attended. A gold-plated Rolls Royce slowly rose in the center of the hydraulically operated dance floor. English Guardsmen in full dress red coats with their distinguished tall black bearskin hats (arranged by Mr. Bernard Sakowitz) brought gifts from within the Rolls Royce and presented them regally to each guest.

Today the Warwick still retains the elegance the Mecoms gave her. And the three fountains outside the Hotel are a gift to the City of Houston, from the Mecom family.

Houstonians and the astronauts held a common bond; both were explorers in time. On September 19, 1961, the National Aeronautics and Space Administration announced that Houston was to be the site of the new space center. NASA would be constructed on a tract of land, donated by Rice University, at Clear Lake, 20 miles southeast of downtown.

Space City. U.S.A. rolled out the red carpet for the new space age personnel that had settled in their town. On July 4, 1962, they were given a rousing Texas welcome with a Bar-B-Que, bands, celebrities and fireworks. The astronauts and their families were overwhelmed. So were Texans.

The Capital Club in the Rice Hotel became the meeting ground of both groups. Once again the walls of the first Capitol of Texas gazed down on a rollicking raucous crowd. Percy Foreman held court daily in his special corner, with his own private telephone—huddled with the newest divorcee to be (they weren't *all* in Dallas).

New names were added to the invitation lists: Donald Douglas (Douglas Aircraft, California), Mr. Mac (McDonnell Aircraft, St. Louis), Harrison J. Storm (North American Aviation). General Dynamics filmed a special documentary on Houston called "Keep Your Eyes on the Stars."

Walter Cronkite came; so did Jules Bergman. The intellectual choices of opinion flew around the Capital Club. Not always agreeable! Michael Landon and "Hoss" were in the crowd. So were Dean Martin, Frank Sinatra and always Bob Hope. The American Fighter Pilots held their reunion in the Albert Thomas Convention Center. Houston committee women and astronaut wives feverishly made flower centerpieces for oceans of tables. All of the United States four star Generals were coming and the Navy flew in its special drum band from Peru. The Bob Mosbachers hosted a pre-dinner cocktail party. Bud Mahurin, Suitcase Simpson and Ernie Gann (author of *The High and the Mighty*) marveled at Houston's hospitality.

It was as if each had met his maker. Houston and its aerospace friends were forming a bond that would remain indelible.

Achievement Rewards for College Scientists (ARCS) was founded in California but the tree rooted in Houston, championed by Mrs. Milo Abercrombie (Grace), Mrs. Robert Gilruth, Mrs. Theodore Heyne, Vira Fredericks, Mrs. Floyd Karsten, Mrs. John T. Jones, Mrs. Alan Shepard, Mrs. James McDivitt, Mrs. Phillip Hoffman, Mrs. Roy Olson and 25 other women.

The lift off from Cape Canaveral (later named Cape Kennedy) was the only national televised newscast of the flight from NASA. It brought waves of Houstonians to Clear Lake where they dove into what was called the "Splash Down" party. And the band played on!

"Shorty" Powers' birthday party was another day to remember. He was 40 years old. The Rice Hotel baked a 100-lb birthday cake, the replica of the Saturn rocket, gantry and all, including images of the first seven astronauts. Sandy Kimbriel, Betty Garrett (Edge), Mary Jo Bell, Wes Hooper, Dick Stedman and Ben James put the surprise party together. All astronauts attended and Denton Cooley's band the "Heart Beats" played. Everyone celebrated because light-hearted Shorty was one of the fun people who had landed on Texas soil.

However, the years of "getting to know you" were not all song and dance. A party scheduled at the elegant Ross Sterling mansion, owned by Paul and Lela Abercrombie Barkley was canceled when the tragic news of the fire aboard the capsule took the lives of three astronauts, Ed White, Gus Grissom, and Roger Chaffee. However, the close bond strengthened because Houston friends deeply felt the loss of these dedicated men who had experimented with life and death for the people of the United States.

But the program continued toward its goals. John Glenn, Alan Shepard and Neil Armstrong became national heroes. Soft spoken Anne Glenn won the hearts of all.

Of course a fatal day finally arrived that would be remembered forever. President John F. Kennedy was coming to Houston.

The Gulf Freeway and the streets of Houston were jammed with people. The Rice Hotel was a crowded shoving mass of humanity, waving box banners "Hi, Mr. President," "Welcome to Texas" hoping to glimpse the new leader of "Camelot."

Hosts and hostesses cleared by security were in their places when the entourage arrived: Vice-President Lyndon B. Johnson and Lady Bird, Senators, buses of press people and, of course, President and Mrs. Kennedy.

The gallery in the lobby quieted down. The President looked more like a sea captain with his tanned face and tousled red-gold hair. He was much taller and thinner too. And he was shy.

Later after the press and the White House guests had eaten, the mezzanine was cleared by the Texas State Cavalry Officers. "Here she comes" they shouted and screamed when the crowd spotted Jacqueline Kennedy. Across the mezzanine an observer caught a look in the eye of a stranger. "There is the loneliest man in the world," she thought. But as the face came into focus, he smiled, acknowledging her fleeting thought. After a welcome at the Albert Thomas Convention Center, the President and Mrs. Kennedy left for Dallas.

But this was not the ending. John Kennedy inspired the courage and adventure that only "Arthur" could have inspired into the astronauts of his round table at Camelot.

And in the 1960s, Houston *was* Camelot.

CHAPTER SIXTEEN

"Downtown Houston is an architectonic forest of buildings that seem to reach for the stars as they spiral toward the heavens."

THE YOUNG generation of the 60s began to mature. They settled down. They began to plan. They began to seek advice from the peer group that had held the control of power and strategy over Houston planning for so many years. They watched R. E. (Bob) Smith, a jovial, great-hearted ex-boxer who owned 17 square miles of Houston (after he had made his fortune in oil) team with Judge Roy E. Hofheinz to build the then eighth wonder of the world, the Astrodome, and the Houston Sports Association. It was built on land owned by Smith.

Plans do not always mature as we envision them. One thing for sure, however, Houston did get a covered, air-conditioned sports stadium. On opening night in 1964, Governor John Connally threw out the first ball. President Lyndon B. Johnson sat in the "skybox" with Roy Hofheinz, and the Astros beat the Los Angeles Dodgers

2-1 in 12 innings. The Astrodome beckoned the world to come and see. The world came.

Houston opened its doors of welcome. Always a town looking for a reason to celebrate, it now became a city where hosts and hostesses planned grand parties with elaborate detail and impressive guest lists. Local columnists Maxine Mesinger and Marge Crumbaker attended all of these parties and events with the vigor worthy of the *Houston Chronicle* and *The Houston Post*. There wasn't anyone who could attend everything so they were able to envision the parties of the night before, through the verbal pictures related in Maxine's and Marge's daily columns.

On Richmond, a young architect built a contemporary office building that was to catch everyone's attention. Then he built another. Gerald Hines and his associates had their eyes on a piece of land on Post Oak and Westheimer.

A small buff-colored school house stood on the corner where Neiman Marcus is now. Houston Independent School District had no takers for the years that it had been for sale. The school house stood next to a popular golf driving range (now Lord & Taylor) with Michel Halbouty's former offices on that same site. Oil patch friends could bag pheasant and quail on the acres in back of Halbouty's rear entrance. Gerald Hines didn't see any of this at all. What he envisioned is what has become a second downtown Houston.

How Harwood Taylor of Neuhaus & Taylor and Gerald Hines combined the excitement of Rockefeller Plaza in New York and the under-one-roof shopping and entertainment center for the international visitor, no one knows. Today, the Galleria shines like a multi-faceted diamond on Westheimer. Its retail stores range from small exclusive boutiques to Neiman-Marcus, Chicago's Marshall Field's, Tiffany, Sweeney's, New York's Macy's and Lord & Taylor. It also offers restaurants, movie theatres, two luxury-class hotels, and a ground floor ice skating rink.

The Giorgio Borlenghi Towers on Post Oak Boulevard between the 610 loop and Westheimer add to the rising significance of the Galleria skyline. Transco Tower, the tallest building out of a downtown area added the legacy of a 64-foot waterwall located on the park area around Transco, and designed by New York's Johnson and Burgee for Houston and her friends who arrive daily from the International cities of the world.

Leon Jaworski, son of a Lutheran minister, was born in Waco, Texas. He studied law at Baylor and George Washington University.

After marrying Jeannette Adam he moved to Houston to join the law firm of Fulbright, Crooker, Freeman and Bates. For over 30 years Jaworski served his profession well. Following World War II Colonel Jaworski was placed in charge of the U.S. Army War Crimes Trials Section in the American Zone of Occupation. In this capacity, he not only gathered the evidence and prepared the cases, but personally prosecuted these trials. (*After Fifteen Years,* Leon Jaworski.) However, Leon Jaworski was to play a more prominent role in world affairs. On October 30, 1973 immersed in a stack of paper work at the office, his telephone rang. It was General Alexander Haig calling from the White House.

International news reports had shocked the world when headlines revealed that President Nixon was withholding tapes which would later levy charges against him and his administration.

Leon Jaworski accepted the challenge as defender of the people and prosecutor of the Government. When told by President Nixon that he had no right to the tapes which President Nixon held in secrecy, Jaworski's famous reply was, "I not only have the right; I have the power." History proved him correct and there is that moment when Alexander Haig, shocked to the core by what Jaworski was revealing, gazed out at the snow-covered White House grounds with tears in his eyes. (*The Right and the Power,* Leon Jaworski.)

Nixon was forced to resign. Leon Jaworski, guardian of our constitutional government and of the citizens themselves, returned to Houston, Texas and resumed his life there with his wife and family until he died in 1983.

Meredith Long left his home in Austin, Texas after telling his astonished father that he wanted to be an art dealer. Long had predicted that one day Houston would be a major city needing major art galleries. Two months later he opened his Gallery on Westheimer exhibiting the works of John Singer Sargent, Gilbert Stuart. He specialized in 19th century art. He married Cornelia Cullen, the granddaughter of Hugh Roy Cullen. Together, as collectors, they moved into the contemporary art world and Meredith Long Gallery on San Felipe attracts the attention of all serious art collectors.

Since Houston has always been a developers' city, new homes and buildings began to stretch into the infinity of the West and the Southwest. George and Johnny Mitchell cast their dreams and plans out I-45 North and called it The Woodlands. More recently, George Mitchell and his wife Cynthia have undertaken the almost indescribable task of the new building and renovation of many buildings in Galveston, Texas.

Walter Mischer carved a career and fortune for himself and his family after moving to Houston from Karnes County, Texas. A contractor-builder for starters, Mischer soon began to form joint ventures in successful development properties. Today, he heads Allied Bancshares and is a major stockholder in Penn Central.

Downtown Houston is an architectonic forest of buildings that seem to reach for the stars as they spiral toward the heavens. Public sculpture, once rejected by the city, now lives easily nestled among the man-made monuments of steel and glass and chrome. Joan Miro's *Personage with Bird* stands in the United Energy Plaza; Claes Oldenburg's *Geometric Mouse* in the Houston Public Library Plaza; Jean Dubuffet's *Monument to the Phantom* on Louisiana in front of Interfirst Bank; Louise Nevelson's *Frozen Lace* in Four Allen Center; and Henry Moore's *Spindle Piece* on Allen Parkway. Prominent artist, David Addickes' controversial *Virtuoso* at Lyric Office Center, also has its admirers.

Hannah Stewart, renowned sculptress from Marion, Alabama, was raised in the colonial home of the Margaret Lea family. Sam Houston married Margaret Lea in the parlor of that mansion before bringing her to Houston. Hannah Stewart's *Libertad* stands at the World Trade Center, but her spiritually symbolic *Atropos Key* at Miller Theatre perhaps best fortells the image of Houston of tomorrow.

The Cullen Sculpture Garden is planned for the spring of 1986, to celebrate Texas' Sesquicentennial year. Designed by Isamu Noguchi, internationally renowned sculptor, the garden is on a one-acre lot between the Museum of Fine Arts and the Glassell School of Art. The Museum will exhibit the finest examples of 18th and 19th century sculpture. Vine-covered concrete walls of varying heights will shield the garden from the street. The land was donated by the Brown Foundation and the City of Houston. The design and construction of the Sculpture Garden was given by the Cullen Foundation in memory of Lillie and Roy Cullen.

Leading portrait artist Robert Joy, who has painted 365 portraits of prominent Houstonians, will have a book on his work published along with an exhibit at the Museum of Fine Arts.

This Day we sailed on. Course WSW.
    —Christopher Columbus

This entry was put down day after day on that first voyage that Columbus made across the uncharted Atlantic. He must have written it in a spirit alternating between blind hope and quiet despair. Perhaps his own confidence was wavering. But . . . he had set his course.

Houston set its course in 1836. Although the course was uncharted at times, mistaken at times, Houston has continued through the faith, the hope, the dreams and the hard work of its people through one hundred, fifty years. Houston's future is as high and as wide as the stretch between James Coney Island and the 21 Club in New York. Houstonians feel equally at home in both.

The vision is still here, in the minds of the young and of those who will never grow old. There will always be a new strength. Houston, like life itself, offers no final answers. An ascendancy, destination unknown, is hurtling Augustus C. and John Allen's village of 1836 into a universe which seems as far beyond man's reach as once was the face of the moon.

Dr. Edgar Odell Lovett's words in his inaugural address at Rice University in 1912 are worth recalling:

"I have felt the spirit of greatness brooding over the city. I have heard her step at midnight. I have seen her face at dawn. I have lived under the spell of the building of the city, I have come to believe in the larger life ahead of us."

E P I L O G U E

B UT, THIS IS not the
ending. We have been
on a journey—a journey in time. We are still on that
same journey—departing on a new day, ready to embark
upon tomorrow.

Building a city is really like building a ship, and travel
on that ship has the essence of dreams. It takes patience,
care and planning to build with delicacy. As for the city
itself, beauty comes and goes like the ebbtide. We built
wide streets and planted historical trees but then we
scarred them with bulldozers. Yawning pits have given
way to towering buildings that too were aspirations of
man in the last two decades. Houston survived the boom
that beckoned thousands of people, cars and builders. It
was 1974 when the Arabs raised the price of oil. That
boom is over and most Houstonians haven't been downtown in ten years.

But, downtown Houston has vitality of its own, and
the vitality of the entire city depends on the new projects
which have become major undertakings. Houston has a
beautiful world-famous skyline. But it needs to bring
that beauty closer to the ground, in the form of trees.
The Living Skyline group is literally doing just that—
planting 5500 trees, bringing life to downtown Houston.

In commemoration of the 150th birthday of the city of
Houston and of the state of Texas, the Sesquicentennial
Committee, chaired by Robert Sakowitz, has selected
two projects. One is the development of Buffalo Bayou

Park and the other is the Texas Museum of History and Technology. Dr. William C. Griggs, president of the Harris County Heritage Society (sponsor of the new Museum), has developed the concept of the main exhibit. A time machine will enable visitors to move backwards and forwards in time over the entire 467-year history of Texas. It is one of a kind. It is world-class.

The 25-year Buffalo Bayou Park rejuvenation project is underway while celebrating Houston's 150th birthday, the Sesquicentennial. The Task Force committee will decide what can be done to include Buffalo Bayou as a long-term and short-term asset. One day, a Midway, with restaurants and retail shops will be positioned along the waterfront. A national competition for the design of the Bayou Park is under the directorship of Central Houston, Inc.

For those who can give a defiant look backward, I say, "Look forward!" Whatever existed before still does exist in eternity. The red sunset viewed from downtown Houston with its ribbons of red and gold against the blue and purple sky is a reflection of the promise of the fulfillment of tomorrow. A mystic chord of memory stretching from generation to generation, from the pulsing hearts of every early pioneer to the living soul of Houston's visionary men and women will bring today's new dawn.

Mary Jo Bell
Editor and Publisher

EARLY HOUSTON HOMES

AT THE TURN of the century, Houston had its equivalent of River Oaks—Quality Hill. It was on the east side of Main Street, bounded by Buffalo Bayou on the north, Congress on the south, Austin on the east and Travis on the west. In this small area were the County Court House, Christ Church, white-columned houses and raised cottages. It was elevated above the rest of the town physically and socially.

Builder Charles Grainger's rambling home and garden occupied a quarter block facing Christ Church at Texas and Fannin. There the first Shell Oil Company building would one day rise. Grainger is said to have paid $800 for the property.

He hosted the finest wedding for his daughter, Georgia, that the town had ever seen. He laid a red carpet from his front door across Texas Avenue to the portals of Christ Church. The entire block between Fannin and San Jacinto was roped off against carriages. The groom,

Alfred Ryland Howard, was no newcomer to Houston. His grandfather, George Capron, whose parents were guillotined in the French Revolution, came to the village in 1837 and lived in a small white cottage on Main Street, on the future site of the First City National Bank. The bride and groom's descendants live in Houston today, among them, the Saffords and McCorquodales.

Over on Austin and Rusk, Cesar Lombardi's house and gardens covered an entire block, now occupied by parking lots serving the Houston Center development. Lombardi was publisher of the *Galveston News,* the *Dallas Morning News,* and was a trustee of Rice Institute. Banker Charles Dillingham's white-columned mansion with regal ionic columns still stands on Austin, as the Child Guidance Clinic.

Rusk was a popular street. Here, during the Civil War, General Magruder established his headquarters in the W. R. Bakers' big colonial home. Baker was Mayor of Houston from 1880 to 1885. Also on Rusk, was the A. P. Roots' large house. The entire block, today's Root Square, was given to the city by their Houston descendants, Laura Kirkland Bruce (Mrs. George) and William Kirkland.

W. D. Cleveland, a wholesale grocer and leading cotton exporter, built his charming yellow house, with handcarved gingerbread and white trim, on Rusk at San Jacinto; its neighbor today would be the present Texaco building. Among Cleveland's many descendants in Houston are Tina Cleveland Sharp (Mrs. Dudley L.) and Cleveland's grandson, Dudley L. Sharp, Jr.

The J. Waldos lived at Rusk and Caroline. Later, the mansion was dismantled, brick by brick, and moved to Westmoreland Place, where it has been restored by the Vernon Frost family. The Waldo sisters ran one of the town's early private schools. They taught democracy as well as Shakespeare. One of the sisters reprimanded one young student basketball captain for her way of choosing her team: "Everybody whose mother has fine cut glass, line up on my side!"

Captain Joseph C. Hutcheson's home was on McKinney Avenue. Before he resigned from the United States House of Representatives, he introduced a bill authorizing a federal survey for deepening the ship channel to 25 feet.

Thomas M. House built his house amidst stately palms between McKinney and Lamar, an area now filled with skyscrapers. Succeeding to Hutcheson's Congressional seat, House urged action on the Hutcheson Bill. The Rivers and Harbors Committee finally inspected Buffalo Bayou in 1897, just after some big rains. The swollen bayou looked impressive. The Committee reported favorably on the bill. On June 13, 1902, President Theodore Roosevelt signed the bill appropriating the necessary funds for the survey.

Banker Benjamin A. Shepherd spread his home over land bounded by Lamar, Dallas, Travis and Milam. It was so big that when his daughter married, he cut it in half and gave one section to her as a wedding gift. Foley's Garage occupies the site today. Many of Shepherd's descendants live in Houston.

Back in the 1860s, in what is today the city's downtown, the town's first shoemaker, Fred Gieseke, had his big white house, then on a hill where the Civic Center is today. He made shoes for the Confederate Army. With five children of his own to shoe, Gieseke gave every new baby in town his or her first pair of shoes. Every minister, priest, rabbi or nun who came in his shop got his or her first pair free. Gieseke's descendants living in Houston today include Francis Sarah Gieseke Boone.

A good distance out Main, Mayor Scanlan built a big turreted house where he lived with his seven daughters, Alberta, Carolina, Charlotte, Kate, Lillian, Mary, and Stella. The oak tree out front became one of the town's most famous landmarks. When Main was widened and the huge oak was cut down, you could hear the wails of outrage all the way to Galveston. Houston had begun to sacrifice its trees.

The house was eventually moved south of town for a Roman Catholic retreat. Interestingly, the tombstones of the seven daughters in Glenwood Cemetery show no birth date, only the death date.

The W. R. Eckhardt home of many towers stood on Jefferson Street. It was to become the Houston Art League, forerunner of the Museum of Fine Arts. On Holman and Caroline, Houston *Tri-Weekly* Editor Edward P. Cushing and his family occupied a three-story mansion amidst ten acres of gardens. He was so vehemently opposed to the carpetbag regime following the Civil War that Governor E. J. Davis recommended he not be pardoned but hanged.

───────────►◄ ►◄───────────

Main Street, in the first decade of the 20th century, was lined with large, imposing homes. Unlike the period mansions of Galveston and San Antonio, Houston homes were built more with an eye for utility. They spread over a large portion of the block; three-storied, galleried, and turreted; built for big families and for more than one generation. Carriage houses at the rear looked like good-sized cottages. There was a cow, a matched team of horses, vegetable garden, and a smoke house. In some carriage houses, the new steam mobile was parked beside the Victoria.

Interiors of these homes were on the dark side, often with stained glass windows, heavy draperies over beaded glass curtains, deep-toned Brussels and Oriental carpeting, with white fur rugs flung about, heavy oak-stained furniture, sometimes with an incongruously dainty gold leafed French parlor. Greek maiden statues stood about beneath potted palms. A favorite one for the hall held aloft a tray for calling cards. There was a fireplace in every room. The inside halls, closed off by heavy, sliding doors, were always cold.

One of the homes in this period was at 2210 Main Street. T. L. Hackney built it of cypress in 1902 for $8,000. He had bought the quarter block in 1894 for $5,500. Ollie J. Lorehn, who designed many of Houston's early homes and buildings, was the architect. The house changed hands three times in the next five years. The final owner was J. J. Sweeney, founder of Sweeney & Co. Jewelers, owner of Sweeney-Coombs Opera House. Sweeney's granddaughter, Marian Mellinger, lived in the house 24 years until her marriage to James Lanier Britton, son of another prominent Houston family. In 1969 the fine old home that had seen so much living vanished under the wrecking ball.

Another mansion was the Abe M. Levy home at 2016 Main Street. Also designed by Ollie Lorehn, it cost $150,000, a high figure for those days. "The three story house had twenty rooms, numerous fireplaces, a living room paneled in imported leather, and all of the furniture custom-made in Europe." (*The Houston Post,* February 5, 1967) Levy owned Levy Bros. Dry Goods Department Store at 35 Main Street. It was the mecca for carriages carrying their mistresses to buy hats, gloves, corsets, laces, table linens.

The last owner of the Levy mansion was the late financier-philanthropist Leopold Meyer. When Harriet Levy sold him the house, she stipulated that at her death it was to be torn down should he no longer live in it. The Meyers followed her wish. Meyers' apartment building, today a condominium, stands on the site.

Main Street held other galleried, three-story houses fronting a grassy esplanade where we children galloped our horses. They were houses to stir the creative juices of youngsters. At Judge John W. Parker's house his granddaughter, Dorothy, and I laid plans to run away, devising a different plan in each hiding place.

Northwest of Court House Square heavily-forested Houston Heights was the highest point around the town. O. M. Carter, who came to town in 1892, saw its great potential. As president of the Omaha and South Texas Land Company, he charted its residential development. He bought H. F. MacGregor's mule-drawn cars and converted them later to electric streetcars.

In these days too, well tailored gentlemen and exquisitely dressed ladies rode thoroughbred horses. Houston's young men rowed on the Bayou. Long a Southern city, Houston was starting to take on a more Western flavor under the stimulus of industries: lumber, railroads, oil, and its always flourishing cotton market.

———————————————◄ ►———————————————

The first house on Heights Boulevard was built by Daniel Denton Cooley, Treasurer of the Omaha and South Texas Land Company. The three-story house, built of cypress, had galleries, a cupola with hand-carved balustrades, ruby-glass windows, a speaking tube to every room, and parquet floors. Cooley installed the first electric lights in the Heights by hooking up his wires to the electric trolley on Heights Boulevard. Every time the trolley rattled by, his lights began blinking.

Cooley little dreamed that his grandson would become one of the world's famous cardiovascular surgeons, Dr. Denton Cooley. Daniel Cooley's son, Ralph, graduated from Dental School and became a prominent dentist. Dr. Cooley invented new treatment medicines and pharmaceutical linings for fillings that were revolutionary and have been manufactured and nationally distributed since 1933. Daniel Cooley's great-grandson Talbot Cooley is manager of the firm, in Houston today. A few years ago, the Cooley landmark was razed, in spite of its elevation and natural beauty.

At the turn of the century many believed the town would grow eastward toward beckoning breezes from Galveston Bay. Colonel John T. Brady, a developer of the Ship Channel, was one. Many years ago, I drove out Harrisburg Boulevard with his daughter, the late Mrs. William Sperry Hunt, granddaughter of General Sidney B. Sherman. She was going to visit the century-old family home in which both she and her son, the late Judge Wilmer B. Hunt, had been born. It was common in this era for several generations to be born in the same house.

Harrisburg Boulevard was lined with dilapidated warehouses, boarding houses, eating joints. Once it had been Harrisburg Road, bordered with great oaks and pines. High-stepping carriage horses, traps, and gigs kicked up the dust on their way to the race track.

Going home after the races, the rigs had to cross the International and Great Northern Railroad track, the I & GN. According to law, if the train delayed a carriage at the crossing longer than 3 to 5 minutes, train officials could be called into court. Each time Colonel Brady's carriage was held up, with his horses rearing, he kept his eyes on his big gold watch. This made his coachman so nervous that after 3½ minutes he would commence yelling, "Break that train!"

The Brady house is still there on the corner of Milby and Wilmer Street. Sold long ago by the family, its former white columned beauty now hides behind drab, asbestos shingled siding.

There is also no trace of a dream the Colonel had of a park to rival New York's Central Park. He built Magnolia Park northeast of the city on sixty acres he owned on the San Jacinto River. The land was forested with huge oaks and 3,750 magnolias! The trunks were so big, the Colonel boasted, it took two of his carriage reins tied together to encircle one tree trunk.

He created small lakes and built enchanting sun houses with names like "Fern Glen." He cut bicycle paths and sailed "pleasure boats" along Buffalo River which ran through the woods. On his main lake, "Estelle," he built a four-story pavilion for dancing, light opera, concerts and private parties.

He constructed a narrow-gauge rail line, "The Houston Belt and Magnolia Park Railway," to bring people to his park. Every Sunday, the train and carriages were filled.

Today there is no trace of the Colonel's dream. The giant oaks and magnolias were bulldozed long ago. The pavilion where Houstonians once romanced to strains of Mozart and Strauss and drank from the artesian springs of flowing crystal water lie buried under the industrialization of the area. Colonel Brady's granddaughters, Lennie Estelle Hunt and Lucy Catherine Barada, live in Houston today.

Eugene Pillot's cottage on McKinney Avenue was respectable. Pillot came to Houston from France at the age of twelve. Starting as a carpenter, he became one of the town's first builders and leaders. Pillot joined Houstonians Paul Bremond and Colonel Thomas House in chartering the Houston East and West Texas Railroad, the first narrow gauge R.R. One trunk ran from Houston to Marshall to Texarkana while another ran southwest to Laredo. Ultimately the hub of the three-foot railroad was Houston where 420 million feet of lumber passed through by 1899. He built the Pillot Opera House and was one of the Founders of the Houston Direct Navigation Company. He married Zeolie Sellers and raised twelve children.

One day I went to see his grandson and namesake, Eugene Pillot, who still lived in the original cottage. A pair of great iron dogs, famous Houston landmarks, guarded the rusting iron gate. His grandfather had brought them all the way from New York. The narcissus that had bloomed for 100 years along the handmade brick walk filled the air with fragrance. For a moment, the carbon monoxide fumes of McKinney were dispelled and the air was sweet and pure.

On the front gallery a small man in a high-back wicker rocker waited. On first sight, you would surmise that Eugene Pillot was President of the Houston Poetry Society. With a delicate, old world courtesy, he bowed toward a high-backed rocker beside him. I had to lean close to hear his low, gentle voice above the thunder of traffic on McKinney.

A bachelor in his late 60s, he talked of how he had never known any other home. He had spent his life writing religious chorales for the Poetry Society, weeding, watering, and feeding his grandfather's beautiful narcissus, scrubbing and freshening his grandfather's famous iron dogs, "a matter of duty, you understand."

As Pillot talked, he made a little tent with the tips of his frail fingers. He kept his small narrow feet side by side on the porch floor like a well-brought-up child. Under the spell of his gentle flow of words, I felt 20th century McKinney Avenue fade away.

It was easy to see the narrow-gauge railroad running along McKinney Avenue, laughing faces at every open window, and hear the rails singing under the wheels. Windows of faces staring in awe and delight at Mr. Pillot's huge, red-tongued, flarey-tailed, glaring-eyed iron dogs that had come all the way from New York! The bell was signaling the interurban to stop; the children were jerking free from restraining hands, running to mount the dogs; others were racing to tear up a lily pad in the garden pond to use as a whip on the back of the dogs. Faster, faster! The race went on until the conductor called, "All aboard!"

Eugene Pillot, rocking gently, smiled over the memory of these children. "I never recall a year when a child didn't ring our bell and cry, 'Run for the tail mender, Mr. Pillot!' The iron tails were yearly torn off. We mended them. We didn't mind. Somehow, the dogs belonged to the children."

His rocker creaked to a halt. He sat in a long silence. Then, he spoke as if with effort. "Since I was a child, nothing has ever changed on this side of the street, while over there. . . ." He gestured toward the boarding house, funeral parlors, cut rate shops on the other side of McKinney Avenue.

Sitting there with him on his quiet Victorian island, it felt strange to look out on Houston's dynamic skyline, to hear its raucous, vital voice. I felt for a moment as if a link with my own time had been broken.

"Tomorrow for the first time. . . ." His words came faintly, "all will be changed on this side of the street, too. This will be the first Christmas of my entire life that I will not hang a Christmas wreath around the neck of each of our dogs."

His thumbs made a circle around each other as though seeking warmth and solace.

"Do you know that for some in Houston, the sight of our dogs in their beautiful wreaths of holly was all the Christmas they had? Why, they would come on Christmas Eve and stand at our garden gate. Just looking at the dogs." Now, he had given the iron dogs to the River Oaks Garden Club to guard the River Oaks Garden Club Forum on Westheimer.

"Why did you give up the dogs?"

He gave a helpless wave of one small hand toward the world beyond his wrought-iron gate.

"They want this land. It's time for the dogs to go, too. They wouldn't want to be here without the house, you know."

So, the great iron dogs departed. Eugene Pillot stayed on in his grandfather's cottage, writing his religious chorales, drifting ever deeper into the past. Once the guardian dogs had gone, the evil spirits of neglect and unlove seemed to take over the Victorian cottage. Shutters sagged, unpainted; weeds choked the famed narcissi. Winds blew the empty rockers on the empty porch. Until at last Eugene Pillot went away from the cottage on McKinney. People said, as they always say of the old who have lost their identity, that he was "content." I prefer to feel that in one of the subterranean vaults of his mind closed to the conscious Eugene Pillot was having a serene time with his poetry, his nurtured narcissus and his beloved iron dogs.

Today, the famous dogs, a gift of the River Oaks Garden Club to the Harris County Heritage Society, once again guard the Pillot Cottage, restored in Sam Houston Park by the Harris County Heritage Society. (Author's column, *The Houston Post,* used with permission.)

BIBLIOGRAPHY

Bates, Col. William B. *Monroe D. Anderson, His Life and Legacy.* Texas Gulf Coast Historical Association Publication, Vol. 1, No. 2; February 1957.

Carroll, H. B. & Walter P. Webb, eds. *The Handbook of Texas, Volumes I and II.* Texas State Historical Association; Austin; 1952.

Clark, Judge George C. *A Glance Backward.* Rein & Sons; 1914.

Clark, James A. with Brock, Nathan. *A Biography of Robert Alonzo Welch.* Clark Book Company; Houston; 1963.

Clark, James A. & Halbouty, Michel T. *The Last Boom.* Random House; New York; 1972.

Clark, James A. & Halbouty, Michel T. *Spindletop.* Gulf Publishing Company; Houston; 1952, 1980.

Cotner, Robert C. *James Stephen Hogg—A Biography.* University of Texas Press; Austin; 1959.

De Cordova, Jacob. *Texas and Her Resources and Her Men.* Texian Press; Waco, Texas; 1968.

Edmondson, Emma. *The Nurse and the Spy.* Publisher unknown.

Fehrenbach, T. R. *Lone Star: A History of Texas and Texans.* Macmillan Publishing Co., Inc.; New York; 1980.

Fuermann, George. *Houston: Land of the Big Rich.* Doubleday & Co., Inc.; Garden City, New York; 1951.

Garwood, Ellen Clayton. *Will Clayton, A Short Biography.* University of Texas Press; Austin; 1958.

Gray, William Fairfax. *From Virginia to Texas.* Notes by Fletcher Young; Fletcher Young Publishing Co.; Houston; 1965.

Halbouty, Michel T. *Salt Domes, Gulf Region, United States and Mexico/2nd Edition.* Gulf Publishing Company; Houston; 1979.

Harris County Heritage Society. *Harris County Heritage Cookbook, Vol. 1.* Houston; 1964.

Holley, Mary Austin. *The Texas Diary: 1835–1838.* Humanities Research Center, The University of Texas; distributed by University of Texas Press; Austin; 1965.

Houstoun, Matilda Charlotte. *Texas and the Gulf Coast Or: Yachting in the New World.* J. Murray; London; 1844.

James, Marquis. *The Raven: A Biography of Sam Houston.* Bobbs-Merrill Co.; Indianapolis; 1938.

Jaworski, Leon. *After Fifteen Years.* Gulf Publishing Company; Houston; 1961.

Jaworski, Leon. *The Right and the Power—The Prosecution of Watergate.* Gulf Publishing Company; Houston; 1976.

Kilman, Alice. *Furniture Used in Days of Republic of Texas.* Harris County Heritage Society; Houston.

Lubbock, Francis R. *Six Decades in Texas.* Edited by C. W. Rains; B. C. Jones & Co.; Austin, Texas; 1900.

Nicholson, Patrick J. *Mr. Jim—The Biography of James Smither Abercrombie.* Gulf Publishing Company; Houston; 1983.

Red, S. C. *A Biographical Sketch of Dr. Ashbel Smith.* Ex-Presidents' Medical Association; 1929.

Reed, St. Clair Griffin. *A History of Texas Railroads.* St. Clair Publishing Co.; Houston; 1941.

Ridd, Dr. S. C. "The Day Old Sam Stole Lamar's Thunder." *Texas Magazine, The Houston Chronicle;* Houston; October 16, 1966.

River Oaks Garden Club. *A Garden Book for Houston and the Gulf Coast.* Gulf Publishing Company; Houston; 1975.

Santangelo, Susan Hillebrandt. *Kinkaid and Houston's 75 Years.* Gulf Printing Company; Houston; 1981.

Wharton, Clarence. *Texas Under Many Flags.* American Historical Association; 1930.

Wheeler, Kenneth W. *To Wear a City's Crown: The Beginning of Urban Growth in Texas, 1836–1865.* Harvard University Press; Cambridge, Massachusetts; 1968.

Young, Dr. S. O. *True Stories of Old Houston and Houstonians: History and Personal Sketches.* Oscar Springer; Galveston, Texas; 1913.

Ziegler, Jesse. *Wave of the Gulf.* The Naylor Co.; San Antonio; 1938.

INDEX